Images of Hope

"*This is an original, independent, perceptive exploration of the psychological and metaphysical elements in hope,*"[1] "*a learned and comprehensive treatment of a subject about which there is little available material.*"[2]

The author speaks "*to and about the mentally ill with real insight and sympathy,*"[3] but he also addresses the well. And he does so in an "*urbane, literate style, which contrasts sharply with the sterility typical of works which deal with personality function and disfunction.*"[4]

"*Like its predecessor, Christ and Apollo,* Images of Hope *deserves a place of distinction in the technical literature of ego psychology. Above all it deserves to be read.*"[5] "*Father Lynch's discussion of wishing is a particularly valuable contribution.*"[6] The chapters on the absolutizing instinct and on mutuality are "*minor classics.*"[7] This is, indeed, "*a major book on Christian wishing.*"[8] "*A good wager would be that few who look into* [Images of Hope] *will fail to read it all.*"[9]

---

1. Joseph F. Fletcher, author of *Situation Ethics*. 2. *Library Journal*. 3. J. E. Royce, *America*. 4. N. J. Pallone, Notre Dame University, psychotherapist. 5. Leslie Schaffer, M.D., psychoanalyst, Bethseda, Md. 6. Rollo May, M.D., psychoanalyst, fellow and member of the faculty of William Alanson Institute of Psychiatry, Psychology and Psychoanalysis, and author of *The Meaning of Anxiety*. 7. N. J. Pallone. 8. *Thought*. 9. Joseph F. Fletcher.

Other MENTOR-OMEGA Books of
Special Catholic Interest

AMERICAN CATHOLIC DILEMMA by Thomas F. O'Dea
A well-known sociologist discusses the contributions of his fellow Catholics to American intellectual life.
(#MP404—60¢)

CATHOLICISM   **by Henri de Lubac**
One of the world's leading theologians discusses the social traditions and ideals inherent in the teachings of the Church, and their relevancy to modern problems.
(#MT573—75¢)

DISPUTED QUESTIONS   **by Thomas Merton**
From Pasternak to the monks of Mount Athos, the author of *The Seven Storey Mountain* tells of hermits, saints, and geniuses whose wisdom points the way to integrity and dignity in the contemporary world.   (#MT622—75¢)

THE PAPAL ENCYCLICALS in Their Historical Context,
                         edited by Anne Fremantle
For the first time in one volume, the teachings of the Catholic Church as expressed by the Popes in their official letters.   (#MQ533—95¢)

Images of Hope

Imagination as Healer of the Hopeless

William F. Lynch, S. J.

A MENTOR-OMEGA BOOK

Published by The New American Library, New York and Toronto
The New English Library Limited, London

To Dr. Leo H. Bartemeier

MENTOR TRADEMARK REG. U.S. PAT. OFF. AND FOREIGN COUNTRIES
REGISTERED TRADEMARK—MARCA REGISTRADA
HECHO EN CHICAGO, U.S.A.

MENTOR-OMEGA BOOKS are published *in the United States* by The New American Library, Inc.,
1301 Avenue of the Americas, New York, New York 10019,
in Canada by The New American Library of Canada Limited,
295 King Street East, Toronto 2, Ontario,
in the United Kingdom by The New English Library Limited,
Barnard's Inn, Holborn, London, E.C. 1, England

PRINTED IN THE UNITED STATES OF AMERICA

Acknowledgments

I wish gratefully to acknowledge the generous permission that has been given me to quote from the following works: *Nineteen Eighty-four* by George Orwell, Harcourt, Brace, courtesy of Brandt and Brandt; *Collected Poems, 1909-1962* by T. S. Eliot, Harcourt, Brace and World; *The Wish to Fall Ill* by Karin Stephen, Cambridge University Press; *The Interpersonal Theory of Psychiatry and Schizophrenia as a Human Process* by Harry Stack Sullivan, W. W. Norton; *Poetics of Music* by Igor Stravinsky, Harvard University Press; *The Image, or What Happened to the American Dream* by Daniel J. Boorstin, Atheneum; *On Not Being Able to Paint* by Marion Milner, International Universities Press; *Judgment and Reasoning in the Child* by Jean Piaget, Routledge, Kegan-Paul and the Humanities Press; *Identity and the Life Cycle* by Erik Erikson, International Universities Press; "Perfectibility and the Psychoanalytic Candidate" by Leslie Farber, *The Journal of Existential Psychiatry;* "Schizophrenia and the Mad Psychotherapist" and "Despair and the Life of Suicide" by Leslie Farber, *The Review of Existential Psychology and Psychiatry;* "The Double-Bind Hypothesis of Schizophrenia and Three-Party Interaction" by John H. Weakland, in *The Etiology of Schizophrenia,* Basic Books; "A Catholic Neurosis?" by Sebastian Moore, O.S.B., reprinted by permission of *The Clergy Review.* I would like to add a final word of thanks to the many other authors who have helped me, by their writing, in working out these ideas.

Foreword

I am deeply honored to introduce *Images of Hope* to those human beings who, whatever their professional or occupational designation, minister to mental illness, and to all those human beings who must at some stage receive these ministrations.

Early in my friendship with Fr. William F. Lynch, he was present when I read a paper on despair and suicide—a paper which contained these lines by T. S. Eliot from *East Coker:*

> I said to my soul, be still, and wait without hope
> For hope would be hope for the wrong thing . . .

At the time I was concerned with the demonic appearances of false hope as it tempts, entraps, and exhausts the despairer in his gropings toward relief. But in the context of this preface, T. S. Eliot's lines now seem to me to catch the predicament of an age grown so suspicious of hope that it can seriously consider such an absurd admonition. Wait without hope, indeed! Without hope we not only cannot wait, we cannot even put one foot in front of the other. Our plight, nevertheless, is that we would almost rather do without hope than submit again to those hollow sentimentalities which have passed themselves off as hope.

The author is well aware of the degradation both the word and the experience have undergone, for he speaks of the "supreme irony" that for many people "hope really means despair. . . . When we say that someone has hope we usually mean he is in serious trouble." So I urge the reader to suspend his understandable queasiness as he first brushes against the word in the opening pages of this work. If it will help, I can assure him the author will not *recommend* hope in the manner of all those grinning evangelists from the sciences, churches, Madison Avenue, Tin Pan Alley, and television—who preach optimism and happy endings as the only alternative to our pervasive pessimism. And just as vigorously, he will dispute all the romantic efforts to make of hope a self-induced and interior thing, unrelated to the life we live.

Though it by and large escapes the fashion of despair, psychiatry still shares the general skittishness around the subject of hope. Since hope is seldom mentioned in psychiatric and psychoanalytic writings, it would seem we prefer to take the matter for granted in our theory—which is different from honoring the taken-for-granted quality of hope when it is present in our lives. It is as though we fear that any explicit attention to the issue would subject those of us who deal with mental illness to charges of emotionalism, religiosity, or worse. For example, when therapist and patient—in the face of almost overwhelming hopelessness—nevertheless persist in their therapeutic pact, we describe their mutual dedication in terms of transference and countertransference, meaning these two people could endure this treatment because they were attached to each other. Yet if Fr. Lynch with his usual tact were to suggest such attachment could hardly exist without hope to sustain it, we might reluctantly agree, though still apprehensive our agreement might land us in metaphysical or religious domains outside our competence.

Much of our reluctance, I am sure, would be due to the deficiency this book hopes to remedy: we have no psychology of hope. And without such a psychology, we lack an adequate vocabulary with which to discuss the place of hope in our existence. As a result we limit our considerations to hopelessness itself, about which we have abundant theory and language, and come increasingly—like the rest of our society —to regard hope merely as one of those fortuitous and beneficent feelings which come and go in any successful treatment. Unfortunately, in this emotive view of hope as mere feeling, we injure the necessary dialectic between hope and hopelessness which is true of both ordinary and disordered life. But far more seriously, the actual treatment of mental illness derives its techniques from this same emotive view. However, I must postpone any evaluation of this distressing consequence until I sketch, however crudely and incompletely, the outlines of the psychology of hope contained in this volume.

Hope, according to the author, is "the very heart and cen-

ter of a human being." And with this passionate statement he
has already passed beyond the constraints of the emotive view.
Hope must be tied, he says, to the life of the imagination, for
the nature of hope is to imagine what has not yet come to
pass but still is possible. To use an expression from Martin
Buber, hope "imagines the real," thus distinguishing this form
of imagining from the unreal absorptions of day dream and
phantasy whose object is transient and solitary self-aggrandize-
ment. Moreover, in addition to reckoning with the real which
is still only possibility, such imagining must claim and be
claimed by the imagination of another if it is to fulfill itself in
hope. Since "hope cannot be achieved alone," imagination
must be admitted to be dialogic in character. In other words,
we imagine *with*. Even the novelist or poet grimly describing
the absolute hopelessness of the human condition is still imagining this landscape *with* his reader; and though he conceals
the fact, he must possess some hope to achieve his description. The momentum to hope, in this psychology, is supplied
by *wishing*, which Fr. Lynch employs in the most honorable
sense of the verb. Wishing, as I understand him, would include imagination, mutuality, judgment, passion—in short,
a joining of all that is human in a move toward what is not
yet but could be.

With the outlines of this conception of hope in mind, we
can now return to the emotive view of hope as feeling in order
to consider its effect on the treatment of mental illness. In the
last few decades we have witnessed a proliferation of elec-
trical, surgical, and chemical devices, all of which would dispel the hopelessness present in every mental illness and in its
place provoke a feeling of well-being or hope. Each device
pursues its own characteristic way, but in all these techniques
it is clear that the mood or feeling sought is internal,
private, and unrelated to the world. Shock and lobotomy require a temporary or permanent assault on memory and imagination and perception, the premise being that when there is
no apprehension of the troubled nature of a given existence,
the hopelessness associated with that apprehension will give
way to a more optimistic mood. Implicit in this approach is
another premise which, I believe, both Fr. Lynch and I would
oppose: namely, that hopelessness, having no privileges of its
own, must be considered solely as encumbrance. Instead, we
would propose that hopelessness, being more than a feeling,
raises its own questions—valid and invalid—which must be
contended with if renewal is to occur.

The newer drugs offer to tranquilize our miseries at the same time that they brighten our mood, such improvements usually being accompanied by a dulling of those faculties essential for imagination and relation. Those who advocate these drugs hope that this chemically induced lifting of spirits will provide the beginnings of a responsible life in the world, although there is mounting evidence this is a false hope which cannot be sustained without continual, and therefore addictive, recourse to the drug. It can be seen, then, that the psychology of hope developed by Fr. Lynch inexorably calls into question the actual measures psychiatry has invented to bring hope to its patients. But there are other implications. By grounding hope in imagination and mutuality and wishing he helps to restore its honorable place in the lives of the well and the sick—with the result that the distinctions between health and sickness will prove less arbitrary and therefore less disheartening to patients and therapists alike.

In conclusion, I wish to say something of the author himself, in an attempt to explain why this significant work, which is so relevant to all of psychotherapy, could have been written by one outside the profession. Normally, I hope, I am more reticent with Fr. Lynch, and I trust he will forgive me if I exploit this public occasion to the point of indiscretion. While he is learned enough about the literature my field has accumulated during its brief history, scholarship alone cannot account for his remarkable effectiveness in this volume. So I must begin with a statement which because of its simplicity is difficult to make cleanly: Fr. Lynch is genuinely devoted to our calling. In fact I suspect he is more devoted than many of its practitioners who tend understandably to be more quickly discouraged by its deficiencies. In these days of fashionable get-togethers between religion and psychiatry, I am impelled to add that he has no wish to proselytize or be proselytized—no urge to join us, mollify us, or convert us. His own faith being sufficient, he is not tempted—as is often the case —to borrow our theories in order to bolster his own doctrine. Nor, as also happens, is he driven to expose the practice of psychotherapy as still another heresy. In other words, he is that rarest of human beings—the outsider who can speak as friend. Like every real scholar he is impatient of jargon, whether it comes from religion or science. Or more precisely, his loyalty to the life of imagination would not permit him to indulge in those polysyllabic monstrosities whose visages are as imprecise as they are unbecoming. Knowing the hazards of all the lower case absolutes which beckon us mortals, he possesses a stubborn affection for the sheer ordinariness of life—an affection which Martin Buber in his writings on the Hasidim called "the hallowing of the everyday." Finally, though he is a man of hope in all the fullness he has described, surely he could not so cherish its presence had he not known the anguish of its loss.

LESLIE H. FARBER, M.D.
Training Analyst
Washington Psychoanalytic Institute
Washington, D. C.

Preface

Every book has a history, part of which is hope. I began this book on hope with the hope that I would finish it. Now that it is finished I would like to mention some of its stages, and I would like to give thanks.

One of the most immediate inspirations for writing it came from the reading of a beautiful presidential address to the American Psychiatric Association by Dr. Karl Menninger, five years ago, on the subject of hope. As is always the case in such histories, other things began to happen and to accumulate in this direction. Yet I hesitated for a solid time over such a project and such a commitment, for he who begins a book should know what he is doing and be serious. One of the reasons for my hesitation was that the subject of hope, while it was extremely fascinating and indeed needed to be written about by more than myself, seemed such a departure, at least on the surface, from work I had been doing over recent years on the life of the imagination. It took me a long time to see that inspiration and the spirit had led me aright, and that there was so strong an equation between hope and the life of the imagination. I hope I have made that equation clear in many of the chapters of *Images of Hope*.

Since there is so close a bond between hope and the imagination, it would be good if the new mental sciences would discover, with the passage of the years immediately ahead of us, that there are still broader bonds between their own work on the one hand and, on the other, the life of the imagination. I mean the life of the imagination in the widest possible sense, not only its life as it is more narrowly if wonderfully contained in the arts. Here, surely, is one area where there is room—and need—for improvement among the psychoanalytic writers and theorists. Their courage, their achievement, the extraordinary contributions they have made to the conquest of mental illness, in both the theoretical and practical orders, goes without saying—though more people *should* say it. I do. But the substance of the psychoanalytic contribution to the study of the imagination, of writers and artists, has been a little less than adequate. A certain habitual limitation to the clinical, and a concentration on the relatively superficial, has rendered their work provincial and marked by a certain intellectual vulgarity. Fortunately, the era of that kind of comment seems to be disappearing.

My own exploration of the task and drive of the literary imagination had proposed, in a book called *Christ and Apollo,* that *its* principal drive was through fantasy and unreality into reality, and that its principal task was the finding and the building and the creating of reality. Literature is indeed a totally different thing from psychiatry. But if the new mental sciences drive for the sake of the sick toward the same goal, even if they do so in totally different ways, if they too drive toward reality, then there are profound functional relationships between these sciences and all the fields of what I call the realistic imagination. One can only wish that the psychoanalytic writers of the future, therefore, will yield this unhappy position of patronizing analysis of the imagination and the artists. The hope is rather that they will explore the possibilities of the imagination as competent collaborator in the search by the ill and by the well for reality.

What we ought especially to do together is to study the content of the human with the help of "the human imagination." That is to say, together we must imagine the nature and the range of the human, until we come to include more and more of the human forms of illness, in increasingly satisfactory ways, under the noble word *human.* This is one of the things I try to do in the pages ahead. (I do not mean them to be a theological study of the supernatural virtue of hope, though they can serve as a preface to such a book.)

They are pages which are written with the hope that they will be of help to the sick who are mentally ill *and* to the sick part of the well—for my basic assumption is (as it seems to have become the basic assumption of the new mental sciences since Freud) that there is nothing in the mentally ill which is not present in the well in a lesser way. Throughout the book I have proposed that two conclusions come from this one assumption: 1) that whatever is ill with the mentally ill is human; and 2) that the well can put off the impossible burden of trying to be as well as they think they must be, and can enjoy the privilege of getting tired and being a little mad. In both cases an act of the imagination is called for. And this way lies hope for both groups.

It seems to me that once you commit yourself to a book several things begin to happen. First of all, life begins to be more difficult in a number of obvious and simple ways. But secondly, the commitment seems to put one in the way of the receiving of blessings and gifts.

That at least is the way things went in this case.

For one thing, as the reader will see, I was quite concerned —for the release of both the well and the sick—to help establish a hard-headed and not sentimental theory of a human wishing behind human hope that would have the qualities of unconditionality and freedom. But I was having considerable trouble with the task. My theory of wishing and wishfulness (and their critical importance over against the threat of apathy and the lack of wishing among us) seemed so like the whole phenomenon of willfulness. And there, for a good while, was the rub. At this point of life I met Dr. Leslie Farber and found that he was preparing a book (to be published as *The Ways of the Will*, Basic Books) that had a study of the willful act as their center. This was such a collaborating help that I can hardly exaggerate this gift of knowing the enemy. Again and again this helped me to find the firm, friendly ground I was searching for, while I held on to the unconditionality and freedom I sought.

I cannot possibly do justice to many other gifts.

There was the generosity and friendship of Dr. Winfred Overholser, who directed the growth of St. Elizabeth's Hospital in Washington for a whole generation with so learned a competence, and there was the equal generosity of his present successor, Dr. Dale C. Cameron. It was through their kindness and interest in the work that I was enabled to live and write for the best part of a year in residence among the actualities of the mentally ill in St. Elizabeth's.

I wish to thank other friends at St. Elizabeth's—three zealous chaplain friends who could not do enough for the sick but also found the time to help my own work: Fathers Wilbur F. Wheeler and Joseph A. O'Brien, and the head of the Protestant chaplains, Ernest E. Bruder. There were several doctors, and especially Straty H. Economon and Katharine Beardsley, who read solid parts of the manuscript as it moved toward completion, and helped with suggestions. There were the intern chaplains of the different faiths who listened to talks of mine as I tried to think the book out loud before them in several lectures on hope. And I give thanks to St. Elizabeth's librarian, Mrs. Elizabeth H. Reavis. So far as those precious people called librarians are concerned I add my grateful acknowledgments and thanks to those at Stockbridge, Massachusetts, the Psychoanalytic Institute in Washington, and the Jung Institute in Zurich. And it was in the beautiful country a little north of Zurich that a wise friend, Dr. Norman Elrod, introduced me to the mind of a wise man, the Lutheran theologian Martti Siirala. I have stolen some of that mind in this book.

As with hope itself, no writer could survive without his editor friends. Nor could a book. In this case they were Joseph Caulfield in Baltimore, and William and Mary Louise Birmingham in New York City. And I am grateful for the generous help of Ethne Tabor in preparing the Supplement.

The reader should ask himself how often he is given a chance to thank his friends in life for many things. And therefore he will generously allow me to think, as he might choose to do so himself for a moment, of a few more friends before the chance dies forever. Since this is the only partially medical book I will have had a try at in my life, I wish to end by heartfully thanking my medical friends, Dr. Thomas A. Lynch, Dr. Harold X. Connolly, Dr. James P. Casey, and especially Dr. Leo H. Bartemeier, to whom I have respectfully dedicated this book.

WILLIAM F. LYNCH, S.J.

Contents

SUPPLEMENT

Introduction

The City of Man

This is a book about hope.

I have divided it into three sections.

Section I is a compact but necessarily limited attempt to describe the actual structure and concrete forms of hope and hopelessness.

Section II is an exploration of *a psychology of hope,* the beginning of an investigation of what psychic forms and dynamisms move most toward hope and against hopelessness.

Section III is an analogous effort to suggest the outlines of *a metaphysics of hope.*

I

We human beings, who need hope more than anything else in life, have written little about it. This is itself a striking phenomenon. The fact is that today we are attracted more toward the hopeless than toward hope; we are passing through a period of fascination with despair. I do not like to use an ugly word so early, but I do say that the hopeless is not only a terrible human problem but it is also, for some writers, a professional occupation.

In the proper place I shall pay my meed of sincere respect to those who have worked on the subject of hope, but it can be repeated even now that they are few. Dr. Karl Menninger, one of the most distinguished of those who have, notes humorously that even in the *Encyclopedia Britannica* there are many columns on love, and still more on faith, but not even a listing of hope. He thinks that the theologians have done more than the scientists, and that the latter incline to conceive of hope as either a purely "psychological" term or as something that corrupts objective judgment by wishful thinking. But, I fear, he is charitable and not scientific in saying that theology has been more productive than science. And what objections to hope the theologians might have I cannot even begin to imagine!

Hope has, apparently, a bad reputation; few people want to have anything consciously to do with it, much less write about it. There is, I suggest, a supreme irony going on around and about it. It comes down to this, that for many people hope really means despair. As we use language, when we say that a man has hope, we mean that he is in serious trouble. When we say that someone has hope, we usually imply that he has nothing else, and that he is close to despair. And I find myself understandably possessed by the strong wish that some people in despair might pick up my book on hope. I certainly hope they do.

The subject of hope got off to a far from perfect start when St. Paul insisted that hope has nothing to do with what can be seen: *hope that is seen is not hope: for who hopeth for that which he seeth*. That is part of the truth —and an essential part—I would gladly agree. Too many, however, have concluded from it that, if hope is eternally beyond the evidence, if it is always stretching beyond the observable facts, then it is a completely romantic and non-scientific idea.

Further, those who have been told to hope have been offered more of the same vinegar and gall they already have, and less of the real hope we shall try to discover in this book. They have been told by Shelley in *Prometheus Unbound:*

> To suffer woes which hope thinks infinite;
> To forgive wrongs darker than death or night;
> To defy powers which seem omnipotent;
> To love and bear; to hope till hope creates
> From its own wreck the thing it contemplates.

That hope, if it be hope at all, is not the hope of this book.

Then again it is difficult to determine what hope is (though that has not prevented books on far more difficult subjects). I shall give a set of preliminary definitions of hope; but they will be skeletal, and it will take the total movement of the book to put flesh on these bare bones. (Hope is indeed an arduous search for a future good of some kind that is realistically possible but not yet visible.)

Hope is none of these vague or negative things. It is something very definite and very positive. It will take generations to explore it and I will therefore mention here but a few of the central ideas I will try to apply to it in my own exploration.

1. First of all I incline to equate the life of hope with the life of the imagination, that is to say, with the realistic imagination, with an imagination that, in the language of Martin Buber, imagines the real. This, too, will take time to explain as we move along. Let us only say now that hope imagines, and that it refuses to stop imagining (or hypothesizing), and that it is always imagining what is not yet seen, or a way out of difficulty, or a wider perspective for life or thought. I do not introduce the equation of hope and the imagination as another non-scientific concept, but rather as one sharply related to the whole scientific method of hypothesis.

This method is simple.

A man is in trouble. There is a way out. What is it? He does not yield. He imagines and hypothesizes. He waits. He continues to imagine and hypothesize.

2. The second and related part of my version of what hope is carries this act of the imagination one step further and insists that it be or become an act of collaboration or mutuality. Hope not only imagines; it *imagines with*. We are so habituated to conceiving of the imagination as a private act of the human spirit that we now find it almost impossible to conceive of a common act of *imagining with*. But what happens in despair is that the private imagination, of which we are so enamored, reaches the point of the end of inward resource and must put on the imagination of another if it is to find a way out. This it must do, or it is lost. Despair lies exactly in the constriction of the private imagination. Whereas a more public act of the imagination comes far closer, I think, to describing the saving process that goes on in the modern psychotherapies; two imaginations, that of the patient and that of the doctor, work together to discover and enlarge the possibilities of a situation. The techniques of the new mental sciences have for their principal intention helping the sick imagine what they cannot imagine by themselves; they are an attack on rigidity and entrapment.

Hope cannot be achieved alone. It must in some way or other be an act of a community, whether the community be a church or a nation or just two people struggling together to produce liberation in each other. People develop hope in each other, hope that they will receive help from each other. As with the imagination, we tend always to think of hope as that final act which is my own, in isolation and in self-assertion. But it is not this at all; this interpretation is, in fact, one source of its dubious and sentimentalized reputation. Hope is an act of the city of man, an act of what I call the public order, not in the external sense of that word but in the sense that it must occur between persons, whether they be man or God. As it occurs among human beings it represents or forges the very bonds of human society, meaning nothing less than that men can depend on one another. According to this understanding of the matter we would rightly expect that human societies and hope would rise and fall together. I shall not elaborate on this question now, save to ask that the principle be taken in a broad and flexible way; that is, in so flexible a way that it can include the life of nations and the living together of a mother and a child. We now know enough from clinical explorations into maternal deprivation to conclude that even babies can become mentally ill from hopelessness when they can no longer depend on their mothers or a substitute equivalent.

3. A third constant supposition is that there is a strong relationship between hoping and wishing. The substance of my exploration will move toward the centrality of wishing in human life. When I begin to discover what my wishes are I am well on the way toward hope. When I cannot wish, I am moving toward despair.

Wherever I use the words *wish* and *wishing*, I wish to indicate something deeply positive. The sense is that of the *Book of Daniel*, in which the angel says to the prophet: God has loved you because you are a man of desires. We must take man as essentially a wishing, desiring being who, in this exalted sense, must at all costs be in contact with his own wishes. Where there is no wishing there can be no hope. One of the most brooding forms of illness and hopelessness among us seems to be that of apathy, which we may define for the moment as the death of wishing. What do I wish? Nothing.

Here again we will find progressively that real wishing, as hope itself, is deeply bound up with imagination and relationship.

II

If this is a book about hope, it is also necessarily a book about hopelessness. There would be no need of a book on hope if today there were not so much hopelessness. There is indeed such a thing as hopelessness. In fact, many of the intellectuals of our generation boast, with Albert Camus as their model, that they have really confronted the monster. I will say a hundred times that we must confront hopelessness. But there is a huge difference between confronting it and falling in love with it.

We shall study hopelessness, describing its concrete forms, origins, pain. We shall study it at its habitual worst, in the world of mental illness. For if anything characterizes all the forms of mental illness, it is hopelessness. There, this monster that dismays all human life—whether it occurs in the concrete form of apathy, or entrapment, or confusion, or the sense of the impossible—can be seen and studied in its sharpest and most visible moments.

More often than not we shall explore the hopelessness of the mentally ill. But we do so with a sense of risk and involvement, since—let it be said for the first of many times—their hopelessness is our own.

For it is a fact, and it is the greatest hope of the sick, that there is nothing wrong with them that is not human and is not present in some degree in every member of our race. This is their hope, that they are human, a hope men stifle as often as they build too high and dig too deep the psychological walls and moats between the well and the ill. We do this out of fear, to convince ourselves of the enormous differences between ourselves and them, and we build a corresponding vocabulary of contempt. What is done out of so much fear is forgivable, but we must understand that these attempts at profound separation add not to our own hope but to our hopelessness. For the well impose impossible burdens of wellness upon themselves by widening this gap. It is ourselves we thus condemn to hopelessness.

As I see it, we are always faced with programmatic alternatives:

We can decide to build a human city, a city of man, in which all men have citizenship, Greek, Jew, and Gentile, the black and the white, the maimed, the halt, and the blind, the mentally well and the mentally ill. This will always require an act of the imagination which will extend the idea of the human and which will imagine nothing in man it cannot contain. The idea of the human and the idea of the city of man will have to remain eternally open and flexible, ready to adjust itself to the new, to new races and, above all, to new illnesses. How many men are up to the building of this kind of city always remains to be seen. There will always be millions who will say No, for the simple reason that they cannot face their own humanity or their own sickness.

Or we will decide to build various absolute and walled cities, from which various pockets of our humanity will always be excluded. They will pose as ideal cities, and will exclude the imagination, the Negro, the sick, the different. These totalistic, these non-human cities offer an extraordinary fascination for the souls of fearful men and we are fools if we underestimate how strong and seductive they can be. For as Robert Jay Lifton points out in *Thought Reform and the Psychology of Totalism,* ideological totalism may offer a man "an intense peak experience: a sense of transcending all that is ordinary and prosaic, of freeing himself from the encumbrances of human ambivalence, of entering a sphere of truth, reality, trust, and sincerity beyond any he had ever known or even imagined." [1] Whatever form these non-human cities take they will always have to be self-enclosed, will always have their own defenses, and their own weapons. The citizens spend their time reassuring each other and hating everyone else. Actually they will never be safe and the final irony will be that they will have to make war on each other. Only the city of the human would have been safe.

These two alternatives go far toward explaining the secondary subject of this book: A study of the human and the absolute in mental illness. Our subjects indeed are hope and hopelessness; but it will turn out that one of the great hopes of all men is that they shall be human and belong to the city of man—and one of the great sources of our hopelessness will come from these rigid and absolutized, these non-human constructions that lead to the self-enclosure of despair.

These constructions are built by what I call the absolutizing instinct.

It is the great enemy of man and of hope.

To its revelation and control, I hope, in the name of hope, to make some small contribution.

part one

TOWARD AN UNDERSTANDING OF HOPE

Chapter 1

On Hope

It is impossible to break hope if it chooses not to be broken. But that is no excuse for placing impossible and hopeless burdens upon it.

The first of these burdens—all of them the creation of an absolutizing tendency in man—would be to declare that hope is a final interior resource, which needs nothing but itself. The sick, who have never been asked, know that this is absolute nonsense.

The fact is that hope is a relative idea. It is always relative to the idea of help. It seeks help. It depends. It looks to the outside world. There are no absolute heroes. That is not the way hope works. The absolute heroes are afraid of help. But hope is not.

I want to say two things about hope in this first chapter.

Hope comes close to being the very heart and center of a human being. It is the best resource of man, always there on the inside, making everything possible when he is in action, or waiting to be illuminated when he is ill. It is his most inward possession, and is rightly thought of, according to

23

the Pandora story, as still there when everything else has gone.

But it would be an intolerable burden for the well or the mentally ill if hope turned out to be a rigidly and exclusively interior thing. The sick, who have reached the limit of their interior resources, are often told to hold on to this completely inward kind of romantic hope. There is a whole literature of such eloquent rhetoric. It speaks endlessly of the absolute and interior spark in man that cannot be overcome and that needs nothing but itself. I shall discuss some of its concrete forms. Medically or spiritually it is nonsense and harmful—especially to the sick when they are told it is there and they know it really is not.

If we did not know that hope is a relative idea, related to the outside world and to help, we would all become sick or sicker than we are. Hope is a deeply relative idea. The well hope for a response from the world, whether they are breathing or working or in love. If the response is not there, trouble starts. With the ill, there is less relationship, less call, less response, more fear of help or response when it is there, and therefore far more trouble. Hope, since it is not in every sense an absolute, must rediscover the other half of itself, the outside world and the idea of help.

Thus we analyze and attack a first form of the absolutizing instinct. We relieve hope of its burden of being an absolutely interior thing. Though deeply interior, it is also, fortunately, a relative term.

I

I define hope, at this earliest stage, as the fundamental knowledge and feeling that there is a way out of difficulty, that things can work out, that we as human persons can somehow handle and manage internal and external reality, that there are "solutions" in the most ordinary biological and physiological sense of that word, that, above all, there are ways out of illness.[1]

What we are already saying is that hope is, in its most general terms, a sense of *the possible,* that what we really need is possible, though difficult, while hopelessness means to be ruled by the sense of the impossible. Hope therefore involves three basic ideas that could not be simpler: what I hope for I do not yet have or see; it may be difficult; but I *can* have it—it is possible.

Without this way of feeling about ourselves and things, we do nothing. We do not act or function. There is no energy. There is no energy because there is no wishing. And there is no wishing because there is no sense of the possible. This second sense of things, this hopelessness, is so painful and intolerable that in the great majority of cases it goes underground. It becomes repressed or denied, and often appears under the guise of its opposites: overactivity, boastfulness, arrogance, even violence. The thought immediately occurs that some degree of the lack of hope is behind one particular facet of our national character, its broad tendency toward running, toward activism, toward overmasculinity. We have not faced and handled our hopelessness. We conceal it under its opposites.

Let me make a few more simple statements about hope.

It seems to me that, no matter what instances and types of hope occur to me, they all of them try to transcend the present moment. (We shall begin with the word *transcend* and find a better later.)

Hope looks to the next step, whatever it is, whatever form the step may take. If there is hope, I take it. We are too much inclined to think of hope as an emergency virtue that saves itself for a crisis (one that is really meant for use in moments when there is not much or any hope at all!). The truth is that it is present in each moment as it looks to the next. It is present everywhere, in the flowing of the bloodstream and in every small action. I would not breathe if I did not hope that the air around me would respond to my call.

I would not begin this sentence if I did not have the hope that I could finish it. I would not begin this book if I did not hope that I could finish it and that something would come of it. Everything in the body works for the same reason. We hope that the muscle will work, that the eye will see if we look, and the ear hear if we listen. We also have hope in our culture, that, for example, our families will survive and our complex political institutions will work. One need but look down from a height at a highway intersection to see what hope in our automotive civilization each driver must have. Traditionally, it is true, we have recognized only the hope in arduous acts, but there is a value in seeing how much more universal than this is its range. Moreover, there is no contradiction here. The arduous thing called life needs hope, and if we did not have hope for this encompassing thing we would not do the simpler things.

It is, in fact, highly probable that people who do not attend to detail are poor in hope. They do not believe that anything will come of detail. They rather expect that the pattern will form of itself, without the detail. This is contempt, which is the opposite of hope. The mentally ill frequently find it extremely difficult to have hope in language, in talk, in the use of one word after another, in actually saying to the doctor, step by step, word by word, what they think or feel. I have the image of many of them, sitting in apathy, without a word. Apparently the fundamental feeling behind this refusal to talk is: what is the use? It must be all or nothing. I want the cure but will not pay the price of the intermediate words. I do not hope in words. Thus the basic principle that Freud proposes for curing within the doctor-patient situation, that whatever comes to the mind should be talked about, is countered with a non-belief in words: what is the use? The tongue has no hope. It refuses to take what we are calling the next step. Modern medicine found it hard to take the step of listening to the sick. Now it is the sick who find it hard to take the step of talking.

We can summarize St. Paul himself, who underlines this universality of hope in all that we do and every step we take. It could not be stronger: *We live by hope.* We can interpret this as meaning that everything we do in life is based on the hope that doing will get us somewhere, though sometimes we know not where. Even our hopelessness probably contains the hope that it will reach some objective. The man who commits suicide, thus ending hope, has the hope that it will solve some problem.[2] We would not do anything if there were not the hope that something would come of it. Hope, therefore, is energized by belief in the possibility of getting somewhere, in the possibility of reaching goals; the "somewhere," the goals, can be as many as the wishes and things we propose to ourselves.

We move into the future, therefore, to the degree that we have hope. This must be taken literally. It literally means that we will not get out of bed in the morning unless there is hope. Apparently hope is something midway between knowledge and willing. For no one can know the future, or know what will happen if one does get out of bed or try to do anything, and yet there is a knowledge from the past, a past that we hope will repeat itself. Here, where absolute knowl-

edge fails, wishing and willing intervene in a creative act, to
take the chance or the risk, knowing full well that the very
wishing and willing will themselves remove the risk. It is
hard to explain, this transcending the present, this constant
decision to move into the future. Hope seems to be the
substance of it.

Another and parallel form of transcendence, or getting
beyond, is the transcending of difficulty. This is our classic
image of hope: overcoming difficulty, liberating the self from
darkness, escaping from some kind of prison. The sense of
hope is: there is a way out. The sense of hopelessness is:
there is no way out, no exit. It is the sense of impossibility,
checkmate, eternal repetition. When we come to the next
chapter on hopelessness, and as we pass through this book,
we will meet form after form of the hopelessness in which
the mentally ill are caught. We will see that no matter what
they do and all the more that they do it, they are caught
in various prisons of the impossible. It is not that they are
not trying and using their wills to the point of desperation. But they are caught in structures of action that are
hopeless. It is enough to say about them now that the in-
creased hope of the ill lies in the fact that we know so
much more about these structures of hopelessness, and so
many more ways out of them.

This great traditional meaning of hope as that which helps
us transcend our endless forms of impossibility, of prison,
of darkness, is complemented by an equally classic understanding of the word *imagination*. For one of the permanent
meanings of imagination has been that it is the gift that en-
visions what cannot yet be seen, the gift that constantly proposes to itself that the boundaries of the possible are wider
than they seem. Imagination, if it is in prison and has tried
every exit, does not panic or move into apathy but sits
down to try to envision another way out. It is always slow
to admit that all the facts are in, that all the doors have
been tried, and that it is defeated. It is not so much that it
has vision as that it is able to wait, to wait for a moment of
vision which is not yet there, for a door that is not yet
locked. It is not overcome by the absoluteness of the present
moment.

Harry Stack Sullivan had the habit of asking a simple
but saving question of a patient who was overwhelmed, in a
preoccupying and panicking way, by a particular incident.
He would ask him at what precise time in the last few days

it had occurred. Any one who is asked this question must think of the surrounding series of moments of non-agitation to which the moment of agitation relates itself. By being placed within its context of time in the imagination the moment and incident becomes less absolute and preoccupying, more relative, more actual. The imagination has fought its way outside the particular instant of time, outside the prison of the instant.

Fortunately, nature and time resolve agitation and despair for most of us. I have myself tried the experiment of polling a group with the question, Do you remember what was badly worrying you three weeks ago? Not one could remember. (One did later, after considerable effort.) In this case again, with the help of time, the imagination has liberated men who were ill from the troubling event, not by denying it but by enlarging the areas of reality. This psychic experience of agitation and preoccupation, accompanied in its darkness by hope, is not too different from the experience of imprisonment where all visible doors are locked and we do not yet submit. Both wait in hope, for the extension of reality and the death of a current absolute.

In fact, one of the principal ways in which hope becomes steadier and more mature, less subject to rise and fall as life moves on, is that it develops precisely this quality of being able to live contextually. It comes to know that things have contexts and are not absolute, atomic units. What happens—like that which happened three weeks ago to my group —is seen in context. This is the great importance of the psychological and sociological thinking of Kurt Lewin, that he has underlined this for us. Everything occurs in what he calls a *field*, a field of life, of time, of goals. And the more mature the life, the larger is the time range and the scope of ideas and intentions within which man lives and breathes. We shall see that a child's attention is consumed by a flash of time—with the inevitable consequences that his hope rises and falls with it. But a man, who has more time, despairs less, and has more hope.

Lewin suggests that our image of future time (what he calls the psychological future) actually has much to do with hope:

The structure of the psychological future is closely related . . . to hope and planning . . . The time perspective existing at a given time has been shown to be very important for many problems such as the level

of aspiration, the mood, the constructiveness, and the
initiative of the individual.[3]

If we expect something in the future, if we have hope, we
actually suffer less. The present moment is less preoccupying.
I would stress that this is a matter of *time* and of *context*
and not of transcendence. *Transcending* difficulty and darkness has a connotation of denial. The ostrich can be said to
transcend the coming storm when he puts his neck in the
sand. But that does not make the storm go away. We all hate
people who go around transcending things. And one analyst
has said that the deepest pains of hell are not too much
for those who will say to the mentally ill: don't worry, transcend it. But it is another matter to look at a fact and to
create a context or a field for it with the help of the realistic
imagination. So that when a moment comes which is impossible we can at least wait for the emergence of a larger
moment and a larger time.[4]

The third permanent part of our understanding of hope is,
of course, that it is the great gift of being able, in an emergency, to act as our last, best and deepest inward resource.
Let us take a longer look at this truth, even if it turns out to
be only half of the truth.

An older culture, like the Italian, close to nature and its
deep resources, is able better and more often than ours to
express this kind of hope in works of art. As often as it
succeeds in such expression, it brings into the area of the
visible something that is present at the deepest levels of the
human personality. In the film *Nights of Cabiria,* we see a
woman, a prostitute, who, after a long life of failure mixed
with little bursts of hope and self-respect, finally—yet only
for an hour—attains an apparently successful and respectable relationship. But the suitor betrays her, steals all her
money, and leaves her in a state far worse than before. Now
what is interesting in the technique of the artist in this case
is the structure of the closing moments. Not a word is
said as she trudges off. There is no further action. But she
begins to be caught in an environment that does not have to
speak: the breath of the trees; a few dancing figures; a
grinning boy cycling by; the rhythms of daily life in a
town; nature going on—as though something there was there
all the time and had not changed at all. The same note is
struck at the end of *La Dolce Vita.* In *General della Rovere*
the rock-bottom situation of strength and dignity is again

created, though in a more complicated way. For "the general," who on the surface is a poltroon exploiting every friend, has discovered his goodness and his true desires—but he covers them with a modest depreciating humor that always mocks a little at the hidden hope; nevertheless, he does let it come out and that is the important thing.

This is the special gift of much true comedy. Comedy has always been able to penetrate the more superficial categories of human life and to have a fine, revelling time in the satisfactions of the more solid reality that it finds underneath. And so, comedy has been the artistic food, so far as art goes, of the poor, the distressed, the market-place, and of all those who have to find out what they have in order to counterbalance what they lack. In a number of rollicking scenes in that great classical comedy *Don Quixote*, Sancho Panza boasts to his pretentiously mighty "lord," Don Quixote, that he has all he needs—himself and enough food: he needs no invitation to the table of kings. We are given a similar figure and structure of reactions in the Falstaff of Shakespeare. This is loud-mouthed, obstreperous, uninhibited comedy in which the world pokes violent fun at our false hopes.

It is found in a more subtle and less magnificent way in the Russian film *Ballad of a Soldier*. The opening moments of this picture are typical of the level on which its comic spirit works. A young Russian boy assigned to front-line duty as a telephone signal man finds himself and a companion suddenly attacked by four enemy tanks. His companion flees. But he finds himself staying and sending the news. Then he flees as never man fled before. The tanks pursue him relentlessly, inevitably, over the open fields. He drops at the point of exhaustion and complete fright. He finds himself using his thin rifle against the pretentious monsters. One explodes in flames, then another. The other two are routed. A slow, half-believing grin begins to break out on the face of the boy. The belief in his heroism comes halfway out, as well as the dawning realization of hope.

Even in these few examples, all the way from Falstaff to the young soldier, one recognizes many degrees in liberating hope, in acknowledging it, in expressing or *asserting* it. We have already found simple illustrations of the *simple* difference between the well and the sick. For the sick hardly dare to discover hope at all. We have the phrase "running for cover." The ill fear to expose themselves, their wishes, and their hopes, or they peer out timidly and then run for cover. A technical vocabulary would say that they create defenses. And many of these defenses are defenses against the deeply inward hope and resources we have been talking about.

II

It would indeed be a limited, even a false understanding of the nature of hope to leave it at the descriptive stage we have thus far reached. For the implication would be that it is a deep inward resource (completely inward in every sense of that word), which has the strength to save us once we succeed in tapping it. But, the implication would continue, somewhere, on a later level and at a later time, it gets into trouble and needs temporary assistance in order that it may again go on its merry way unassisted by the undignified thing called help. The final implication might well be that if the fellow had been a real man he would have beefed his way through in the first place. Like most human statements this one contains some truth, but in its substance it contains a broadly prevalent clinical, philosophical and theological lie. It is also a lie that is broadly operative in our national culture. It is a romantic notion that will make more people sick and sick people sicker still if it is not qualified. It is the notion that help is not basic to the idea of humanity. It believes that hope, wherever discovered or rediscovered, is an interior, self-sufficient absolute. Such a belief would be a real reason for despair for the mentally ill.

The truth is that hope is related to help in such a way that you cannot talk about one without talking of the other. Hope is truly on the inside of us, but hope is an interior sense that there is help on the outside of us. There are times when we are especially aware that our own *purely inward resources* are not enough, that they have to be added to from the outside. But this need of help is a permanent, abiding, continuing fact for each human being; therefore, we can repeat that in severe difficulties we only become more especially aware of it. Our civilization tends to associate a sense of shame with the need for help, as if all real "life" must come from within. If anything need come from the outside there is something wrong with us! Such a view of the human world, which is profoundly pelagian, requires careful clinical and theological analysis.

In a short yet indispensable book on the treatment of schizophrenia, M. A. Sechehaye has firmly and carefully emphasized this extraordinary relation of the outside to the inside. What she is dealing with in great detail in this book is her long treatment of a young girl whose physical deterioration and degree of hallucination would have surely warranted her being catalogued as "hopeless." The courage and tenacity of the doctor is a remarkable thing to sense as this life history moves on its discouraging way. But the courage and the tenacity would not have been effective unless the doctor had made what became for her a central discovery. She discovered that in a sense the growth of a new interior life (and the healing that would come with it) must come from the outside. For example, it was not enough that there be food available; the important thing was not merely the objects but the total human situation, the how given and by whom given of the objects:

> The symbol had to be applied directly, by a being of flesh and blood. If I had simply given the apples to Renée, even bit by bit, and had then left her alone, she would have remained passive in the face of these precious goods. The really indispensable factor was the dynamism, and it was necessary that it be communicated to her from outside; it was necessary that her evolution be upheld by someone living. The patient had to be connected emotionally to a being who gives, because it is not the apples themselves that count but the fact that it is the mother or her substitute who furnishes them. The patient must receive them from a person who is another reality, and it is this person who gives a dynamic reality to the symbol.[5]

I would add only that the act of taking help from the outside is an inward act, an inward appropriation, which in no way depersonalizes the taker or makes him less a man. This is a very important speculative problem to work out for the treatment of mental illness, because so much of it is characterized by an inability to take help.

Here I wish to express a conviction of mine. I believe that our need for help is deeply inscribed in every part of us and is identical with our human nature. The need and the fact is so strong, powerful and characteristic that it can be frightening (especially if its first childhood manifestations have been traumatic or sharply frustrating). The result is that this need, this deep relationship to help, tends to go underground, as I think it has in our national culture. (We force people to go around desperately proving they are men.) But what is underground is still operative. This relationship to help will break out in bizarre ways; we will look for help where we really do not need it at all, or where we cannot get it.

The simplest example I can think of to illustrate this bizarre breaking out of the need of help can be drawn from the area of friendship. We all need a few good and close friends. Sometimes, in an emergency, one will do the trick. But if we are really denying the need of this form of help, if we do not really let anybody get close to us, if we do not really satisfy this need, the denial will often evidence itself in the collecting of a hundred friends, none of whom are really such. The process of collecting gets to be exhausting, and each friend becomes a distraction from the other. Moreover, this kind of friendship does not really help at all. Unfortunately we have been further hindered here by Freud's doctrine that affection and tenderness are really disguised forms of defeated sexuality; here is a good example of the need to examine every concrete, clinical suggestion on its own merits. For one thing we should be aware that Freud himself was no great genius at either friendship or collaboration.

I suggest that in our national culture there is a deep repression of the need for help. We dodge the fact that help is part of the nature of hope. And we pay a price for such a repression.

The child needs external help. He is helpless, but not altogether. He has devices by which he calls for help. Let us imagine the statistically normal situation in which to the usual call there is the usual response. A growing sense of the mutual interaction between call and response is part of the growth of hope. If I ask I shall receive.

It is fashionable to think that such interaction belongs only to childhood, and we are quick to assert that *we* have outgrown this kind of thing. But the hopeful relationship between inner and outer worlds has not changed in adulthood. Only the terms have changed. The difference is that now we ask ourselves what help is needed and what is not, what call is appropriate for this age and condition and what is not. This is one definition of maturity. But to nullify the whole relationship of hope and help in the name of maturity involves a vast denial and can only have painful consequences.

A typical example of failure to accept this permanent reality in the general situation of man is the very great difficulty males in some national cultures have about public prayer. Many Latin nations have this particular problem. The men do not go to church because the going involves the possibility of being caught in an unmanly act of dependence.

Mankind's awareness of its dependence and its relation to help is itself a thing of many degrees. We shall see that one reason for blocking this awareness or for shunting it off to some superficial level of the mind where it is both recognized and not recognized is that dependence is interpreted as a threat to human autonomy and freedom. It is not such a threat, but it is so interpreted. It is no more a threat than love is, yet both can be dealt with fearfully, because seen as dangerous. If this denial moves into the broader atmospheres of religion and art, then we are in even greater trouble.

There have always been a number of areas where artists and writers have managed to create powerful images of human dependency and the human need of help. As often as they have succeeded, they have helped create an atmosphere of perception, without which it is difficult to live. Here my thoughts go toward the forms of tragedy and their contribution to the idea of help. They are a set of epochal achievements in our culture, so many monuments spread thinly here and there to confound our denials. I say "spread thinly," because we cannot stand too much reality. But we need their reminders. Their rhythms, images, and words, if we get to know them, move through the bloodstream and take hold, to be used as truths really perceived.

Richard II says: "For God's sake let's sit upon the ground and tell sad stories of the deaths of kings." Cordelia, looking upon her now wretched father Lear, cries out to all the forces of heaven and earth:

All blest secrets, all you unpublished virtues of the earth, Spring with my tears! Be aidant and remediate in the good man's distress!

And a little later Lear, wishing to help a Cordelia now dead, cries back:

And my poor fool is hanged! No, no, no life!
Why should a dog, a horse, a rat have life,
And thou no health at all? Thou'lt come no more,
Never, never, never, never, never!
Pray you undo this button. Thank you, sir.

These are extreme moments, but we need them as occasional monuments which may help us recall the truth of all the lesser moments in which we need help. They are the few moments which fall back on no suppression or sublimation of a fact, and they help us face our smaller, more constant facts.

For even if a man wishes to sit down he is dependent upon a chair and reaches for it. His body and its relational laws call out for it and the chair is an answer to those requirements. He cannot stand or walk unless the earth and an endless series of factors respond to his "internal" situation. The muscular action of breathing is a call to which the atmosphere responds. All our senses, the eyes, the ears, the tongue, the touch, take these relationships for granted. The senses express real needs, so real for the most part that the lack of their external counterpart—the lack of a response from it—means we cannot survive. Obviously there are many ways of describing the true situation—it is a relation of call and response, of drives and objects, of subjective and objective, of internal and external, of hope and help. But the important thing is that the image of the absolutely self-sufficient man is a mockery of physiological and psychological fact. Yet we must keep asking the question: Are there not a number of powerful forces in our culture which encourage a denial of the fundamental fact of our dependence, even to the point of making it an object of shame and guilt?

The truth is that the most fundamental and universal drive of man is toward objects, toward reality. We hope that we can reach this goal, we hope that there will be a response, physiological or psychological, from the world. When there is none, we find some one of the many forms of desperation.

The second truth we must add is that this relationship of hope and help must be one of mutuality. I must not be in such a relationship to objects that I vanish out of the picture, I am destroyed. And the reverse is also true: ideally the object in coming to me must find itself. It is the hope for this mutuality that is the secret of all our hopes; it is its absence in substance that makes us hopeless. Therefore our task over the years and the generations is to examine our situations, clinical and cultural, to see which are creative and which destructive of this hope.

Let us consider a brief example, one that is deliberately ironic, so that we may have some taste of the need and the hope for mutuality. Why do so many people resent being helped, especially after the fact? The probable answer is that it makes them feel, mistakenly or not, less than themselves. Clearly this may not be true at all; it may be merely a false comparison to past situations where the outside world was doing more harm than good. But it may also indeed be the case. Sometimes "help" is more destructive than creative. Sometimes it is outright interference. Too often it is an attempt to make us more dependent than ever. This is certainly one of the keys to the nature of neurotic friendships and love. What the giver is really saying is: I will help you if you consent to needing me. I will help you in order that and if you will love or serve me.[6]

It is this kind of smothering relationship that children often fall into with an immature mother. Because of their helplessness and absolute need for survival, they have no alternative but submission. To those, then, who do not understand mental illness and the collapse of hope, the one question could be put: What other alternatives did they have? And if the retort is made: But they have other alternatives now, then the further answer to that should be: Yes, that is true, but that is exactly the task of analysis to reveal, that there are other alternatives besides submission, nor is the alternative to submission defiance or rebellion (though there will have to be some of that). For defiance and rebellion are simply playing within the system, taking for granted the permanent presence of this kind of object, playing into its hands.

Hope searches for alternative objects that will not be destructive and that can partake in a relationship of mutuality. Therefore those who are well must ask themselves whether their attitudes and actions will be creatively helpful or destructive. Are they themselves an alternative hope may choose? The thought of the mentally ill reminds us of all our own infirmities. We can solve that problem neurotically and destructively by making the ill outcasts so that we may belong more exclusively to humanity. We would in that way literally *take it out* on the sick, and this is an example of the remarkable accuracy of some homely idioms. For *it* means ourselves, or that part of our humanity which we cannot acknowledge, and *out* means that we locate that part of us in the sick, we push it out of us. By every such action we again reduce the alternatives for the ill to the original situation of helplessness and hopelessness. Whereas by every form of self-knowledge we attack them less and become an image of hope for them.

Let us now take a longer first look at the world of hopelessness.

Chapter 2

On Hopelessness

There is nothing as strong as hope when it knows how to limit itself.

Its first victory was to discover that it was a relative idea, related to help, and could cast off the burden of being an absolute. Now it discovers, with relief, that its range is not absolute.

The human world must be divided between hope and hopelessness. Since there are many things that are hopeless for men, hopelessness is a fact. This is a second reduction in the burden of hope.

The important thing is not to think that all things can be hoped for, but to keep the hopeless out of hope.

What is hopelessness? Granted that it can be the worst of human evils and the most painful, and granted, therefore, that words cannot measure it, let us speak of hopelessness by way of approximations.

There is a creative kind of hopelessness, and a high place and use for it in human life. I shall say many things about it, in analysis and praise of it. But first we speak of the kind of hopelessness and the use of hopelessness that assails the mentally ill and that is perhaps the most characteristic mark of mental illness.

In the commentary that follows, however, it will be good to remember that there is nothing wrong with hopelessness as long as it does not get into our hope. What I mean is what G. K. Chesterton meant about wine when he said: "I don't care where the water goes if it doesn't get into the wine." Hope and hopelessness must keep their absolute identities and not contaminate each other. It is equally important, on the other hand, that hope not be seen as absolute in its range. Not everything can be hoped for. Nothing leads to more hopelessness than the naive theory that everything can indeed be hoped for. These two principles, the uncontaminated identity of hope and the limitations of its range, will permeate our discussion.

I

What, then, is hopelessness? As it strikes the mentally ill it is one or a combination of a number of powerful human feelings that are found to a lesser degree in the well.

One of these feelings, most habitual of all in hopelessness, is the sense of the impossible: what a man must do he cannot; no matter what he does it leads to a sense of checkmate; he is in a trap. With the sick this feeling is generated by some fundamentally hopeless tactic they are pursuing and that cannot work.

A second such powerful feeling is that of *too-muchness:* life is too much for us; there is something there that is too big to be handled; again and again, where this is the case, our fantasies fill the environment with people, things and tasks that look like giants; the task of the realistic imagination will be to reduce these to their actual size.

A third powerful feeling at the heart of hopelessness—it is really a powerful lack of feeling—is that of futility: what is the use? There is no goal, no sense, no reason; and so I do not hope or wish or will. As the poet says, nothing connects with nothing. The present moment has no connection with the next. I therefore do not move. I stand still. We call it apathy. It is something like death.

In the first case—the heightened sense of the impossible—there is a tendency on the part of the mentally ill (but the well do it, too) to keep trying the hopeless way. We use the phrase, *knock your head against a stone wall.* Sometimes we have the impression that there is an actual fascination with the hopeless way, as though the sick one were looking and looking and looking over the edge of a precipice, not able to stop the process of looking, not able to stop the constant nagging effort of working out some problem. The important thing is to stop working the matter out, to move away from the precipice, to end the fascinated playing with the impossible and the hopeless. The sense of impossibility often takes the form of what we may call constant cancellation. It is as if in the same personality two opposing forces were constantly playing a tragic pair of cards, *A* proposing and *B* disposing. *A* hopes and *B* injects an element of hopelessness into the same action; *A* wishes and *B* inserts nonwishing. *A* plays a card and *B* trumps it. *A* acts and *B* spoils everything. Of its very nature the process is hopeless. It is such structures of hopelessness as these that I will elaborate in the next chapter.

Then there is the hopelessness that senses that things are too much. Its victim lives in the perpetual presence of giants. The ill face images of tremendous magnitude, and this is very frightening. The giants may represent their inner feelings; too strong to handle, they command the tactic of repression. Or they may represent figures in the outside world, the parent, the doctor, authority. Fantasy feeds on size and seems to love to magnify it even further. Six-foot people become ten-foot people. We have all seen pictures of the enormous balloons floated through Manhattan during Macy's annual Thanksgiving Day parade. This is the kind of world in which the mentally ill live. The feeling of hopelessness, of non-manageability, created by this world should be clear enough. And of course it is intensified by the relative smallness of the image of the self, even if its body is big. This, too, is fantasy and unreality, because the self is in actuality as big and as good as anything around it. But what is real, psychically real, is the intense, the very intense, the intolerable fright of the ill in the face of such images. No matter what the effort of the will, the project of managing such a world, of functioning within it, seems hopeless unless the imagination, the instrument of reality, learns to correct fantasy, to restore a proper human size to everything. There is only one God. Nothing else is that big, save in fantasy.

But there is a third element. Let us sketch the sense of futility. Picture an inward situation complicated, as it always is in mental illness, by too great a sense of evil in the taste of the self and the taste of reality. Things taste bad, are sensed as worthless or contemptible. Picture further that this is the image of every action and of every detail. They all taste bad. Hope led the imagination to image a future, but hopelessness lacks this central image; or, if it is there, it is highly restricted.

Indeed we can say in general that hopelessness does not image and it does not wish. Hope does, but hopelessness does not. It is characteristic of the latter that it does not have the energy for either imagining or wishing. It is deeply passive, not in any of the good senses of that word, but in its most unhappy sense. Its only fundamental wish is the wish to give up. In particular situations it cannot imagine anything that can be done or that is worth doing. It does not imagine beyond the limits of what is presently happening. It is closed in on itself and is itself its own prison. In such a closed world the manner of life is based not on possibility (which is always open) but on three assumptions which dictate the interpretations of all events:

Hopelessness assumes that, in any difficulty, there are *no interior resources* a man can call upon. (Frequently, when a man feels this way, he is really demanding that some one else do things for him. He may very well feel the same way even about something as simple as tying his shoe laces.)

Hopelessness does not imagine that there is a *possibility of help,* whether on this or the other side of the horizon.

Hopelessness decides that—even if there were interior resources and even if help were available—*there is no use,* no good, no sense in action or in life. Here we are up against the lack even of a wish to do or to live. The life of wishing is so deeply related to hope, and the death of wishing is so deeply related to hopelessness, that our images of hope must include an image of wishing.

The apathy, the sense of futility that we have been discussing, is among the major forms of illness invading human society. Allan Wheelis remarks, and he is not alone in so doing, that futility is our new sickness. "As clearcut symptoms of neuroses disappear, vague conditions of aimlessness and futility become present." [1] I would only add that this is a form of hopelessness.

The apathy we are talking about, whether it is pervasive or not, is marked by negativity, nonwishing, noninvolvement, retreat into the private imagination, absence of feeling, absence of concern. There is a good deal of this among the well. People do not want to be bothered by reality. In the order of politics they do not want to be bothered by the public order, by the public reality, by the common good, by government. At this moment in history, for example, they resent being bothered by the existence of Negroes.

When these principles of negativity and privacy dominate, action and detail, wishing or willing, seem feeble and hopeless.

As I write these words, the world is talking about two completely public events where a horrible crime was being committed against a helpless victim, where a large number of people could have done something about it and did not. In one case as many as thirty-eight persons, and over an extended time, saw the repeated, finally fatal stabbing of the victim, or heard her screams, without so much as calling the police. Certainly some of the thirty-eight could have helped without the slightest danger to themselves. Now the community is explaining to the world that it is really a group of very fine people, and it is begging the world to forget about it, not to bother it with commentary. It still does not wish to be bothered, either by the event or the commentary.

There is present here a wish to deny even the reality of the event. The denial begins by saying, "it could have happened in a lot of places," and concludes, "Therefore do not say that it happened here." So with Dallas. The cry went up: it could have happened in many places. Why, therefore, should Dallas be ashamed? You must, finally, not say it happened in Dallas. In fact, it has not happened at all.

One gets the further impression that behind these situations of non-action and apathy there is some growing contamination of wishing and hoping and acting. If so many things are hopeless and beyond our managing, men seem to have concluded, then so, too, is the smaller, more human, more manageable thing. The area of futility tends to extend itself because the distinction has not been made between what can and cannot be done. The area of hope begins to be contaminated. The area of futility grows. I have voted for twenty years and did it do any good? So what is the use of picking up the telephone to prevent a murder? The hopelessness closes in on the little things—where even a child could see the hope.

If we could only confront this principle of negativity and acknowledge its existence as a wish, we could handle it better. It has been there from the beginning of time, this passive principle, this wish not to act, not to exist, not to have been born. Every wish toward existence seems to have an opposite wish, a wish not to be bothered by it all. We ask profound questions and look for profound answers to such questions as, why people act so, why they can be so monstrously passive in the presence of need or tragedy. But with all our questions we skip the obvious, that just as a human being is indeed born to wish he is also inclined toward the opposite: I do not wish, I do not wish to wish, I do not wish to be. What is so terrible about this? But we have decided in advance that it is hopeless to handle hopelessness and its characteristic futility. And it is, allegedly, not Christian. It is not fashionable. So it goes underground, growing, like every neurosis, in the darkness.

If the wish not to be bothered and not even to be is not acknowledged it grows beyond its place and takes over. Under excessive repression the idea of *I do not wish* can become consuming. In the end only an enormous struggle can contain it. But even here both the sick and the well maintain a disguise against the real issue—which is apathy and negativity. Even at this point they still say that the struggle is hopeless, when what they should say is that the struggle is against the spirit of hopelessness. This would be to place the struggle, unfashionably, at the inmost heart of the self, between the I wish and the I do not wish. It would mean dealing with this basic human split between hope and futility, wishing and not wishing.

Apparently wishing, willing and hoping cannot contact themselves—and the self cannot contact the self—until they recognize the existence and strength of their negatives. Unless the latter are confronted the wishing and the willing can become mere words, and are finally laughed at or mocked by the apathetic principle. People go around deciding, not realizing that they have not decided. This is what Samuel Beckett is saying at the end of the first act of *Waiting For Godot*, where the two actors have just been talking of the uncertainty and futility of all things. The act then ends with the following ironic lines, the third and last being a profound stage direction:

> Shall we go now
> Yes, let's go
> *They do not move.*

II

So much for the hopelessness that lives on the inside of man.

But it seems to me that one of the major causes of this interior hopelessness and futility is the inability or the refusal to face all the forms of actual hopelessness as they occur in real life. The hopelessness of the sick comes largely from an over-extension of hope, an absolutizing of its range. We must explore the place of actual hopelessness, its position among the things we call human, its history in human life.

Hopelessness is always intruding itself into our lives. It is going to be there permanently, to the end of life, to be used creatively and positively, or to be allowed to take over a negative and total perspective until it finally becomes the monster it is traditionally thought to be. It takes time to handle hopelessness; the process will have its vicissitudes, its sharp ups and downs.

But it is critically important to know that this *is* the human story, for otherwise we would think ourselves inhuman whenever we encountered hopelessness in our lives, and we would reject from the human race the mentally ill, those who are for the moment without hope.

We strike here at the importance of the general social atmosphere of ideas for the generation or healing of illness. I have said that when we talk about hopelessness we talk about a human drive which is usually labelled as unacceptable before God or man. It seems that in any given society there are acceptable and unacceptable human weaknesses. Are our weaknesses fashionable? I have heard a chaplain in a mental hospital harangue the sick to the effect that they need not worry about any other human failings, but that if they have the feeling of hopelessness or despair they should panic, rush to the chapel, and throw themselves before the altar, beseeching the forgiveness and mercy of God. The social idea clearly operative here is that some ideas are permitted to the human mind but others are not. The idea is pernicious, for it amounts to saying that some temptations or problems are *respectable* but others are not, and that the feeling of despair is among the latter. I cannot think of an idea less Christian than the notion that temptations must be respectable, or that there is some temptation which places us outside the good, the beautiful society of men. The temptation of hopelessness or despair seems again and again to be placed

in the category of the inhuman. This may very well be one
reason why the mentally ill are so thoroughly isolated by the
well—since there is nothing more feared or less faced by
the well than the possibility of despair. Hopelessness is a
more usual and more human feeling than we are wont to
admit.

The plain fact for all of us is that many things are without
hope, many people we are inclined to depend on cannot give
hope, and many isolated moments or periods of life do not
themselves contain hope. I repeat that hope is not absolute
in its range. Part of reality belongs to hopelessness.[2]

What are some of the things that are impossible to man?
Obviously they are almost without end, and they only come
to an end in himself and in his own possibilities, in the things
that are human. Within this universe man occupies a single
island of possibility, which is an island of possibility and not
of condemnation. Among many other things it is certain
that he must be born of woman and that he must die; it is
hopeless to hope for anything else. The wish not to be
subject to time, minute after minute, tick after tick, is a
hopeless one. It is impossible not to be subject to detail and
the taking of measures and means. There is in all of us a strain
of what I shall now and then call the gnostic imagination,
an imagination which will try to tell us, up to the very
end, that the human reality is really a dream, or that this or
that cannot really happen to us. Surely, we should anticipate
violence as part of the human reality in or outside of a mental
hospital. Yet I know one psychiatrist who finally *was*
punched by a patient, and even his reaction in that stunned
moment was: it can't happen to me. We are careless in
crossing the street because we say to ourselves: a car can
hit somebody else, but not me. This is to wish for a rari-
fication of reality that is impossible and hopeless. In a
special way this seems to apply to the image of dying. We
all rather expect not to die. But that is a hopeless project.

Many things, I repeat, are hopeless.

It is a hopeless project to think that we can trust everybody. There is no doubt that some people cannot be trusted.

It is a hopeless project to think that people can always be
cool and poised, responding always with the proper bon mot,
flicking a cigarette in just the right way and with the right
timing, knowing the right people, saying all the right things,
never fearing, the legs never shaking, the mind always alert,
the nerves never shredded, the feelings always correct and

reputable—always afraid that someone might discover one has an emotion out of place. This comes close to representing one set of national ideals and hopes; and, of course, they are hopeless.

Nothing creates as much hopelessness as an ideal that is not human, an ideal that seems to be commanded and that is also hopeless. In fact this dilemma—I must but I cannot—is the common mark of many forms of the hopeless. One of these ideals is that a human being should not display his feelings, or, better, have none. I wonder whether this rejection or fear of feeling is not pervasive among the mentally ill. And might we not conjecture that this false ideal has been forced on them?

The sense that it is not all right to have human feelings is a fundamental clue to mental illness. Those who would really help the sick must have the courage to approach this fact in the concrete and from the inside. They must leave their own ideal society. They must have faced and conquered their own scandal at the human condition. Otherwise they add to our hopelessness. If they think it acceptable to be assailed by envy or contempt, they will not be frightened by either and will not communicate fright to others. If they think it acceptable to be angry, they will not be frightened by the enormous rages that lie buried in so much sickness. If they think it acceptable that all human beings identify to some degree with both sexes, and wish in part to be the other sex, they will not be frightened by homosexual fantasies and will not thereby redouble the fear in the sick that all these things are not human. Most important of all perhaps, it is all right to despair, or to be without hope. I know at least one therapist who abandoned the treatment of a particular schizophrenic in despair, only to find that his acknowledgment of despair had cured the patient! In acknowledging some of his own hopelessness he had himself rejoined the human race and had thereby helped to relieve the patient of an impossible burden, the burden of having nothing but beautiful feelings.

The kind of system or ideal I am now talking about does not recognize the hopeless; by this very act of non-recognition it destroys hope. It sets up a self that cannot be reached. The striving self cannot reach the ideal self. The project is hopeless. Thus there can be no taste of the self, and no rest. But *this* project is often to be found full blooming in members of the most reputable systems.

Dr. Leslie Farber has a warning for psychoanalytic societies that they, too, in their training and ideals, are vulnerable to the idea of gnostic perfection. He remarks: "When a man believes in his perfectibility, he experiences his own real being almost as a disease, a fatal sickness whose cure (perfection) seems unattainable for himself, and whose tormenting symptoms can only partially be eased by the exchange of seeming for being . . . the noble dream of perfection makes cynics of us all, destroying our infinite variety, reducing us to our facility for imitation and rendering us despicable to ourselves." [3]

The Benedictine Father Sebastian Moore, writes in the same spirit about the possibility of "A Catholic Neurosis" and warns of the ills of a gnostic version of Catholic life. He imagines a Catholic acting and feeling under the following burden: "Between him and what *he* feels and, fumblingly, thinks about life—'life' meaning girls, money, marriage, fun and drudgery—there comes what great and noble souls have thought about it . . . So he oscillates between two standards. This oscillation is not the same thing as the tension between good and evil, between the dictates of conscience and the importunities of the flesh. It is a division of the mind rather than of the will. It is better described as a neurosis than as a straight spiritual conflict." [4]

This division of the mind, it seems to me, involves these questions: Is it all right to be me? And can my search for perfection be completely within these terms? Or do I have to import some holy but alien self? Do I have to plaster on to myself a system that for me is identical with the hopeless?

Apparently, it is very difficult for human beings to stay away from the fascination of these systems of the hopeless. They have always exerted an enormous attraction over his spirit. They occur in dreams, of course, for neither the unconscious nor the dream has any use for limits. But the attraction has also exerted an extraordinary influence on the waking moments of human history.

There is a fascinating account of some of these moments and of some of the groups who lived their incredible life within them in Norman Cohn's book *The Pursuit of the Millenium*. Sometimes these groups are called the Brethren of the Free Spirit, or the adepts of the Free Spirit. Some of them called themselves *the perfect*. "Many instances have been recorded," says Cohn, "of heretics saying that the Virgin and Christ had stopped short of the perfection re-

quired by the 'subtle in spirit.' " [5] In England there was the
sect called the Ranters. Finally, many of them, released
from a human world, thought they were God and omnipotent.

Every such system is based on some kind of omnipotence.
It cannot tolerate any fact that we human beings call
hopeless. And it seems to me that it is this part of every
human being—the omnipotent or omniscient part, the part
that destroys our hope by driving us toward the fascination
of the hopeless—that is at the root of human anxiety and
fear. For it has conjured up vast, inhuman treasures, all hopeless, and it has everything to lose. I think we are afraid of
the hopeless, wide open, endless spaces of this infinitude.

Therefore, assuming that I understand him rightly, I
would be forced by the logic of my own position to disagree
with Paul Tillich's version of the source of anxiety. Writing
on "What Is Basic in Human Nature?" he says: "It is not a
distortion, but the expression of man's basic nature to be
anxious, or, in other words, to be aware of one's finitude." [6]
My general argument moves in precisely the opposite direction: the action of the omnipotent drive, and its fear of de-
scending into the human, is one of the great sources of
anxiety. Grasping and reaching our finite humanity is the end
of anxiety. I do not think we are existentially afraid of our
finitude.

III

The child begins life in the midst of one of these ideal,
omnipotent systems.

The child is full of hope that everything in life, every
object, every person, will conform to the security of certain
ideal moments spent with a mother acting ideally in terms of
his needs. This is the first dream of hope. But that is not the
way things are. Some things and moments begin to produce
deep frustration. The child cannot reach the toy, or cannot
reach it immediately; but he must, or so he thinks, and at
once, so he thinks, but it is impossible, so it seems. Everyone
has experienced the rages that can develop out of this
"hopelessness." At any rate the odyssey has begun and there
is no doubt that it has dramatic and painful beginnings. The
cause of this first hopelessness may be the fear of permanent
separation from the object. Indeed it is possible that the fear
of separation is the single basic fear in life, in which all other

fears somehow participate. It can be excruciating, beyond all the forms of physical pain. And that no doubt is why it is necessary at times to repeat one refrain: that we must recognize the humanity of the sick and must by every available resource bridge the gap of separation between the ill and the well. For every such gap reproduces the original pain and hopelessness.

The child has been equipped by nature with his own resources for solving this difficult problem of hopelessness and separation. If the problem is difficult, the resources and the helps given him by nature are powerful and usually up to the situation. First of all, there is the charm of babyhood, which naturally attracts help. Even wild animals are instinctively drawn toward children and become less aggressive in their presence. Secondly, children are skilled in demanding. They are indeed demanding in their relationship to help. After all, they have a right to be; they have a right to help, and a right to be angry when its substance is refused. Their hope is a demand; demanding is their way of solving a crucial problem. They did not particularly ask to be brought into this rather complicated human condition, and they have a right to be cared for by those who had the maturity, or the immaturity as the case may be, to bring them into it.

Usually, however, children are reasonably answered by reasonable adults. There is hardly an analyst who would not agree as to what is happening in this situation. The child's hope is responded to with help *because he wishes it*. He has but to cry and the thing is done. He has but to think and wish—the reality appears before his sovereign throne. His complete helplessness is solved by his complete omnipotence: he concludes that it is only necessary to say an inarticulate word and the world moves about him. Frustration of any immediate hope, on the other hand, can throw him into an omnipotent rage, driving him to use still more omnipotent means. He is so absorbed in his own problem, whatever it be, that he cannot be expected, temporary god that he is, to be aware of any other reality save himself. We need not say this in any unfriendly spirit toward children. Actually they could not survive without their omnipotence. This is their hope, that they are gods, and for the time being they know of no other help or resource. I see nothing particularly shocking or scandalous in this, though there will, of course, be some still omnipotent elders who will object and insist that things and children should have been made otherwise. Yet the fact is there: these little people have *a hope that cannot yet endure any kind of accompanying hopelessness*, and that is the way it is going to be until we all begin to emerge full-grown like Pallas Athena from the head of her father Zeus.

The mutuality of call and response sets up the first model of trust and hope for the child. Erik Erikson proposes that this is the fundamental goal of the first stage of life, the finding in embryo of this model of trust. Others have proposed that at every later stage we are seeking some equivalent of such a perfect situation of deepest unity and rhythmic communication, though its terms must continually take on new and appropriate differences. We shall see from Spitz' work [7] that if a child is completely isolated from the response of love which he seeks he will atrophy and die. Only a profoundly manichaean instinct will be afraid to give the response that is needed; it will be afraid on the supposition that if such a model is set up it will lead to a permanent pattern of yielding and demanding on these identical terms. This is simply not true. Whenever this early stage is met with perfect response, it leads to a spontaneous passage into the next stage of life. For example, what we call a mama's boy has never resulted from too much real love from anybody. Rather there has been some deformation, some deep dissatisfaction, in this first relationship, the result of which is a fixation, a constant, nagging attempt, under the deep skin of the mind, to work out the original situation. A "good boy" never had or thinks he never had love. More often than not he has lost confidence or hope.

So the odyssey of hope keeps working through the field of the hopeless. The odyssey may be heroic or comic. It is life itself. A man tries a path in one direction, and it does not work. It is without hope. This is completely commonplace and human. He shifts his aim and tries another path, in a different direction. Flexibility of approach to problem-solving begins to develop; there is an adjustment to being blocked. The block becomes a ground where man sets his heel to spring in another direction, with another solution. Hopelessness is part of the game. It demands recognition. It belongs as much to the pattern of life as to the pattern of all scientific thinking and experimentation, which tests one unworkable hypothesis after another until the problem is solved. [8]

We learn to hold a goal in sight and seek a way. It is a

time of endless motility and exploration. The collapse of the venture is meant to create movement, resourcefulness. Rigidity never wins the game. Each failure of hope becomes a source of energy. It is a time of imagination and freedom. This is especially apparent among children. The function of the parent should be to keep the child from that which hurts, not from freedom to move and conquer the hopeless. A child can be taught to laugh at the lack of hope. Later on he may be able to say: My right is crushed, my left has crumbled, I shall attack at the center.

The important thing about this process is that workable and unworkable means can be found and distinguished. To learn the difference between the possible and the impossible is central to the learning process. The healthy mind is able to learn, to learn especially that some ways are without hope and others are not. At a certain age the child begins to make this distinction.[9]

His next task is to work out the problems of contamination and ambivalence. One way works and another does not. This is a simple but crucial proposition for human life. Man has legs but not wings; he can walk but cannot fly. There is hope and there is hopelessness and our task is to keep them apart, to prevent one from contaminating the other. Men *can* handle hopelessness if it doesn't get into the hope.

Self-discovery is growing, too, in the midst of the new process. I am the one who can walk and not fly. The self is being separated out, is exploring and discovering on its own. Hopelessness helps the process. As the child experiments with hope and hopelessness, he discovers both his powers and his limitations. He begins to be at home with himself, with his boundaries. His hope is increasingly set on success in this second task. I would call the first task the pursuit of unity, of trust and mutuality. I would prefer to call this second task not that of separation but of separating-out. An essential problem of all human life is to become separated-out (to become myself) without separation. It is the great hope of the human heart that its need for autonomy will not conflict with its need for unity. In the light of our present double knowledge, clinical and theological, it is reasonable to calculate that the fear of incompatibility between these two aspirations is a great source of our anxiety, while the possibility that they can be fused in one act is the major source of our hope. We hope that we can become ourselves and yet love; that we can be independent and yet dependent; that we can follow our interior and autonomous wishes without hostility or hatred; that we can love our mother without hating our father; that we can be separated out and still belong to a community. It also means the reverse of all these things: That we can love and be loved without being annihilated; that accepting the fact of human dependency does not mean the end of half our hope; that giving in to love does not mean death; that one can belong somewhere without the loss of his soul or identity. Under no circumstances can we accept one of these poles and give up the other.

One of the best safeguards of our hopes, I have suggested, is to be able to mark off the areas of hopelessness and to acknowledge them, to face them directly, not with despair but with the creative intent of keeping them from polluting all the areas of possibility. There are thousands of things that man cannot do, thousands of things that some can do and others cannot. To keep the two, the possible and the impossible, in place is to stay free of intolerable burdens.

Thus with hope and hopelessness. We must have both. We all have areas of hopelessness, areas where we know that we are helpless or incompetent. We all know that there are situations we cannot handle, things we cannot do, tasks which for us would be hopeless. But it contributes enormously to our well-being to keep all of these areas and problems sorted out from the things we can do, or can at least do with help. Thus, I repeat, the hopelessness does not get into the hope, nor do the areas of inadequacy get into the areas of adequacy. I know what I can do. It is good to come to rest in the possible, letting the other man be, leaving him to the secret of his own possibilities. I stay within the human and leave the rest to fools or angels.

Chapter 3

The Hopeless as Entrapment

Hopelessness is rooted in structures of thought, feeling, and action that are rigid and inflexible. They are absolutized and repetitious structures that have become so many traps.

*If, therefore, one of the central qualities of the hopeless
is the feeling of entrapment, a central quality of hope is freedom.*

*These absolute structures lead to a sense of endlessness. We
analyze this sense of endlessness and begin to look for the
forms of thought and reality that involve endings, boundaries,
rest, determination, peace.*

*In our present chapter I want to study the qualities of
hopelessness that are named by three words: impossibility,
entrapment, helplessness. Usually there is entrapment in
some "absolute."*

There seems to be a sense of impossibility in all the forms
of mental illness. Nothing the sick person tries works; no
tactic he adopts to heal himself is successful. This applies to
the course of the illness as a whole and to particular situations
as well. We have seen that in hope there is a principle of
adaptability, and that it works. There is a sense of possibility.
If a movement to the left fails, a movement to the right is
tried, and finally the venturing finds a way out. But in
illness the very opposite is true; nothing works, though everything seems to have been tried. There is a deep sense of entrapment and helplessness. The question is: how can we
liberate human beings from their traps?

I

There *is* a deep sense of entrapment. Actually every neurosis
is a trap, and much of our technical explanatory language
buttresses this reading of the neurotic situation. Dr. Lawrence
Kubie centers his theory of mental illness on the word rigidity
and on the image of a rigid, negative, destructive unconscious. Holding this in mind we can calculate that the mentally ill may be desperately trying, but they are not really
exploring, in the sense that hope explores. They are bogged
down in some repetitious pattern of the past; they remain
within the mire as they confront every new thing. The quick-
sand traps every experience. This happens with the sick and
the well. For members of the John Birch Society, for example, not some things but every thing falls into the fixed
categories of Communism or anti-Communism. Even the
movement and the struggle for mental health in this country
becomes identified as an attempt by the Communists to
take over our minds. The fight for civil rights falls into the

same category. And this may point up one advantage, for the common good, that comes from illness. For the clinically ill generally know they are trapped, though they cannot identify the source, and they suffer some kind of despair. But not so with the John Birch Society. Not knowing they are trapped they have trapping intentions of their own. Dubiously fearful of being taken over by anything and everything in the atmosphere, they want to take over before they are taken over.

We have other technical ways of explaining rigidity. For the word rigidity we may substitute the idea of fixation, and this in entire agreement with the psychoanalytic theory of stages of growth—the oral, the anal, the Oedipal—within one of which the evolving personality may have literally got stuck.

In every neurosis some thing or wish or situation or pattern or person has become absolutized and fixed. In this context, we can equate the idea of entrapment and the idea of an absolute—a false absolute—of course. What is clearly lacking in every such case is flexibility, freedom, imagination. What is also present is some degree of hopelessness. Hope never quite gives up imagining, but the neurosis is an entrapment and a failure of the imagination. The effect of a neurosis, and indeed of all mental illness, is to narrow the possible range of action, thought and feeling. The trap gets tighter as the range of these three becomes smaller and smaller. The ideal end of the ideal neurosis, if I may use that language, would be to make it impossible to act or think or feel. That would be complete helplessness and hopelessness.

As we know it in history the imagination—even as hope itself—acts differently in every way and has a totally different ideal. It wishes to be free to imagine all the possibilities of man. It is always adding to and refining human feelings. The artist, their best guardian and nurturer, is literally helping to invent the future of man and to extend man's possibilities. Shakespeare's lack of rigidity and range of feeling are remarkable. The ideal artist is in every way the opposite of the ideal neurotic.

If the imagination were really neurotic, how would it act? It would act in such a way as to increase our entrapment, in such a way as to crib, cabin and confine our thoughts and feelings. It would act as George Orwell satirically acted when, in *1984*, he developed the language of Newspeak:

Newspeak was the official language of Oceania and had been devised to meet the ideological needs of Ingsoc, or English Socialism. In the year 1984 there was not as yet anyone who used Newspeak as his sole means of communication, either in speech or writing. The leading articles in the Times were written in it, but this was a tour de force which could only be carried out by a specialist. It was expected that Newspeak would have finally superseded Oldspeak (or Standard English, as we should call it) by about the year 2050. Meanwhile it gained ground steadily, all Party members tending to use Newspeak words and grammatical constructions more and more in their everyday speech. The version in use in 1984, and embodied in the Ninth and Tenth Editions of the Newspeak dictionary, was a provisional one, and contained many superfluous words and archaic formations which were due to be suppressed later. It is with the final, perfected version, as embodied in the Eleventh Edition of the dictionary, that we are concerned here.

The purpose of Newspeak was not only to provide a medium of expression for the world-view and mental habits proper to the devotees of Ingsoc, but to make all other modes of thought impossible. It was intended that when Newspeak had been adopted once and for all and Oldspeak forgotten, a heretical thought—that is, a thought diverging from the principles of Ingsoc —should be literally unthinkable, at least so far as thought is dependent on words. Its vocabulary was so constructed as to give exact and often very subtle expression to every meaning that a Party member could properly wish to express, while excluding all other meanings and also the possibility of arriving at them by indirect methods. This was done partly by the invention of new words, but chiefly by eliminating undesirable words and by stripping such words as remained of unorthodox meanings, and so far as possible of all secondary meanings whatever. To give a single example. The word free still existed in Newspeak, but it could only be used in such statements as "This dog is free from lice" or "This field is free from weeds." It could not be used in its old sense of "politically free" or "intellectually free," since political and intellectual freedom no longer existed even as concepts, and were therefore of necessity nameless. Quite apart from the suppression of definitely heretical words, reduction of vocabulary was regarded as an end in itself, and no word that could be dispensed with was allowed to survive. Newspeak was designed not to be extended but to diminish the range of thought, and this purpose was indirectly assisted by cutting the choice of words down to a minimum.[1]

Honesty requires that we recognize how universal such methods for the restriction and the entrapment of the mind and the imagination are. The weapons of restriction and entrapment are in the atmosphere and immediately available. We let a child know that if he becomes angry he will lose our love, so that his imagination is forever closed to the possibility of anger. We construct our own versions of various ideal societies and declare that all those who break *our* rules within *our* version do not belong. We say that such and such a thought—hopelessness, for example—is not Christian and that it should not enter into the imagination. Others declare, rigidly, what an American can think and not think. Slogans and propaganda help put other seals on the imagination. An American always follows through. An American favors free enterprise. An American never imagines anything but the unconditional surrender of the enemy in wartime. In this way, we create our socialized rigidities and neuroses. Let us now examine the rigid (and endless) structure of an individual neurotic process.

Here is a man who must always be busy and getting things done because this is what he conceives to be goodness and life itself. He admires the busy people, the accomplishers. Anything else, like resting or those who rest, must be bad. He hates the poor because they would not be poor had they been active. He hates the present Negro generation because he thinks it wants favors by legislation and does not want to come up the hard way. He likes important people because it is through them that one gets things done. He hates and is afraid of rest, but is beginning to exhaust himself, and so is driven to rest. But the only escape from the guilt of resting is that absolutely good thing, activity, and the only escape from activity is rest. Nothing he does pleases either himself or the hidden figure or figures whom he seems to have incorporated into himself. They lash him on to work. He has absolutized an idea and must keep returning to its worship. It is an idol and must be appeased with constant incense, else it will slay him. Its contrary—rest—is never taken for its own sake, identity and value, but as the enemy, the contradiction of work. He is trapped. He begins to panic from some degree of hopelessness. He thinks he is going down. This is what I mean by giant effort but no maneuverability. Now he is all will and no imagination. And even his understanding of the will betrays a lack of imagination—for he conceives of it, in the fashion of most Americans, as an entirely active faculty. He has no image of it as passive and receptive, meant as much for rest as for work.

But whichever he chooses, work or rest, under the terms and definitions he has chosen, he is defeated. Not only is *A* cancelling *B*, but *B* is cancelling *A*. Action drives, not to enjoyment, but to rest; rest, being guilty, drives, not to enjoyment but to action.

Probably rest was once forbidden by someone else, but now it is forbidden by some force in the person himself. The resulting process is like a game, but destructive, hidden, of ever increasing tempo. Thus, in the following diagram we can imagine that in each case the upstroke is the act of hope, the wish, the plan, the proposed act (in this case, the passive act of resting); the downstroke is the accompanying cancellation. And so the ill are always saying, I wish and I hope; but my wish, my hope is forbidden—it is evil, or it cannot be handled:

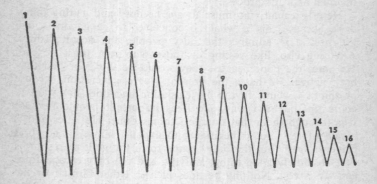

The increasing frequency and growing weakness of the wave indicate the enormity of the struggle the human self is putting up for hope and against the forces that are trying at every moment to beat it down. But we must face the fact that in this diagram hope is not winning the battle, its thrust falls shorter and shorter—and this because it is perpetually in the presence of the opposing, negating thrust. The inevitable result is an accompanying rage and fury, though this is so strong and frightening that it must be kept from consciousness. Granted enough time and enough repetition, every wish and hope can be accompanied by the possibility of rage and the terror of the destructive, so that it seems finally better to such human beings that they cancel the positive thrust in order to avoid the awful negative.

II

Perhaps the most notorious trap of all, because it is the most habitual among human beings, is that which is contained in the vicious circle of dependence-anger-dependence. This form of entrapment is very clearly sketched by Maslow, who rightly sees the process as endless and hopeless. One, two, one, two, and never an end to the neurotic march.

1. Neurotic dependence is the first step.
2. The step that should be taken next is growth and freedom. That step is either not taken or cannot be taken. What therefore and inevitably takes its place is anger, fury, rage, with accompanying guilt, all rooted in neurotic dependence.
1. The anger and the guilt drive the sick person to a new and further dependence and submissiveness.
2. Which leads to anger.
1. Which leads to guilty submission. And we are now in the midst of an endless entrapment.

This is the way Maslow describes the endless circle of this situation:

Complete neurotic dependence implies expectations that must be thwarted. This necessary thwarting creates anger additional to that probably already involved by the admission of weakness and helplessness implicit in complete dependence. This anger, however, tends to be directed against the very person on whom one is dependent and through whose help one hopes to avoid catastrophe, and such anger feelings immediately lead to guilt, anxiety, fear of retaliation, etc. But these states are among the very factors that produced need for complete dependence in the first place. Examination of such a patient will show *at any one moment* most of these factors coexisting in continual flux and mutual re-enforcement. While a genetic analysis may show priority of one over another in time, a dynamic analysis will never show this. All the factors will be equally causes and effects.[2]

We might thus combine this genetic and dynamic picture:

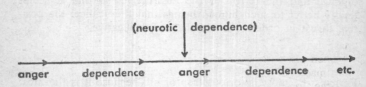

And thus the mind goes round and round in an endless vicious circle that has neither beginning nor end. We all have our small frustrating areas of hopelessness, where we are not free. But in the case of the ill, the circle has been enlarged and intensified; the consequences in pain should be clear enough.

The pattern of endlessness in mental illness takes other forms. (We shall also look at some of the forms of confusion in illness and conclude that these two things, endlessness and confusion, produce most of the despairs of the sick.) Two other forms of endlessness are central: the endless sense of an endless past and the endless taste of an unworthy self. Both have the power to ramify without end.

In hope there is a future. That there be a future is part of the nature of hope. If there is a future to which we can look forward, we can endure all things in hope. Prisoners of war, for example, were able to endure astonishing things whenever they had a realistic expectation of release and return to their loved ones. In mental illness, however, the image of the future is restricted. The future dies as the disease grows. But what then is there? There is only the past, and it is endless. The sick are trapped in the past.

In illness, wherever there is a present, composed of new times, people, things, the past intervenes to cover it up or to deform it. A child wants his mother. He may keep wanting her all his life, in everything he sees and everyone he meets. In later years he literally does not see what is in front of him, so preoccupied is he with childhood dreams and hopes. He only see his mother. He tries to escape. But he cannot. He tries to move forward. But he cannot, as the characters in *Waiting for Godot* cannot. No matter whom he meets, he is meeting the past or is working out some situation of the past that has no relevance for this situation of the present. There is an unconscious nagging principle in him which says, you must work it out, you must work it out, you must work it out, you must do something about it. While doing anything he is always and incessantly thinking of something else. That something else is seldom the future, seldom an act of planning or hoping. Nearly always it is the past. But that past grows dank and dies, and this is the taste of his life.

Then there are the endless ramifications that proceed from the image of the self as unworthy and unacceptable. Behind all the forms of mental illness there seems to lie a generalizing image of the human self as darkly unworthy and "no good." I am talking not of a reality but of a psychic fact; this is how many today think and feel about themselves; it is a deep fantasy and a deep conviction that gets into everything men do. Single events, single mechanisms, single phases of life may produce this image; but once produced *it is this generalized image which thereafter produces every evil and every unfortunate mechanism*. We have reason to think that thereafter there are not independent entities called the perversions, no matter what the latter be, but that all of these are chosen by the self under the burden of this generalizing problem. They are repetitions of the basic evil image, or desperate attempts to work it out and remove it, or manifestations of this negative sense of the self. I wonder if we really recognize how strong and how wide this image, though well hidden, is among human beings. One formula in which we can express it is this: I am not good enough to do good things. I have no right to be good. I have no right to hope. I have no right to act. I am not good enough to love myself. Its capacity to generate endless negative children is endless.

The human being who has concluded within himself that he is no good and has hidden himself underground as not worth looking at with consciousness, also tries in a thousand ways to get rid of his identity in the outside world. The man who is no good and cannot approve of or love himself has to search endlessly for approval in the outside world.[3]

There is a sense of constant, endless urgency, Sullivan tells us, in the schizophrenic condition. There is a constant non-waiting, for they cannot wait. What they are urgent about, and cannot wait for (who could?) is the recovery of their

sense of themselves as human. They have lost their humanity
and must at all costs recover it. Schizophrenia emerges as an
unsuccessful attempt, but an attempt nevertheless, "to cope
with what is essentially a failure at being human."[4] Sullivan
sees the same failure of the same image of the human in
obsessional cases, cases where the endless nature of the efforts to heal the self are clear. I could not agree more sharply: this issue of the human is an essential line of thought for
understanding mental illness and permeates this book until it
receives the analysis of a separate chapter. My own devotion
to it preceded my reading Sullivan's work but has only been
deepened by it. Indeed, I would propose that this lack of
the taste of the self as human is the cause of all other woes
in illness, and nothing will eliminate the exhausting, the
agonizing, the hopeless pursuit of the endless until that image
begins to be recovered.

III

On the one hand, any form of the endless in the psychic life
tends to breed illness and hopelessness; it is this taste of the
human, on the other hand, that always helps enormously to
put an end to the endless.

By the endless I do not mean any positive form of the infinite. Rather, something completely negative is deeply involved. Nor do I intend any religious connotation; quite the
reverse. In theological terms, God is infinite and endless in
many ways, but He is also a completely determinate and personal being, full of identity and reality. The Greeks, however, used the word *endless* to mean something completely
indeterminate, without quality or identity, and needing some
act or fact or form to give it shape, determination, identity.
Psychically, it has no boundaries, or is purely repetitive but
moving nowhere. It has no specific quality in itself, nor does
it have any differentiation or articulation within itself. It was
in these senses that it was called the unlimited or the indeterminate or the infinite.

I have given some examples of the way it operates and
reverberates at the interior of mental illness. But it is difficult for us to understand how frightening it really is, and
how identical it is with hopelessness when it becomes a habitual form of life. Of itself it is always impotent and sterile.

Let us form some partial images of the process of endlessness and the indefinite, first as they operate in the work of a

healthy and great musician, then as they occur in schizo-phrenia.

Igor Stravinsky tells us what he experiences in music, and how he overcomes it:

> As for myself, I experience a sort of terror when, at the moment of setting to work and finding myself before the infinitude of possibilities that present themselves, I have the feeling that everything is permissible to me. If everything is permissible to me, the best and the worst; if nothing offers me any resistance then any effort is inconceivable, and I cannot use anything as a basis, and consequently every undertaking becomes futile.
>
> Will I then have to lose myself in this abyss of freedom? To what shall I cling in order to escape the dizziness that seizes me before the virtuality of this infinitude? However, I shall not succumb. I shall overcome my terror and shall be reassured by the thought that I have the seven notes of the scale and its chromatic intervals at my disposal, that strong and weak accents are within my reach, and that in all of these I possess solid and concrete elements which offer me a field of experience just as vast as the upsetting and dizzy infinitude that had just frightened me. It is into this field that I shall sink my roots, fully convinced that combinations which have at their disposal twelve sounds in each octave and all possible rhythmic varieties promise me riches that all the activity of human genius will never exhaust.
>
> What delivers me from the anguish into which an unrestricted freedom plunges me is the fact that I am always able to turn immediately to the concrete things that are here in question. I have no use for a theoretic freedom. Let me have something finite, definite—matter that can lend itself to my operation only insofar as it is commensurate with my possibilities. And such matter presents itself to me together with its limitations. I must in turn impose mine upon it. So here we are, whether we like it or not, in the realm of necessity. And yet which of us has ever heard talk of art as other than a realm of freedom? This sort of heresy is uniformly widespread because it is imagined that art is outside the bounds of ordinary activity. Well, in art as in everything else, one can build only upon a re-

sisting foundation: whatever constantly gives way to pressure constantly renders movement impossible.

My freedom thus consists in my moving about within the narrow frame that I have assigned myself for each one of my undertakings.

I shall go even farther: my freedom will be so much the greater and more meaningful the more narrowly I limit my field of action and the more I surround myself with obstacles. Whatever diminishes constraint diminishes strength. The more constraints one imposes, the more one frees one's self of the chains that shackle the spirit.

To the voice that commands me to create I first respond with fright; then I reassure myself by taking up as weapons those things participating in creation but as yet outside of it; and the arbitrariness of the constraint serves only to obtain precision of execution.

From all this we shall conclude the necessity of dogmatizing on pain of missing our goal. If these words annoy us and seem harsh, we can abstain from pronouncing them. For all that, they nonetheless contain the secret of salvation: "It is evident," writes Baudelaire, "that rhetorics and prosodies are not arbitrarily invented tyrannies, but a collection of rules demanded by the very organization of the spiritual being, and rhetorics kept originality from fully manifesting itself. The contrary, that is to say, that they have aided the flowering of originality, would be infinitely more true." [5]

Perhaps this experience of the terror of endlessness occurs in heightened form in men of achievement and in the ill.

If we now watch the schizophrenic child, we will discover how frightened he is by boundless, open, inarticulated spaces.[6] When he leaves a house and steps out into vast, open territory, some kind of nameless terror takes hold of him. But there is evidence of a relaxation of terror when the reverse happens and he steps into a world of fields marked and articulated by roads, hedges, fences, directions back and forth. As a matter of fact the healthier among us are sufficiently familiar with degrees of this feeling to make it patronizing to consider it a stigma of the sick. The articulation and formation of space gives some kind of relief to all of us, a relief from the vague threat that seems to emanate from negative indeterminateness. Architecture—I mean good architecture—supplies that same relief from the nothingness of space. On the other hand there is a kind of architecture—like the vast undifferentiated masses of brick in Stuyvesant Town and Peter Cooper Village in New York City—that fails to achieve human effect and only adds to the fright of human beings. This endless massive sameness *is* frightening, if we will permit ourselves to recognize the fear. These places are not for the ill, but they will do much to generate illness.

I think of other things as I try to understand the types of fear and hopelessness that are generated by these versions of the endless and the indeterminate. To be caught for a long time alone at the center of a deep fog, not knowing whether there is anything to the right or left, or whether there is a right or left, can do something of this to the human spirit. It is complete aloneness, surrounded by nothing, without orientation. The same thing happens in the woods when one is lost without a clue to the way out. Panic threatens. Since there is no sense of direction, there is the inevitable fear that any movement might end in the same place, that the effort could turn out to be endless and lead to exhaustion and despair.

The endless and indeterminate bring about a loss of contact. There is some failure of the sense of touch.

Both the body and the spirit of man are constantly reaching out for a sense of touch, so much so that the consequences become serious wherever there is any extraordinary frustration of this drive. To be in a foreign country without friends, to be alone for a long time in a deep fog, or to be in a fogbound plane that is trying unsuccessfully to contact the hidden earth below—these are passing hints of the terror of being out of touch. It is not the sick alone who are out of touch, but all of us. And now we know, more clinically and in greater detail, to what degree men can and cannot tolerate deprivation of actuality. We can put deep gloves on a man, cover his eyes, close his ears, separate him from events, and introduce scheduled monotony; the psychic results of all this will often be extreme, to the point of creating hallucination in the victim. He cannot do without the touch of reality, and when he is this much separated from it, he must do something desperate. Through hallucination, he creates a substitute world that he calls reality.

We may conjecture that, in all those situations of illness where human beings hopelessly thrash about within structures of endlessness, they are seeking that sense of contact without which there is desperation. But the methods of search are always indirect, and intensify the hopelessness. They handle the present by living in a past that screens the present; they try to heal the terrible image of the self by seeking approval in a thousand places but refusing to give it to themselves; they cannot find any beginning or end to their circles of action. It is a thrashing in a vacuum where nothing is touched.[7]

The important thing is that all these endless processes, whatever their concrete or clinical form, create helplessness, partial or total.

IV

It is important to understand that the mentally ill *are* trapped and *are* helpless. To promote that understanding is to fight against several of the deep prejudices of the well. For all too many of the well are convinced that the ill are not helpless, that nobody is helpless, that the ill could help themselves if they only chose to, that God helps those who help themselves. There is one way in which shibboleths are like the problems of mental illness: they are endless.

The image of helplessness is somewhat frightening to everyone. Therefore the imagination closes itself to the image and denies the evidence before its eyes. It cannot imagine helplessness because it does not wish to. In order to make sure that I will never be helpless—God forbid!—I refuse to imagine that others can really and in all honesty be helpless, that is to say, that they are beyond the point of self-help. The spirit of capitalism has been added to the flamboyant convictions of the American frontier. No one is poor or helpless—whether on the East Side of New York or in Appalachia—unless he chooses.

When I say a man is helpless, I wish to convey that he is beyond the point of self-help but is not beyond help.[8] In this sense the mentally ill are indeed helpless, but their own precise and visible situation is only a painful reflection of man's universal helplessness in the face of his destiny. This is the true thing and this is the frightening thing, though if it were not true we would be faced with the yet more frightening and impossible truth that every man must save himself. Christian theologians tell us that man cannot win to salvation, is helpless to save himself without the help of God. God will indeed help us to help ourselves, but that in no way means that He will help us only if we help ourselves. If this were the case, what else would it mean but that we would have to be constituted as absolute atomic units capable of an original and absolute autonomy before God would consent to help us. We would have passed the test with colors flying, drums rolling, eyes aflame, spirit high, heart strong, all comers confronted and defeated—and only at that stage would we magnanimously call in God or a friend or a doctor, to give them the gracious assurance that we appreciated their help. But we would already have quite proved that we did not need it. The only difficulty with this kind of bravado is that demonstrating it becomes, with a special form of irony, another form of the endless; for just a moment before it succeeds in the ultimate and final demonstration, it breaks down and really needs help.

I propose that the sick person *is* really helpless, and that there is nothing more human than to be helpless. He *is* helpless. For he is operating within his own closed system of fantasy and feeling, unable, as a result, even to see or imagine what is on the outside. He needs another's imagination that will begin to work with his own, and then the two can do it together. He must put on another's imagination in order to rediscover his own.

Being helpless, being unable, that is, to help himself, he suddenly finds himself confronted, at so critical a moment, with a culture, and sometimes with a medical situation, which tells him that he must help himself, that the help must come from within. It was bad enough that he be told that hope must come entirely from within when he knows that hope needs the help of the outside world. Now the final blow falls: he is told that even the help must come from within.

This is what a Japanese analyst looking at our culture from the inside and the outside calls a "vicious double bind." The entrapment of the double bind will become clearer as we go along, but our present example is classical: you who need help from another, it asserts, must help yourself—". . . the philosophy of self-help, as it is understood today," says Dr. L. Takeo Doi, "is entirely a Western product."

I believe that the idea of self-help or the intrinsic autonomy of a person gradually became popular in

western Europe during the early Renaissance. One may
perhaps associate the development of this idea with the
saying, "God helps those who help themselves," which
seems to have become popular by the seventeenth century. It was used by Algernon Sidney in his political
essay, Discourses Concerning Government, written
around 1680, and a similar saying appears in George
Herbert's Outlandish Proverbs, first published in 1640.
Interestingly enough, this saying in another form can
be found in old Greek authors, but not in authentic
Judeo-Christian literature, including the Bible. One might
well argue, then, that the "God" of "God helps those
who help themselves," who does not take the initiative
in helping people, but only waits for them to help themselves, is not a Judeo-Christian God. Incidentally, such
an interpretation is quite possible from Sidney's book,
since he uses the saying primarily to point to the grim,
almost cruel reality of the hostile world, and scarcely
to a helping God. Such a God can easily be dispensed
with, because He cannot be depended upon, and what
counts, after all, is whether one helps oneself or
not. [9]

There has been a deep cynicism behind the use of the saying, "God helps those who help themselves," that has reflected a deep distrust of the surrounding world. Why should
not men be doubly afraid of helplessness—of all those situations in which they cannot help themselves—if they believe
there is no help on the outside, from God or man. Such a
belief can depend on nothing and has no hope. (And such a
belief can be strengthened by the existing body of ideas
and feelings in a culture or in a neighborhood; if apathy
grows, and if it decides not to help anyone, it adds to the
atmosphere of our despair.)

The belief that there is no help throttles the gift of being
able to depend. But how many people can admit this to
themselves? It seems better to most that they resort to
frenetic and endless activity, to prove that they are not in
despair, that they need not depend, that they have no use
for the help that is not there.

V

There is nothing more hopeless than this sense of endlessness or infinitude. Freud studied the phenomenon under the

term *repetition*. Long before that Plato had explored it philosophically under the term *the unlimited* and had contributed to philosophy the parallel idea of the defining term, the pause or the limit. There is something deeply frightening about that which is unlimited or has no boundaries. But by finding what gives pause and limit to our thoughts, feelings and actions, we find hope.

We will add to hope as often as we find what gives form and limit to all these pathological qualities of endlessness in human thoughts, feelings, and actions. I have explored and emphasized these structures of endlessness because they are so operative in producing hopelessness and so central to our understanding it. But by the same token—and because this is first and foremost a book on hope—I shall be on the lookout, in all that follows, for those many forms of reality and of psychic life that know how to give pause to the endless, and surcease, small or large, from neurosis or madness. No one is going to come up with a cure-all for the dense and manifold ills of the mind. But we can add, however slightly, to the weight and number of ideas that are counter-agents to the forces of illness. One of my recurring questions, accordingly, will be: what gives pause, or boundary, or end, to the sick forms of the infinite? What are some of the absolute (but not rigid) points at which the human spirit can rest?

In finding answers to those questions, one of them that we will uncover is what might be called the *psychology of the immediate*. This phenomenon shows how what gives pause or limit gives hope to the thoughts of the sick, and leads them out of entrapment.

One temptation of those who are ill is to think that they must wait until they are "cured" before they can take on the rights of those who are well. This can be an endless procedure because there is a sense in which this ideal moment, romantically conceived, never comes to anyone. By the psychology of the immediate I mean simply that here and now the sick person has the right and the need to conceive of himself as human and as permitted to act positively and creatively. The sickness is at every moment a real sickness and very painful, but in itself it is a fantasy, a fantasy image of the self, which leads to thoughts, feelings, actions. This image may be absolutely preoccupying and intense, but it is still and for all that a lie, without rights. To say that we must get well before we deal with this image is to put the cart before the horse. The illness has no rights.

Do I mean then that even the seriously ill, the severely neurotic, the pervert, the addict, the homosexual, all have the right to hold their heads up in pride and dignity? I do indeed. Not because of what they seem to themselves to be at the moment, and upon which they act, but because of what they really are and do not yet see. (Hope acts in the name of what is not yet seen.) They are human and can love; everybody can. But some do not give themselves the right to be human, or have had the right taken away from them by others.

It would be naive to think that this psychology of the immediate will work without delay in the case of the sick. What is important is that the right and the quality of the human is *immediately there* as a fact, and that its opposites, the illness itself, the fantasies and the perversions, painful though they be, are constructions, lies, irrealities.

To choose the way of fantasy is endless. To choose oneself as human even in the dark, to choose such an absolute point in the midst of the indeterminate, can be a beginning of hope. But it will be equally incumbent on the well to exend their notion of the human and of the city of man, so that it includes these first thrusts of the sick.

In our darkness there are many other points that can conquer the endless. These points will emerge with greater clarity if the darkness is seen as common to the sick and the well, and not seen patronizingly from the outside, from the glory of our hygienic, microbe-free light.

Chapter 4

Hopelessness and Confusion

Confusion is a necessary part of the human but when it passes beyond a certain degree, it tends toward panic and hopelessness.

The essence of this confusion in the ill is that people, feelings, and things which should have their own absolute

identities, limits, boundaries, begin to dissolve and lose them-
selves in each other. Instead of helping to create and liberate
each other their movement is toward blurring and destroy-
ing each other.

There is no more powerful or destructive a weapon than
the creation of this kind of confusion in and among people.

The most painful forms of hopelessness and entrapment in
mental illness come from a set of psychic experiences that
we can bring together under the name of *confusion*.

We say of the sick: they are confused. And this is a truth
that could not be more true. But in order that we may remain faithful to the main task we have set ourselves, we
must avoid a patronizing attitude. Let us locate confusion
within the city of man, and not outside. For the confusion
of the sick is the confusion of man.

In his lifetime each human being must negotiate the straits
between the Scylla of confusion and the Charybdis of extreme forms of clarity. Each brings its form of distress.

On the one hand confusion *does* lie at the heart of mental
illness. There *are* forms of confusion that are unquestionable
enemies of the human spirit. We must discover and analyze
the pathological, the sick, inhuman forms of confusion, the
forms that have no rights in the city of man and that should
be attacked by all the arts and sciences. And it will be good
to recognize clearly those points at which we ourselves introduce these inhuman forms of confusion into the human
atmosphere, literally using them as weapons, terribly destructive weapons, against other human beings.

On the other hand there are the diseased forms of clarity
which must be kept constantly in mind if we are not to
deal too simplistically with this question of confusion. We
must be forewarned against certain reachings toward clarity
and certainty that are inhuman and dangerous, themselves
as severe forms of illness and hopelessness as the very confusion they fight.

There is the man who needs certainty in everything and
constantly strives to eliminate possibility. He cannot deal
with possibility by simply letting it be. He does actually say
to himself: there *might* be a Communist under the table.
He does actually look. He is now looking. He does not in
this case find the Communist but that proves nothing. For
it still remains true that there may have been a Communist
under the table. He will spot a number of tables during the

day, all to be carefully investigated. You can never be too sure.

We may smile at this character, yet he is only following a bent toward clarity and the absolute elimination of possibility that seems to be on the increase among us, though it tries to take more socially acceptable forms than looking under tables. With the widespread collapse of our belief in an order of providence it should have been quite expected that men should have tensely adopted every manner and means to eliminate possibility on their own hook. Control and calculation are good things, but absolute control and precaution are a hopeless, exhausting venture that is doomed to failure. Now and then the human race stands appalled at the sudden intervention of possibility, readjusts itself to that kind of world, and tries to go on. That is what happened with the assassination at Dallas in 1963, where evil and the irrational and the merely possible erupted into the world of calculation and control. There was the sense of an unknown horror breaking in upon the expected and breaking the human heart with tears.

What happened there to us is what happens to the sick. The difference is that they suffer more surprises and more eruptions into the world of *their* expected. They expect more, and are therefore hurt more; they expect less, and are therefore more taken by surprise.

Over against the terror of confusion, therefore, there is the search for an impossible control and clarity. Thus, while we now deal with the hopelessness that comes from confusion, we will in our next chapter discuss what I call the absolutizing spirit, the spirit that abides nothing ambivalent, nothing confused, nothing conflictual; it will demand absolute feelings, absolute clarity, absolute thoughts, absolute actions. It has the absolute vocation of rescuing human beings out of the frying pan of confusion into the fire of the absolutized. It is the common denominator of all the hopeless projects of the human race.

That being said, we must now look at the terror of the confusion of the sick and our human confusion. We will attempt a series of successive explorations into the nature of this monster.

I

There are a few things, first of all, that confusion is *not*.

Confusion does *not* mean that such contraries as dependence and independence, passivity and action, are present
together, for why should they not co-exist without confusion?
Nor does it mean that contradictories like good and evil
are there in co-existence, for that, too, can happen in perfect
clarity. The both/and of many contraries can co-exist in a
creative relationship, and the mature spirit can tolerate it.
Indeed, human beings can also to their profit endure the
warfare of good and evil.

Confusion is not identical with conflict. It goes a step
further and is worse than conflict. It may include all the
problems inherent in conflict, but no conflict of any kind,
no matter how severe, and no matter what the quarrel between opposites or between good and evil, has ever of itself
defined mental illness. The different or added element in
mental illness is confusion. And it always seems to involve
an intermixing of things, a running into each other, that is
destructive rather than creative.

This confusion of the ill is no mere intellectual confusion,
in which ideas are not quite straightened out. Their confusion is far more existential and painful than that. For their
confusion occurs right at the center of their own identity
and their own most basic feelings. It is as actual as one
person getting inextricably entangled in the existence of another, to the point of the psychic loss of the self, as actual
as love and hate getting into and spoiling each other. It is
deeply related to the intolerable state called hopelessness.

By confusion, then, I mean that kind of situation, in the
real or the psychological order, where elements so coexist
and intermix that they blur or distort or destroy each other's
identity. Where *A* is becoming confused with *B*, they are
both evaporating.

It is difficult to think of anything more conducive to despair and hopelessness than the deep and continuing confusion of the sick. How should they handle confusion? By
doing something about it? By doing something about what?
For in his confusion the sufferer cannot name the question,
much less answer it. Since this is the fundamental character
of confusion, its capacity to render human beings helpless
and impotent is obvious.

It is hard for us to understand that the sick do not know
what is the matter with them. People hunger for exact and
simplistic explanations of mental illness and feel they are
themselves threatened if the explanations are not there in

full and consoling panoply. Confronted with uncertainty they demand simplicity, not yet knowing that this very demand has made other people ill. For example, they demand that confusion have no rights, that a purely moral reason be able to explain illness away. They forget that, though their heroism in facing and accepting the sinner, even to the point of pretentiousness, may be endless, their courage in facing the fact of mental illness is minimal. The religious man may boast of welcoming a sinner at a cocktail party yet remain unashamed that his knees tremble in the presence of the mentally ill. It is the simplest of proofs that we fear confusion more than evil. It is, in fantasy, that great a monster.

So there is the first fact about confusion. The mentally ill do not know what is the matter with them. Freud gives his version of this kind of ignorance in the sick. He gives us a picture of a consciousness and an unconscious that are bringing confusing influences to bear on the same act and that are simply not on talking terms. Freud puts it clearly:

> The pathogenic conflict in a neurotic must not be confounded with a normal struggle between conflicting impulses all of which are in the same mental field. It is a battle between two forces of which one has succeeded in coming to the level of the preconscious and conscious part of the mind, while the other has been confined on the unconscious level. That is why the conflict can never have a final outcome one way or the other; the antagonists meet each other as little as the whale and the polar bear in the well known story. An effective decision can be reached only when they confront each other on the same ground. And, in my opinion, to accomplish this is the sole task of the treatment.[1]

No, nothing is more conducive to despair than a deep and continuing confusion that also contains the basic element of the unknown. Human beings seem to prefer any situation to the forms of confusion we now begin to discuss.

Let us suppose that in a given case there is an unconscious sense of guilt, real or imagined. Let us further suppose that its gnawing quality, in addition to being unknown, is powerful and endless. This is the haunting confusion that Franz Kafka portrays in *The Castle* and *The Trial*. The human being who is so weighed down with confusion will often prefer to commit a clear crime, a definite robbery, or rape, or act of arson—an act, at any rate, that will reduce the confusion to definiteness. Up to that moment the sense of something wrong had been getting into every thought and act, to blur it, spoil it, distort it; now the wrong seems to be only where it has been placed, in this specific act or crime where the human spirit has a fighting chance. Man prefers at all costs to create his own definite terms rather than deal with a heightened degree of confusion.

II

Let us widen our search for a moment before we return to an attempt at a sharper clarification of our own definitions.

Clearly we may call the negative unconscious unveiled by modern psychoanalytic medicine the place of confusion. It is often enough referred to as the place where there is only "eternity," where there is no time, no contradictories, no contraries, no boundaries. Everything in it can be confused with everything else. That is one reason why the thought of the ill, who are under the domination of the unconscious, is so often arbitrarily symbolic. One thing can suggest or symbolize countless others, even though there is no actual relation between them. We would say that in them the darndest, most ornery things become connected. In "The Wasteland" T. S. Eliot makes the criticism of our civilization that "nothing connects with nothing," to the point of general intellectual fragmentation. It is just as serious a matter, however, when everything connects with everything, when everything runs into everything else.

We also know enough about that mysterious disease called schizophrenia to be able to say that it is deeply vulnerable to the panics that come from the confusion we are beginning to explore. One way of describing schizophrenia is this: a few rigid and absolute categories are set up in the mind to describe and handle reality; when reality is widened, when life introduces some new element, the schizophrenic is unable to reconstruct his managing concepts to the point of adjustment; the resulting confusion will be proportionate to the amount of unassimilated material from the world and people that thus accumulates. Reality becomes a place of confusion and is to be avoided.

Paul Schilder's theories on the common elements in all mental illness also help us understand confusion. He sees two basic confusions in mental illness: the sick cannot inte-

grate the parts of any situation, with the result that the
parts remain so many scattered members and never form a
whole; or they cannot break a whole down into its parts.[2]
The parts would then, I take it, remain undifferentiated and
confused. The whole remains an undifferentiated absolute.
It is this confusing inability to differentiate that I would
like to examine further.

To the degree that the parts of wholes remain undifferentiated, they run into each other and destroy each other's
identity. This can occur in the most multifarious and astonishing ways. Take the hypothetical whole or unity called
passivity, which has such meanings as being passive, not
being active, being receptive or on the receiving end, not
doing anything, or being helpless. For the mentally ill, unfortunately, this unity remains undifferentiated.

> Now I wish to go to bed and to sleep,
> or I wish to listen to a musical concert,
> or I omit a task which is a fundamental duty in life,
> or I receive a gift,
> or take help.

The ill perceive each of these things as one and the same
thing. Whether good or bad, human or inhuman, of slight
or great resemblance, they are linked together as passivity.
The absoluteness of the unitary thinking triumphs. The
kind of imagination used here is blurred and blurring, is
not up to the task of mastering and preserving the sharp,
differentiating edges of things. The unities that are operative,
in this case *passivity*, act like so many steaming clouds of
fog that rise or descend to wipe out the outlines of trees,
houses and hills in a landscape. The passivity of going to
a concert will reproduce in the sick the same reverberations as the passivity of omitting a fundamental task.

One of the simplest and noblest acts of the human mind
and imagination is to be able to discern, to pronounce that
this is this, that is that, and this is not that. It may be
simple, yet it is also the task of a lifetime to learn, to break
down identifications between this and that.

This power to differentiate is no mere "mental" gift. Psychologists are now able to describe with increasing precision
the various affective forces that operate in the unconscious
and either do not care or do not know how to differentiate.
Our wishes, especially where they are not known to us, can
be remarkably competent in breaking down the edges of

things and in creating confusion. They are no respecters of persons! We can be so anxious to see a particular person that we can make a hundred people look like him or her.

Most important of all, we can be so preoccupied with the past that we break down the edges and identities of each thing in contemporary reality and make it all look like the past. Time is a unified continuum in anybody's lifetime, but we destroy its individual units when we make past and present run into each other. It is wonderful to be able to say: that is past, this is new. We have not nearly explored the sentence of Christ: Behold, I make all things new.

The present is not the past. That sentence could not be clearer on the surface or more obscure in its depths. If it were truly grasped, and grasped affectively, there would be no mental illness among adults. But the past keeps running in upon us, obscuring and even obliterating the freshness and newness of everything we do.

I now repeat our generalization.

Pathological confusion, the confusion in illness, always involves a relationship within whose terms an affective act of blurring, or of distortion, or of spoiling, or of destruction is going on. These processes often involve a back and forth; *A* is destroying the clarity and identity of *B*, *B* is doing the same to *A*. When played between persons, the game is deadly; it can become a battle to the death.

We have already had an extended taste of this process in discussing the way in which hopelessness can enter the very guts of hope, bringing it to the point where hope is no longer distinguishable from hopelessness. As long as we can keep them at all separated we have a chance; if we can go further and keep them at once separated and creatively related, we can accomplish great things; the trouble starts when they begin to contaminate each other and cannot be differentiated. When they do, there remains only some further unnameable kind of hope that commands the struggle and the resistance called waiting. Hope shares at least this much with confusion: it cannot see; but it can wait.

III

If this confusion can occur between hope and hopelessness, it can also occur between many other pairs. It can also occur between people.

Here we can begin with that broad human area in which

ordinary wishes and feelings tend to lose their identity and to become confused with the wishes and feelings of other people. The confusion can be partial or complete, ten percent or a hundred.

Some fraction characterizes all of us, without a possible exception. (Let us be charitable and say a ten percent level of confusion is "normal.") Social life requires a solid degree of conformity, but there comes a point where confusion begins: whose feelings and wishes are present in me, my own or another's. I begin not to be able to distinguish. A lady from the suburbs describes the painful but lesser degrees of the problem:

> Out here in this split-level or ranch type society, you've got to belong to the group. If you don't belong to the group, you're treated as if you have typhoid and their children won't play with your children. That means you have to like what they like and do as they do. You're not even supposed to entertain friends they don't know, unless you invite them in to be introduced. Lord help you if they catch you reading a book by somebody they never heard of, like Dylan Thomas. That means you're a freak, or maybe a Communist. It's not like that in the city. That's why I can't wait to get back there.[3]

That is bad enough. At a further point of intensity the confusion moves toward the point of fury. We see such a situation in the novel *Arturo's Island* by Elsa Morante. Here is the way one character thinks of his mother:

> When she can't enslave you, she cheers herself with the old tale of the martyred mother and the heartless son. You, of course, can't stand that old tale, and have a good guffaw at it: other tales and other hearts are what you're after . . . So she weeps and gets more boring, older, sadder for herself. Everything around her's soaked with tears. And so, of course, you keep away more than ever. The minute you turn up, she starts accusing you in the most highfalutin Biblical way: the mildest insult is *frightful murderer!* Not a day goes by without her chanting this litany. Maybe she hopes to make you hate yourself with all these accusations, to rob you and set herself up as a gloomy usurper of all your glory and your pride. Wherever you escape to—

miles away into town—you can't escape that everlasting parasite, her *love*. Suppose you hear thunder in the sky, or it starts raining, you can just swear that at the precise moment she'll be in a state of despair at home in the old hovel. *He'll get wet, he'll catch cold, he'll be sneezing* . . . But if the sky clears, you can be perfectly certain she'll be moaning: the dear, now that it's fine that wretch won't set foot inside the house before nightfall . . .

No natural or historical event means anything to her except in relation to you—and so, the whole of creation threatens to turn into a cage. That's what she wants, that's all that *love* of her dreams of. What she'd really like would be to keep you always prisoner, the way you were when she was pregnant. And when you run away, she tries to pull you back from afar, to set her stamp on the whole of your world . . .[4]

Now the battle is on in earnest. Between the events described in these examples and other extreme situations there is every manner of degree. But there is always a battle, a battle between human beings. The other human being may not be there. He or she may even be dead; but the past and the dead are incorporated into the sufferer, and the desperate battle for one's own feelings and wishes goes on.

For the time being it is a losing battle. But if the sufferer meets the right and liberating relationship, the situation is at most points reversible. Fortunately there are innumerable points of peace as well as battle in our atmosphere. That is one great desideratum for the sick, to find a point of pause or rest or peace in a person who does not strike back, who brings the endless battle to an at least temporary halt. The religious representation of this relationship is contained preeminently in the image of Christ.

We know that human feeling and wishing can be transferred to another person, or stolen by another, or lost through a mutual conspiracy with another to the extent that confusion is complete: is this my thought or feeling, or does it belong to another? A woman comes up to me in a hospital and says: "Father, I am in agony, I have no identity." This is agony, so to melt one's thoughts, wishes, feelings, and self into those of others that one completely loses the taste of self. If we can say it without raising any moral implications for the sick, I think that this is the psychic parallel of the terror of the loss of the soul. It is *not* the loss of the soul;

in fact, the sickness may ironically turn out to be salvation, but it causes reverberations similar to the terror of this loss.

IV

Our exploration is leading us to the conclusion that there must be a vast difference between the creative and the destructive ways in which human beings share and fuse their identities, thoughts, feelings, wishes. It is the way they share them that leads to health and peace, or to various forms of apathy, or to confusion and illness.

At any rate the blessing or the problem is going to be people—and the way they relate—creatively or in destructive confusion.

First of all, the issue will always be people, and the issue of illness will always occur whenever there are people. The place may matter, but need not matter too much. "I have frequently cited a group of Scotch-Canadian woodsmen," Dr. Kubie says, "who enjoyed economic and physical security and lived a physically challenging and toughening existence, in comfortable seclusion and yet with ready access to others. During a period of seven weeks in which I lived in the midst of two such families, I was consulted professionally by every member of both families. Not only was it evident that the neurotic process was universal in the group but even more impressive was the fact that the quality of their neuroses was indistinguishable from that which challenged me daily in my private office and in the psychiatric outpatient clinic of a general hospital in New York, the origins of whose patients were predominantly Italian, Jewish, and Latin-American." [5]

It will indeed always be people, for good or bad. I was having a cup of coffee with a strappingly healthy young man at St. Elizabeth's Hospital one day and complained that it was a very bad day, as it most certainly was. Whereupon he began to make me blush for my vocation by giving me the following sermon:

"Father, when the Lord sends me a bad day, I take it and don't complain. When he sends me a good day, I take it for what it is. There's just no use complaining." There was a pause, and then he burst out angrily, "The one thing I can't stand is people."

It is indeed people, and people coming together, with straightness or confusion.

Where there is maturity in and love between two people, there is no confusion. There are closeness, strong ties, a mixing without confusion of personalities, feelings, wishes. Ideally they feel for each other and they wish with each other. So far as we can judge, the reason such closeness is possible without confusion is that each is an independently existing person. *A* knows that he is *A*, with all his differentiations, and *B* knows she is *B*, with all her differentiations. There is no absolute in the middle which would melt them both down. There is self-acceptance and a minimum of envy. They may and indeed do have common feelings, but each also knows that the common feeling is his or her feeling, a genuine, internally possessed feeling. The same is true for their wishes when they are common, close, and united; they may have a common wish to spend a day in the country, but the wish is also separately and genuinely present in each. There is a degree of confidence in their separate identities which gives them a certain ease in allowing a close relationship to grow. Therefore they know that love will not mean suffocation or death. The way it works is not that two half human beings unite to form a single person, but that two whole human beings form one single, unified relation in which both grow even more. They know how to let be and how to let go.

Such is the ideal. Intermediate between this ideal and the extreme situations of mental illness where all is battle and confusion, there are, of course, all shades of grey area in which most people do reasonably well and reasonably badly at life in the city of man. (They manage to fight off the advertisements that urge them to gnostic perfection, to the perfect serenity that comes with an odorless body and the perfect belonging that is given to those who think young.) What happens at the other pole, where illness grows, has extraordinary surface resemblances with our ideal; the differences seem small; in reality they are decisive and enormous.

For the ill, there is not only closeness, relating, mixing, but confusion has also entered every part of the picture. It tries to grow and take over. As it does, it produces impotence and hopelessness. Let us look at a common clinical version of what can happen.

Because neither *A* nor *B* can take care of himself and because neither wishes to be involved in the public order, they begin to feed on each other. They desperately and dependently need to be related to each other. Any suggestion that they are in any way unrelated is catastrophic. If either keeps anything private it is taken as a threat by the other. *A* completely invades the privacy of *B* and vice-versa. There is an ontological confusion in the way they act toward each other. *A* is living in the midst of *B* and cannot stay out. *A* is literally spoiling *B,* and *B* is doing the same to *A.* Now neither can find his own existence: on the one hand, *A's* has been thrown into the existence of *B;* and on the other hand *A's* has been invaded by *B's.* In panic they are trying to secure themselves and save themselves in life by lives of clinging and invasion.

In such displacements the sick really lose the sense of existing in themselves. The schizophrenic seems literally to feel that he is part of someone else, in the pejorative sense that there is contamination of his being by someone else. He never has an experience of wholeness, that is, of just plain being himself and no one else. One key to understanding the sick, therefore, is to understand that they do not feel free and that they are not free with the ordinary fraction of real freedom and autonomy which the well have. Everything is or seems a back-and-forth battle with somebody who will not let go, or let them be, or, literally, let them be born as separate entities.

This kind of closeness leads to hatred. For neither will let the other be or help him become his differentiated self. What they should do is take a chance in this direction and now and then let the other be; they should stop invading, stop exploring; they should master their fascination with the private. They must struggle to understand that their "mutual" loves and invasions are producing hatred and distance. Now the closeness becomes hateful and produces distance; but the distance, any kind of distance, becomes frightening and redoubles the need of closeness. Two people have literally run into each other, in confusion. The closeness becomes absolute, the separate people nothing.

Where lives and thoughts and feelings and wishes thus press in on each other, they do so in battle and confusion, each element gradually losing its identity. The battle and confusion contract all the elements involved and constrict the vision of the range of reality. It is hardly necessary to indicate the difference between this kind of life and the life of hope and imagination. These two liberate things and enlarge reality, whereas confusion contracts and entangles everything it touches, and moves toward helplessness.

Hope and the imagination create freedom; confusion creates traps. Hope and the imagination widen possibility; confusion shrinks it.

We can now circle back to the basic confusion that occurs in the individual act or wish or emotional experience. That, surely, is where the trouble lies. If life were an abstraction it would be no problem. But life is composed of nothing save actual moments and actual feelings. The problem is always in the actual moment or actual feeling, and the point or place of confusion is going to be there. The ill can always find the most spiritual, otherworldly reasons for thinking that the problem must lie elsewhere; but that solution is a defense. The trouble, whether we like it or not, always lies in the actual. Confusion will always be located in an actual experience.

The sick want to fly to eternity and say that *their* questions lie there and not in time, *their* troubles are "spiritual" and not actual, *their* troubles and confusion lie with God and not with men. They deny that the issue can be located in the moment that has just passed or the person they have just met. It is for this reason that the sick often prefer to rush to a priest rather than a doctor: their problem is "spiritual" if it needs a priest; it is, therefore, not actual; it does not need an actual examination of the issues at stake. It is a vast relief to decide that the question is moral, a question of guilt, a question of values. It is anything but a question of the actual and what goes on right now between me and him or her.

The hate gets into the love: in the actual moment that is what happens to the ill and, in their difficult moments, to the well. Neither the hate nor the love are generalized; an actual bit of hate gets into an actual bit of love.[6] There is no doubt about what happens. In his unconscious a man says to or about someone he loves: "I hate you," or "I resent what you just did," or "I have nothing but contempt for a certain part of you." This may be, or may have been, a perfectly reasonable and understandable *part* of his reaction and attitude, but many people in a close relationship find it an intolerable thought that threatens to shake their universe. The repression or denial they now resort to (anathema on the very idea that I a Christian or a dearly loved child or a

conscientious parent should have negative thoughts toward
my best friend, my parents or my son) produces an effect
that is even worse. The negative thought enters the unconscious, an underground that does not discriminate, and remains operative for all that it has been cast out. No re-
specter of the boundaries, it begins to operate everywhere.
When isolated and identifiable, hate is all right and has a
definite job to do; but now it enters everything and spoils
everything; above all, it contaminates or seems to contaminate our attempts at love.

As a result of this confusion three things happen to the sick
person:

He cannot love with clarity;

He cannot hate with clarity;

He now thinks totally of himself as *one who hates, one
who destroys,* one whose love will do harm.

At stake here are the fundamental few clarities that seem
—like bread, wine, water, air—to be necessities of human
life. There are a certain few clarities a human being must
have, or perish. There are a few forms of darkness that it is
impossible, beyond a certain degree, to sustain. One clarity
which we must to some degree have is that which distinguishes love from hate. For the healing of illness this
seems to me to be much more important than that more
usual dictum: love or perish.

Everyone experiences something of this confusion, or
doubt, or hesitation; the danger is that it not be controlled,
that it go too far. When it goes too far, when the core of
love becomes infected and confused in substance by its
opposite, we must imagine the sick making desperate efforts
to vomit out the source of the confusion, to purify the love,
to get it to work. We must imagine that this point where the
human positive feelings are so infected, or seem to be infected, is a point of profoundest psychological darkness.

As he makes his great pilgrimage through *The Divine
Comedy* Dante is constantly discoursing with Virgil on light
and darkness, since light is the life of the soul as darkness is
its enemy. The growth of light sparkles and glows everywhere
through the poem, and in every form. And there are many
studies of their vast journey through the regions of purification. In the Purgatorio they are anxious to be on their way,
even though it is sundown. Sordello, the fellow Mantuan
whom they have met, warns them that it is impossible, and it
develops that he is talking not so much of a physical as of a

psychological impossibility. There are forms of darkness that
immobilize the will.

> "What is it you say?" my guide asked. "If one sought
>   to climb at night, would others block his way?
>   Or would he simply find that he could not?"
> "Once the sun sets," that noble soul replied,
>   "you would not cross this line"—and ran his finger
>   across the ground between him and my Guide.
> "Nor is there anything to block the ascent
>   except the shades of night; they of themselves
>   suffice to sap the will of the most fervent."

We must try to calculate what effect this darkness can have,
to what extent it can immobilize a man when it takes the
form of negative feelings and gets so deep into the place of
love that they cannot be sorted out. I have suggested earlier
that the ideal goal of every neurosis, over against the contrary workings of imagination and hope, is that there should
be no thoughts, wishes or feelings. Hope and imagination
have the goal of unlimited expansion; now we are coming at
last to the opposite goal of absolute contraction. Arieti gives
us a picture of what can happen at this point. We may smile
at the kind of man he describes, but after all it is only ourselves written out in large letters.

Let us think with him of this catatonic patient standing
rigidly immobilized in the middle of a room, and let us add
our own guesses as to what goes on at the interior of this
man. He cannot move forward or backward, to the right or
to the left. He cannot move arm or leg or eye or tongue. Such
is his imagined responsibility and such the possible harm he
might do should he but breathe, that he cannot calculate the
consequences of anything he might do. He had best not
imagine or feel or think, for terror of what might come of it.
A thought might push the button to destroy the world. At
all costs that must be prevented, and it can only be prevented
by immobility. He will not act because vast possibility has inserted itself into his action. There is only one thing he will
let himself do, seeing that it is the only thing that is in accord
with this confused image of his love, and that is to do harm
to himself, to commit suicide. In the face of these contaminated images, he decides that suicide is his only possible
point of freedom and expansion. With this exception, his
hope and the imagination have reached a pinpoint of constriction and entrapment. Anything else that is positive or

creative, since it is confused and contaminated at its source, involves an immediate interior act of cancellation. So he must stand in the exact center of that room, without blinking an eye.

That is one of the final pictures of what we mean by confusion.

V

Mental illness occurs only in society, not apart from it. The social atmosphere of ideas and affectivity that helps to generate illness and confusion must never slip from our sight. There are great generating forces and there are powerful methods of spewing confusion into the air. But we must face the fact that society is not an abstraction: we are society; it is ourselves who do the spewing.

The ability to create confusion is one of the most destructive weapons one human being can use against another. The use of this weapon can be professional and universal; it is sadistic; it is always seeking the amateur as its victim. How does it work? That is to say, how do *we* do it?

There have been a number of serious studies of the nature and use of one version of this weapon, that of the "double bind." Dr. John H. Weakland describes the double-bind situation as "that of one person giving another two related but contradictory or incongruent messages, presenting conflicting injunctions of importance, while also acting to forestall escape and to inhibit notice and comment on the inconsistency by the 'victim.' "[7]

In still simpler language, we may say that the double bind describes a situation in which someone who has a position of indispensable power or advantage is creating confusion in someone who is weaker; the binder is doing something negative to the victim under the guise of the positive. The victim is bound inwardly through confusion and in helplessness to the binder, who strikes and makes it impossible to strike back.

1. The binder is saying to the victim:

"You know how much I love you, and how much I do all things for your good."

But his act of "love" is accompanied by unmistakable gestures and intonations of hostility.

And the victim is in such a state of dependence or need in relation to the binder that he cannot even afford to let the second part of the message enter his consciousness; or if he does, he cannot act properly upon the awareness. He is a child in the presence of parents who are absolutely essential to his life; or a dull person in the presence of a sharp mind; or a pious person in the presence of a priest who clearly could never do evil. He is in the presence of a contemptible misuse of power.

2. Or, someone says:

"I need you badly, you must work with me.

"But I will also show you in a thousand ways that you are completely unnecessary.

"And so important am I to you that you will not be able to discern the contradiction or have the courage to reveal my truth to me. For I am the master of all you survey. You need me."

3. Or, there are all the little moments of created confusion in life, where we are all guilty every day. We say to someone:

"You want that window closed, don't you?"

It must not seem to be our wish, but the other's. If he dare express his wish, he can anticipate our reply:

"Oh come on. Every time I say *anything* you get annoyed. Do, do close the damned window."

So he pretends our wish is his.

What becomes clear from even so few examples is that in all such cases the one using power in this way is, in reality, the weaker and the more dependent. He *must* bind the other party to him. He does this by using confusion as a deadly weapon. He stings his victim into helplessness. He takes away hope.

The sick are especially vulnerable to such tactics because of their impression that they have an absolute need. If they were free, they would become aware of the tactic of confusion in a flash. The image of hope for them is that they should come into the presence of adults who are not dependent on them, who will not bind them, who will leave them free. The spiritual and emotional freedom extended by a mature person will help to free their minds of confusion.

This, then, is that efficient instrument of confusion, the double bind. We shall gain victory over it only as we become increasingly conscious of its structures and intentions and increasingly aware of the way it is used against us and by us, especially *by us.*

For no one is exempt from its use, not even the best or the holiest of people. Its very structures lead to deliberate or accidental use by the best and the holiest of people, since they are least vulnerable to the charge of using it. Its very nature, like Satan, is to appear under the guise of an angel of light. Who would question an angel!

Religious groups should be especially conscious of the temptation to use and exploit contradictory messages, for people incline to receive these messages with reverence and to accept the painful confusion that goes with them. That religious groups can—and often do—give contradictory messages and prevent discovery or response we must unhesitatingly admit. For example, they can tell their members, as many religious orders do, that they must accomplish great and daring and adventurous things for God; but simultaneously and subtly, they can—and often do—threaten those same members with the direst consequences if they show any initiative or imagination in the pursuit of these goals. In or out of religion this is a contemptible procedure, and the simplest thing to say about it is that it should stop. It is one cause of apathy and hopelessness in many very good people.

VI

This leads us to our further question: What happens when responding and not responding to a situation, or wishing and not wishing, get caught up confusedly in a single act, or in an attempt to act?

I am about to have dinner. Shall I enjoy it? Or shall I take it and not enjoy it? That is to say, shall I have it and not have it?

I am in love. Shall I really love this person?

Whoever first taught human beings to ask such questions created crises of confusion that did not exist before the questions were asked.

And at this point we come to a kind of crisis in our contemporary thinking, all the way from the order of the psychic to that of the political. It involves defining the nature of absolutes in human thought, and deciding who shall run off with the prize.

Before turning to the crisis, let me put forth a paradox: Every chapter of this book will attack some absolute that has invaded the forms of human thinking, feeling, wishing. Yet each will with equal firmness defend the ideal of thinking absolutely, feeling and wishing absolutely, clearly, firmly, without block, check, confusion, or inhibition.

There are many absolutists in our midst who proclaim that they alone can teach men really to think and feel absolutely, with clarity and without confusion. They wish to save us through absolutisms. The question is: Can we wish absolutely without the perpetual and destructive wishing of absolutes. These are the two poles I wish to study.

I want to attack the invasion of absolutes into the human order.

I want to defend the human order as the only order in which we can wish absolutely. *I want to defend absolute wishing, but not the wishing of absolutes.*

I ask the patience of the reader as this argument develops many times in many ways.

It is interesting to recall, for example, that during the election campaign of 1960 John F. Kennedy was criticized for wanting to be president while many endorsed one of Kennedy's rivals for the Democratic nomination as too modest, too fine a person really to want with all his heart to be president. Apparently it was wrong to have an unabashed, absolute wish, one that did not pretend to be indifferent and that did not have to be coy.

At this juncture, we reach the line of demarcation between a healthy and unhealthy emotional life as well as the difference between a true and a false spirituality. There is the supposition in a certain kind of spirituality that no object or person or situation may be yielded to completely and absolutely, that the emotional and spiritual life of man must always be inhibited, always on its guard, always on the alert. It is clear how closely this way of talking resembles some parts of the vocabulary of Christian asceticism—and therein lies its spacious strength.

The truth is that no object, person, or situation, when seen objectively according to both the fullness and the limitations of its reality, needs any inhibition in the hope for it or the response to it, as long as the hope and the response is for exactly what each is. It is dangerous for human beings that we ask them to half respond to the world. It would be akin to the following description of child-training among the Balinese.

From about five or six months of age, and steadily becoming more definite as the child grows older, the mother continually tantalizes and teases the child. She stimulates him to show emotion, love or desire, jealousy or anger, and then turns away, as the child in rising

passion ragingly and despairingly implores emotional
response from her. This discouragement of the interpersonal emotion is systematic. The child never attains
a climax of emotional response, and the resulting withdrawal is seen in a lack of responsiveness which is
established by the age of three or four. The relationship
to people remains distant, wary of the expression of too
much feeling.[8]

The full response to a thing, correctly perceived in its
reality, is satisfying and gets the matter done with (or establishes the hope of its repetition). An inhibited response,
an impoverishing response, the Balinese system, produces
withdrawal or endless ineffective repetitions of the act. Such a
response has nothing to do with Christianity. Certainly it requires a good deal of discipline and education to establish
the reality of things and to act accordingly, but this is totally
different from the pernicious assumption that, once established, the reality is not to be given the response it demands.
Such an assumption, once it is deeply internalized, causes
illness. It produces stunted human beings. At the very least
it means the death of all spontaneity. Unfortunately, the
assumption has an important place in our atmosphere of ideas.
It involves a destructive confusion of wishing and not wishing.

How pernicious in all its effects this assumption has been
will not be fully clear until the Last Judgment, though one
can calculate pretty accurately without that final evidence.

It will probably prove to have been particularly pernicious
to religious people who have been victims of similar distortions of a truly Christian ascetical theology. This will be true
for a large number of men and women in the formally
religious life of the Church, seminarians, priests, nuns, who
somehow or other have convinced themselves that they may
not yield to complete interest in their studies, may not have
real and strong friendships, may not really enjoy food,
may never "let themselves go" according to the demands of
reality. Such people are not in the least helped toward God
by these attitudes and inhibitions; indeed the very reverse is
true, for such an inhibiting pattern affects the very core of the
religious life. It reduces the capacity in good men and
women to hope.

*Such inhibitions introduce an element of hopelessness into
the very structure of hope, and an element of nonwishing*

into the very structure of wishing. There is nothing more confusing than such an addition to conflict, especially when it is nurtured by superficial resemblances to Christian asceticism. The negative, disciplining tradition in asceticism is altogether essential, but at all costs it must be kept out of the positive.

What are some of the important distinctions to be made between realistic, acceptable inhibitions and the kind of inhibition that is neurotic and contaminates our hope?

I think that the most important distinction is the following. The realistic inhibition is usually a clear dictum of a mature consciousness and conscience, a dictum that can be specifically located in its object. There is no doubt about its absoluteness and strength. It says: thou shalt not do this—and it means it. Such a dictum of the conscience can be welcomed as a first cousin to positive wishing, matching the latter in its precision, definiteness, clarity. Something else is true of it. By denying our wishes in certain areas it leaves the rest of our interior and exterior world open for uninhibited wishing and acting. In fact it reinforces the latter. It increases the possibility that our positive wishes be absolute. These wishes need no defense.

The neurotic inhibition of hopes and wishes is altogether different. A real inhibition or prohibition, as we have seen, can be sorted out and exactly identified. It leaves the rest of the world to wishing and acting. Therefore it will never do psychological or spiritual harm. It does not contaminate or spoil or blur anything else by its own negativity. It keeps to its place. The operation of neurotic inhibition is entirely the reverse. Its ambition is to become absolute. It does not take over a determined, unquestioned, locatable and limited province for its own action. Instead, it takes over an ever-widening area of hoping, wishing, and movement toward goals, contaminating these by its presence. It establishes a mixed state of wishing and nonwishing, hope and hopelessness, movement and nonmovement toward goals, in such a way that it becomes increasingly difficult to extricate any one of the members of these pairs from the other. I want to have dinner and not have it. This means the introduction of essential conflict not between good and bad, where it would belong, but right at the heart of the good and the real, where it has no place. The more intense degrees of hopelessness produced by such confusion are the special and unique kinds of hopelessness that characterize the pain of mental illness.

So much for absolute wishing. It is an ideal to be aimed at.

But there is all the difference in the world between it and absolutism, between the spontaneity and freedom of absolute wishing and the rigidities and hopelessness of *the absolutizing spirit*. We can also call the latter the generator of the hopeless project. Let us have a look at the monster.

Chapter 5

The Absolutizing Instinct

Though we have been dealing with it from the beginning the following chapter is a more formal and explicit study of the absolutizing instinct.

The fight against this instinct can become a meeting ground for understanding and collaboration between religion and the new mental sciences.

The instinct's whole drive is to make absolutes out of everything it touches and to pour floods of fantasy into the world about it. It is the father of all hopeless projects and of hopelessness. It is the enemy of the human and of hope.

By the absolutizing instinct, I mean something very literal and nothing complicated. I mean the instinct in human beings that tends to absolutize everything, to make an absolute out of everything it touches. I ask indulgence if for the moment I let the matter of an exact definition go at that, and allow a fuller statement to emerge as this instinct reveals its own nature by marching with its habitual magnificence into its many concrete forms. It will not be shy about revealing itself. For it is never subtle, but always loud and boisterous, always magnificently present on the scene. It is also a world of false hope which counterfeits the reality of hope.

The best way of understanding the absolutizing instinct is to look at the world through its own glasses. How does it see things when it absolutizes?

I have just finished talking and walking with a mental patient, and what happened was an instructive example of how those glasses work.

Most of us would call this patient not perhaps a giant but certainly very, very big. I think he was about six-feet-eight.

As we talked and walked in one direction, another man, about five-feet-ten, passed us in the other direction.

My friend turned and looked at him in astonishment and fear.

"Did you see that giant?" he asked.

"I saw him, but he's no giant," I answered.

"But he is, he's a giant," he insisted.

I threw the comfort back at him that really he was himself much bigger and could easily handle the other man.

"Oh no, I could never handle that giant. I fight like a soldier. I'm a marksman."

I did not try to tell him that he was the victim of an absolutizing imagination, but it certainly made me reflect historically and sadly on the kind and the size of objects that marksmen sometimes see.

Whatever is seen (or wished) as an absolute through the glasses of this instinct receives an enormous discharge of fantasy. The absolutizing instinct magnifies. In its presence each thing loses its true perspective and its true edges. The good becomes the tremendously good, the evil becomes the absolutely evil, the grey becomes the black or white, the complicated, because it is difficult to handle, becomes, in desperation, the completely simple. The small becomes the big.

But above all, everything assumes a greater weight than it has, and becomes a greater burden. I wish to emphasize this quality of weight in everything that comes from the operation of the absolutizing instinct, and I want to forewarn about the burden it makes of everything. The absolutizing instinct is the father of the hopeless and adds that special feeling of weight that hopelessness attaches to everything it touches. It is, in general, the creator of hopeless projects and the creator of idols.

According to the stricter terms of the vocabulary I am using in this book the absolutizing instinct is not really an action of the imagination. Rather, it is a creator of fantasy, distortion, magnification; it is invariably in full and violent operation before it ever meets its object, and by the time it is finished nothing much is left of the object's boundaries or edges or identity. The object has been elevated to the status of a dream and has lost its own name. This instinct is a maker of dreams and does not give a tinker's dam for objects or people.

Let us imagine it at work on a bar of soap. It will magnify, blur and distort and, in the end, there is precious little soap left. The soap has become all the things that the instinct desires: the creator of beauty, the winner of friends, the answer to problems, the sharer of the life of Marilyn Monroe, the giver of sleep and of peace, that which is accompanied by music and life. A powerful stream of fantasy has rushed into—and destroyed—the soap.

Let us imagine it in the presence of the love for a girl. It now declares that it is in love with Love. We can guess the reaction of the girl in the presence of this absolutizing act. She has been elevated to a magnificent status that she knows is false. Her eyes, though blue, are not blueness itself; her hair, though red, has a touch of the carrot; there is a real blackhead on her forehead. The absolutizing instinct has nothing but contempt for her reality. In its presence nothing measures up. And so nothing is wished for.

Let me choose a more solemn form of the way this instinct spews fantasy into the air and adds to the sense of weight in life and death. In fact, I wish to choose death itself.

There is a controversy among religious thinkers concerning the moment of death—which is indeed a critical moment for anyone. Some theologians would make it a numinous, completely critical and absolute moment. At that critical juncture the soul, they say, must choose between the world and God. Notice the increasing projection of unnecessary fantasy into this moment. The issues are enormous, they insist, and must be faced. We may not see what is happening on the deathbed, but something extraordinary is occurring. A special light will be given to all, to see the great issue and to choose. Thus, a moment that is already difficult enough for ordinary human beings becomes completely demanding and even more frightening than the ordinary human reality of death as we see it.

Now suppose that none of this is either true or necessary, and suppose that the moment of complete insight does not come: the thunder does not roll nor do the trumpets blare; angels and devils do not appear to demand a decision one way or the other; then imagine the terror at discovering no terror, no moment of absolute climax. The dying man cannot make the moment divine, because, to put it mildly, he is having enough trouble as it is. But at this moment he is required to become a Dante or a Shakespeare, nothing less.

There is, after all, nothing wrong with dying according to a purely human mode in all its weakness and simplicity. Our decisions have been made innumerable times on the long road of life. Death is but another limited moment, even if it is the last. In the theological struggle to keep absolutes where they belong, Christianity must always remain realistic, even about death, and should refuse to increase its burdens. Therefore, it will not demand a surcharge of fantasy at the very moment when that is least possible. At such a time, nature is so exhausted that its deepest wish is to be passive and to do nothing. There is a place for that kind of wishing, too. A human being, because he is exhausted, is not for that reason without hope. But he will be hopeless if at this moment he knows he *must* do what he cannot—if, that is to say, he must produce a divine flood of fantasy- and decision-making which is completely beyond him.

Many other modes of the operation of this instinct will occur as we move along, but it is already clear that it is a magnifying, and over-ebullient, over-enthusiastic principle, never content to leave anything in its plain human setting. I for one have difficulty in deciding which it is, a completely ridiculous and childish exaggerator of things that always moves toward nonsense—or a distorted, distorting and misdirected part of a powerful movement of the soul toward the absolute. Perhaps it is something of both, with the worst features of both, and it is not necessary to choose between them. Ultimately we will conclude that it is a form of false hope. But before we reach that development in the argument I should like to insert a parenthesis relevant from both the medical and the theological point of view.[1]

II

By introducing the idea of the Absolute into a book on mental illness, I do not intend to compound the already grave difficulties of the sick by making their problems religious in the burdensome sense of that word. There are always zealots who are ready at the slightest mention of such words as religion or the absolute to say, "I told you so: I always knew that the problem of mental illness was religious. If they had kept the law of God they would be well. If they fall down on their knees and make a good confession, they will be cured." Actually, most of the sick should get off their psychological knees.

Ironically enough, this incorrigible use of purely moral

categories to explain mental illness is itself another mode of
the absolutizing instinct and is one of the most persistent
forms of the neurotic need to have certainty and clarity in
everything. Actually we only *seem* to be religious when we
attribute all suffering to some purely rational categories of
the understanding, to moral causes, to justice, to retribution,
to a theory of rewards and punishments. We need not eliminate these ideas from the relations between God and man,
whether the latter be well or sick. But the important thing
is that to impose this exclusive set of rational and absolute
answers is no great compliment to the absoluteness of God
or to the dignity of the final relations between God and man.
(And why must we settle every question!)

I am inclined to call this moral theory absolutely false as
a proposition. It runs counter to our knowledge that even
small children (under a single year) can be grievously sick
mentally. It is, incidentally, ironic that many of the pro-
ponents of this moral proposition are in too much of a hurry
to make an absolute distinction between physical and
mental illness, ascribing the first to misfortune and the
second to sin. (They wish to create the ideal society of the
well.) But science is rapidly associating more and more of
our physical ills with our mental and emotional histories; the
results of analysis might embarrass those holy souls who go
about glorying in their physical ills and denouncing those
whose ills are "mental." As Fenichel says: "Every disease is
'psychosomatic' for no 'somatic' disease is entirely free from
'psychic' influence . . ." [2] That mental illness necessarily involves moral causation seems nothing other than a twentieth-
century form of a Calvinism which would proclaim that the
just are blessed on earth with health and wealth and may
God have mercy on the rest of us. The healthy and the
wealthy do not need mercy.

Here the central issue of the Book of Job is, or should be,
decisive. Job suffers, and greatly, as we all know, so that
his name has come to represent the idea of suffering. His
friends berate him and command him to accept his woes as
given him by a just God for his sins. Job protests and will
not accept so easy a solution. God himself becomes angry
at such counsellors. The one, Job, senses and the other,
God, knows, that such a simplistic solution is a fundamental
attack on the deepest relations between man and God. It
reduces these relations to nothing but recognizable and rational categories, it is an attack on the transcendent mys-

tery of God and is an attempt to reduce the purest religion to a matter of sin and justice. The greater truth is that God wishes to get below and above all the categories of our understanding. He does this, not by crushing man but by purifying all the categories and powers of the pure understanding. Thus the Book of Job is an appeal, not for an irrational theology or for placing God beyond reason (for that is not the question under discusson); rather it is an appeal for recognizing a personal relationship between God and man that is not satisfied by the statements of reason and justice. Justice is a noble form of reason, but it is not enough to explain the mysteries of suffering.

As I understand the fundamental logic of the Book of Job, it runs as follows:

The friends of Job insist that they know the mind of God and insist with Job that his sufferings are a justice meted out to his sins:

> How can a man be just in God's sight,
> Or how can any woman's child be innocent?
> Behold, even the moon is not bright
> and the stars are not clear in his sight.
> How much less man, who is but a maggot,
> The son of man, who is only a worm? [3]

To which Job replies, with a sarcasm that many of the sick, less innocent than he, would deeply appreciate:

> What help you give to the powerless,
> What strength to the feeble arm!
> How you counsel, as though we had no wisdom;
> How profuse is the advice you offer! [4]

Job maintains his innocence and speaks out in unmistakable protest:

> This is my final plea; let the Almighty answer me! [5]

And another friend, ascending higher in his view of suffering, warns that it must be accepted as preventive or medicinal:

> He opens their ears to correction
> And exhorts them to turn back from evil. [6]

Finally, God not only attacks the friends with their glib and rationalistic answers, because they have questioned the innocence of Job; he also attacks the innocent Job for demanding that innocence be untouched or vindicated. God asserts a higher ground than either, his own incomparable wisdom. He does not attack the innocence or justice of Job, but his rationalism, his need for absolute clarity, his self-imposed declaration of innocence. The hypothesis, therefore, is that he attacks the friends of Job and Job himself for their religious rationalism and their absolutizing.

III

The central point I wish to make is that *the new mental sciences and religion can share in this attack on the absolutizing instinct, to the enormous advantage of the ill and the well. Their separate paths can reach the common goal of freeing man from absolutizing forms of thought.*

We often wonder whether these two human fields cannot only act together but really think together. Here, surely, is a large area where they can, in separate but deeply related ways. There are indeed difficult questions. Psychiatry and religion may view differently the nature and the role of the absolute, but they should be able to agree on the role and the nature of the absolutizing instinct.

It is difficult for modern man to "place" the absolute. On the purely intellectual level of settling problems both scientific and literary, minds have inclined to assign the absolute an external, irrelevant and innocuous position in their own universes.

Intellectually, conceptually, we have not been able to work out this question of the relation of the absolute to the world. We cannot understand how it is possible that we ourselves will function with freedom and inwardness, as we must, if we are in any way possessed and moved by the absolute, as past ages insisted that we were. To put these things together, complete inwardness and complete dependence, is still too difficult a dialectical task for us. Nor do we yet see any dialectical, or conceptual, or scientific need of it. The ages that recognized such a need, the argument would run, were not nearly as aware as we of the enormous drives in things and their capacity for inward action and achievement. We are today much more in the presence of absolute things that do not need the absolute. Things seem able to take care of themselves.

My own view of man and of mental illness is built on another kind of dialectic. Proposing that inwardness is *the* great human gift, it will also consistently propose that we cannot have inwardness without being given it, and that this inwardness is always the result of a kind of grace, whether natural or supernatural. If I were to add a study of natural theology (which I will not!), I would talk of a God who does not make things impotent, or annihilate their resources and their identity, by entering so deeply into them. The final test of his powers, as of all healthy human relations, is that he communicates autonomy: he does not destroy but creates by entering in. If, therefore, we really wish to imitate God, let us make men free.

My second point concerning the place of the absolute in our day would skip the intellectual question. I would propose that, just as we tend to deny dependence, so we tend to deny the internal presence of many forms of the absolute in our emotional and passional life. The advance of the medical sciences in our time has accumulated evidence for this extraordinary phenomenon. One set of sciences has tended to make the absolute irrelevant and external to us, at the same time that another set has rediscovered its distorted, disguised and repressed presence on a vast scale in our most inward being in the form of the absolutizing instinct. The absolute breaks into light in many forms, not in any intellectual way but in emotional reverberations that have much to do with mental illness. In the case of religion there is no doubt at all, once the matter is well understood, that its entire good is to fight this instinct and to keep the absolute in the right place.[7]

Some false religion or some false drive within true religion has fashioned a god and an absolute out of almost everything imaginable: sticks, stones, cows, serpents, the sun, the moon, the heavens, emperors, little children, fire, statues, fatted calves, places on and under the earth. All of these and many more besides have been formally and explicitly pronounced divine. Again and again true religion has made war on these creations, always struggling to isolate the notion of divinity, to purify it, and to keep it segregated from the whole created world.

Again, the history of religious asceticism is a constant attempt to keep the spirit of man from worshipping false gods of a less explicit but more baleful kind. There is no end to the need to fight against them, in whatever form they take as internal drives of the human spirit. The evidence points to some common absolutizing root that is capable of producing a thousand fruits in the best of men. One of them is power. Some people must consume the whole atmosphere around them, incapable of enduring any resistance, demanding that everyone, including the sick, submit to them. Another need that is easily absolutized is that of money and possessions. Another is the need to know, the need for certainty in everything, the inability to endure not knowing. Religious faith has always taught man not only to know, but to be able to live in waiting, in a kind of darkness, making war on the desire of man to reduce the whole of reality, supernatural and natural, to his own limited ways of knowing.

Another instance of the idolizing instinct of false religion is drawn from the political order. In fact, it is hard to think of any other order which sets itself up more regularly in forms dictated by the absolutizing instinct.[8] Periodically, it insists on drawing everything to itself and becomes the object of all the absolute fantasies of man. It announces itself as the alpha and the omega of all man's energies, leaving its own limited place and invading the total human spirit, demanding unconditioned and demonic dedication. The notes of Wagnerian music peal out. The ritual develops. The resulting passions are absolute and consume every other possible dedication.

IV

If the attitude of religion and theology is clear, there is as little doubt about the hostility of medicine toward the absolutizing instinct.

One of the principal vocations of the mental sciences is to deal with and unravel a form of the unconscious with which man is not blessed but plagued and which, accepting the terms of good clinical books, I have characterized as negative, rigid, and destructive. This unconscious impedes our movement—not only toward the absolute, but toward everything else that is good in life. It is the source of the absolutizing instinct that we have been at some pains to describe. It is operative in every human being, but for most of us does not interfere with substantial functioning, so that we can afford to do little or nothing about it. In the seriously sick, however, its power and grip and destructiveness are overwhelming.

Remember that by definition the unconscious is neither available nor open to consciousness. But we have resources to help us reach it and bring it into the light. These resources belong not to religion, but to medical science. They help to unveil the absolutizing energies of this unconscious and they have the task of bringing them into the light. It is by such a process of illumination that we restore hope to the ill. Until then, the absolutizing interior giant produces the hopelessness that is the hallmark of mental illness. The mentally ill are in the constant company of absolutes, having lost the more comfortable human world.

The absolutizing forms which medicine battles are so numerous that we can attempt only brief explorations of a few of them.

1. One of the most common of all, to which we are all subject in some degree, is the human tendency to expect a single, simple way of thinking and feeling in any human situation. One may call this the desire for some absolute in the situation. If we love, we think that we should have no negative feelings. If we are angry, we tend to fear that love cannot coexist with the anger. In brief, we fear that if we hate we do not love. We want to be in the presence of one feeling, one thought.

Let us take a simple example. Someone dies who is very dear to us. We feel an immediate sense of guilt, though we may not recognize it as such. The negative feelings felt on past occasions for this person seem, in retrospect, more important than they were in fact. The occasion of death becomes a demanding moment; it demands perfect nobility and purity of feeling toward him who is dead. But that is impossible, as this kind of interior situation is impossible in all things human. Nevertheless, the absolutizing "conscience" demands that it must be so. The mourning continues for years, in an attempt to satisfy the demanding conscience, to hide and repress the negative feelings—often the most natural feelings in the world. The mourner may even withdraw from the world to prove his love for the dead—and in reality to punish himself for an anger that he cannot face as a human being.[9]

2. Another common example of the same demanding, absolutizing instinct, is the supposition that children must love

their parents perfectly, without a shadow of hostility. Such a doctrine (it arrives at such a status with many people) produces incalculable pain and, if the involved parents persevere in the doctrine, potential mental illness. The child grows up in a completely absolutized atmosphere. Nothing short of the pure contemplative love of a St. John of the Cross is demanded of him. If, later in life, in an attempt to recover his humanity, he goes to a psychiatrist, other absolutizers may feel that a doctor who encourages him to discover his hostility toward those parents who gave him life itself is over-permissive.

3. Actually, the psychiatrist is trying to create or restore in him a capacity to tolerate ambivalent feelings in ordinary human situations; to make it possible for the man to love and hate, like and dislike, approve and disapprove at the same time. He is attacking the absolute project that has been set up by the sick person, or by others for him—attacking it because the project is hopeless.

Some medical men would say that learning to tolerate ambivalence is a decisive struggle for the sick in their conquest of hopelessness.[10] Such a position tallies remarkably, though analogically, with the findings and the goals of true religion.

By ambivalence, in this sense, we mean a number of things: the ability to accept negative and unpleasant feelings as well as positive and pleasant ones; the end of a life of habitual denial, because now when one loves he need not deny the drawbacks and the difficulties. Decision now becomes possible, because formerly decision had been impeded by the unconscious negative feelings that went with it: the wish not to do a thing as well as the wish to do it. Now a man can commit himself strongly and absolutely to things without needing to believe that there must be no negatives and that he must be in the constant presence of absolute thoughts and feelings. I can choose more freely, knowing well that another's contrary choice might be just as good as mine. As I am in the presence of fewer absolutes, I am in the presence of less magic and fewer absolute commands from the outer world. The sick person will conform less and submit less. The result may be, especially at this precise moment in our culture, that he will be hated by a few more people, who now take his new course as a criticism of their own absolute ways, but he will have the love of friends who count.

This new interior ability to tolerate the fundamental ambivalences that belong to the heart of the creative world will effect a corresponding ability to handle those pairs or sets of realities that must be held in equilibrium in external human situations: the demands of the past and of the present, of the old and the new, of one's own needs and the needs of others, the truth of science and the truth of religion, the needs of the body and the needs of the spirit, the needs of the nation and the needs of the world, the need of giving correction and the need of giving love. These are only a few examples of the recurring need to live with more than one reality.

The process of healing by making ambivalence possible is an agonizing one. Men set their hearts on love, on love pure and simple and absolute. Now, it *seems,* they must watch it turn to hate, must see it as a corruptible and corrupting thing. The myth of the absolute is being exploded, and the absolutizing part of us is in despair. All will be well in the end, however, because love will be recognized as love, and hate as hate, while each will prevent the other from becoming an infinite frightening giant. The path to this ambivalence is through hopelessness to hope. Because, when it is surmounted and accepted, the sick leave the nightmare world of unqualified, absolute feelings to revel in the valley of the human. It is a valley of peace guarded by a purgatory of fire.

To move through the fire into the valley of the human is to move right through a whole camp of these absolutes. Everything the self turns to for salvation actually dissolves and gives no grip upon itself. Everything is at first a fire, yet it turns out to be not fire but balm. The whole question is, how that can be? To give up an "absolute," to give up a "necessity," to give up that with which one is absolutely identified, to give up what was a point of absolute security, to give up a black-and-white world—each of the surrenders is a trial by fire. But each turns out to be a balm because these things were weights that burdened us and brought no taste of freedom. The single points of safety are gone, but now we sense that they had been dead weights. We must discover how such change occurs.

The sick want a simple answer and they cannnot have it. What they want they do not get. They want just one psychological certainty, one self-enclosed absolutized point of feeling and thinking, but there is none. So they enter upon

a period of hopelessness, for this had been their hope. No
idolatry of the psychological order is gratified. There is nothing that does not call for its opposite. They decide to be independent, and their souls dive into a veritable ocean of
dependence. And the reverse will be true if they start with
dependence. They learn that they are too aggressive and not
aggressive enough. They want to love and they find hate
there, too. They are narcissistic but they do not in fact
think well of themselves. They secretly rant and rave, they
rave against the medicine. They want to hope and are forced
to face hopelessness. Every idol, every strong infantile hope,
seems in the process of being dethroned. Now two, three,
four, five, six things, so many points of view, can be true
at the same time, and none is an idol. What is first an agony
is then a relief. (But we still do not understand at what
point, or how, the difference occurs.)

The idols are falling, and the false hopes, and what re-
places them seems the sheerest chaos, and hopeless. This
is the point of the fire, and the apparent hopelessness
through which the human being must walk.

Perhaps this is, at least in the psychological order, something of what Dante must have meant by the passage of the
soul through the fire in Canto XXVII of the *Purgatorio*. To
give up so many hopes seems hopelessness itself, and a passage through a fire. But the peace and rest of the real
order is on the other side. The reader will recall that in our
first chapter, on hope, there was a theme of apples given by a
living hand to a very sick human being. It is beautiful to
watch this same theme in this ancient canto. Virgil finally
persuades Dante to walk through the fire (". . . he wagged his
head, as at a child won over by an apple"). And at the other
side of the fire he can pronounce:

> "This is the day your hungry soul shall be
> fed on the golden apples men have sought
> on many different boughs so ardently."

V

As it moves through the fire, the human journey is retracing
its steps. It started with hope. It had run into the hopeless.

Instead of confronting the hopeless as a possible ally, it
invented the mechanism of denial, rejected the idea of

hopelessness, and launched into years of false hope, years in which the absolutizing instinct took over.

Now the idols, the rigidities, the fixations, the absolutes, are collapsing. It is the return of the repressed. The human spirit is asked to return and confront hopelessness again.

In the confrontation with hopelessness, a number of things can happen.

1. The stay with hopelessness can be too short, the period of waiting refused; some form of the absolutizing instinct now takes over more powerfully than before, this time in the guise of a savior, of an angel of light. This is true for the individual, and it is true for the political order. Fantasy or tyrants take over. Our greatest writers have studied the process.

Plato tells the story of the takeover by the tyrant in the Fourth Book of his *Republic,* and he analyzes it in terms of both the psychological and the political orders. The tyrant's despair is perceived as strength and he moves to victory because too few can tell the difference.

The gnostic imagination, too, lacks patience. Throughout its history, it has leaped from what seems an impossible actuality to tremendous apocalyptic visions. Each time, it has leaped to a freedom and a form of hope that will collapse at the slightest touch. Norman Cohn explains how the medieval gnostics faced a crisis like our own: "From the standpoint of depth-psychology," he proposes, "it could be said that orthodox mystic and heretical adept both started their psychic adventure by a profound introversion, in the course of which they lived through as adults a reactivation of the distorting fantasies of infancy. But whereas the orthodox mystic emerged from this experience—like a patient from a successful psychoanalysis—as a more integrated personality with a widened range of sympathy, the adept of the Free Spirit introjected the gigantic parental images in their most domineering, aggressive and wanton aspects and emerged as a nihilistic megalomaniac." [11]

The modern political order has suffered at the hands of the terrible excesses of the gnostic and absolute imagination. We hardly need review the story, so terrible and familiar has been the course of its absolutes. Is it too much to say that we have produced more mad tyrants than any other age? Are not we in America faced constantly with the possibility of the success of extremism? The situation would be better if these forces could see that their drive toward power is generated by despair and weakness. But this is the very thing they dare not confront in a waiting way.

Few figures in literature tell us more about the absolute imagination and the absolute will than Captain Ahab in Melville's *Moby Dick:*

"The whale [Moby Dick] has become, in Ahab's mind, an incarnation of the world's evil," says Charles H. Cook, "but of himself Ahab has projected upon the whale the evil inherent in mortality. By killing this monster he would bring mankind into the millenium. In his desperate pursuit, intent upon what he supposes to be the greatest boon to humanity, he surrenders human values and enlists the aid of evil in its own pursuit. He obtains his crew by deception, leading the members to believe that they are embarking on a regular whaling expedition to seek oil for the lamps of mankind. When the men comprehend the true purpose of the voyage and develop an obvious reluctance, Ahab leads them on by sheer power of will. Employing the mass-psychology of Hitler and the scientific deception of a magician, he awes the men. . . . At last he plunges to the depths of inhumanity when, for fear of losing the hot track of Moby Dick and consequently the chance of blasting evil from the world, he refuses to join the search for the lost sons of the captain of the *Rachel*. . . . The outcome of this madness is the destruction by the angered whale of boat, crew, captain —all except Ishmael, whose survival is justified partly by the practical necessity of saving the narrator of the story but also by the questioning humility of his personality, which prevents him from committing Ahab's tragic error of allegorizing. To Ishmael the whale is doubtless a symbol, but a symbol of infinitely multiple significance beyond the full comprehension of any man. To Ahab, filled with monomaniacal egotism, the whale is an unmixed incarnation of evil and therefore, by Melville's standards, a hideous and intolerable allegory." [12]

Many artists in many cultures have worked on the theme. It has been the story of two distinguished films, *Lawrence of Arabia* and *The Bridge on the River Kwai*. It will always be fascinating and frightening, this story of the absolute man, unable to live with reality and therefore constructing his own world with powerful consuming strokes of fantasy and the will. Goethe has told it in *Faust*. Camus has studied it in *The Rebel*. William Golding tackles the absolutizer in *The Spire*.

The Spire is, under the skin of a romantic style, a relentless and savage revelation of an absolute will and imagination, dreaming and acting over the well-hidden surfaces of the human. Jocelyn, the absolute willer and dreamer, is the Dean of the cathedral and has set to the task of building a spire for it. His is the story of an act of the will, the self-adoring will, that has no relation to imagination or reality, for it is heedless of warnings that there is no foundation, that what goes up four-hundred feet must go down as much; his friends say the spire may and will fall upon the church and destroy it and all with it; but his will, he feels, will build and raise and hold it. He has had a vision. He has an angel with whom he talks. He has had a call from on high and must be about his Father's business:

> The singing of the stones pierced him, and he fought it with jaws and fists clenched. His will began to burn fiercely and he thrust it into the four pillars, tamped it in with the pain of his neck and his head and his back, welcomed in some obscurity of feeling the wheels and flashes of light, and let them hurt his open eyes as much as they would. His fists were before him on the stall but he never noticed them. . . . At last when he understood nothing else at all, he knew that the whole weight of the building was resting on his back.[13]

This is the terrible sense of weight and fixation that we have been talking of since the beginning of this chapter.

2. Somewhere, somehow, by some miracle, there is another path that leaves from the point of confrontation with hopelessness. It is good though hard to comprehend. This path leads the ill over the hump of hopelessness and the collapse of absolutes toward some acceptance of ambivalence and the world of the human. It has not yet been fully charted, either theologically or medically. My own explanation of it is tentative.[14]

VI

Dante, who was talking about a moral purification, a purification from the seven capital sins (so many P's or *peccata*), talks of the path through *his* Purgatorio as involving a constant sense of increasing *lightness,* or removal of weights. If we will remain in the psychological order of a Purgatorio and will remain faithful to the idea of an increasingly successful

war on the absolutizing instinct, we will still find that his
phenomenon of lightness is accurate and we can apply the
metaphor.

> We were going up the holy steps, and though
>   the climb was steep, I seemed to feel much lighter
>   than I had felt on level ground below.
> "Master," I said, "tell me what heaviness
>   has been removed from me that I can climb
>   yet seem to feel almost no weariness."
> He answered: "When the P's that still remain,
>   though fading, on your brow, are wiped away
>   as the first was, without a trace of stain—
> Then will your feet be filled with good desire:
>   not only will they feel no more fatigue
>   but all their joy will be in mounting higher."

There is, then, one difference, the difference between
weight and lightness, in this decision and process. There are
other explanations. Fantasy has been purified. Instead of
achieving a return, as in the gnostic imagination, the monsters have been slain or reduced to size.

But for a further explanation I think we have to look in
the direction where the special genius of the American
achievement in mental medicine lies—that is to say, in the
sphere of human relations proper. We must, I think, surmise
that the relationship between the patient and the doctor (or
his equivalent) reaches a point that is transforming. It
is a moment of trust. Trust transforms the evidence. Before
the moment of trust, evidence suggested that an attack was
on, that a bull was being baited, that every clear idea was but
an introduction to the hopelessness of its opposite. There was
nothing to face but the despair of ambivalence and the
death of absolutes. Now, the same evidence, with trust behind it, is transformed; now it proves the possibility of
hope and freedom and the end of the enormous claims of
the absolutizing instinct.[15] In a sense, *the relationship comes
first and the evidence comes second*, produced or illuminated
by the relationship. Of this dynamism of faith and trust,
Freud himself had declared in ringing terms that are never
cited by his religious critics:

> When the patient has to fight out the normal conflict
> with the resistances which we have discovered in him
> by analyses, he requires a powerful propelling force to

influence him toward the decision we aim at, leading to recovery. Otherwise it might happen that he would decide for a repetition of the previous outcome and allow that which had been raised into consciousness to slip back again under repression. The outcome in this struggle is not decided by his intellectual insight—it is neither strong enough nor free enough to accomplish such a thing—but slowly by his relationship to the physician. In so far as his transference bears the positive sign, it clothes the physician with authority, transforms itself into faith in his findings and in his views. Without this kind of transference or with a negative one, the physician and his arguments would never even be listened to. Faith repeats the history of its own origin; it is a derivation of love and at first it needed no arguments. Not until later does it admit them so far as to take them into critical consideration if they have been offered by someone who is loved. Without this support arguments have no weight with the patient, never do have any with most people in life.[16]

There is little difference between this trust in Freud on the one hand and hope in St. Paul on the other. The startling thing to note is the temporal relationship of both trust and hope to the moment of the amassing of evidence. Neither of them depends on the evidence of what is seen but together they create the evidence of what is seen and give it its structure. If we wait till all the evidence is in before we trust, we will never trust—because it is trust that gives the evidence its structural existence. But the relationship of trust and hope is a hard-headed *fact*. And we have said from the beginning about hope: "hope that is seen is not hope: for who hopeth for that which he seeth?" [17] Freud and St. Paul agree.

Trust and distrust, hope and hopelessness, create two different kinds of story and two different types of evidence. There is no such thing as pure evidence, untouched by the spirit of man.

A last question occurs in this context: must the trust be absolute? Is it wishful thinking before an absolute? Do we substitute an absolute for an absolute?

We would indeed still be absolutizing if it were not also true that we only so trust those who will refuse, and refuse with skill, to become an absolute. Dr. Daim suggests that the last thing that must be dethroned for the sick is the doctor [18]—and, I would add, the thousand equivalents of a doctor in this life. But it must not be by force. He or they must voluntarily dethrone themselves, by a dethronement that is ascetical and not sufficiently frequent in this world. For he and they are up against the absolutizing demands of the sick, demanding the impossible and the hopeless from these who would cure them. They would seduce us onto the throne. And there is no more beautiful, more comfortable seat in the world than a throne. It seems the part of charity and pity, in such harsh circumstances, to take the throne. If, however, we refuse this throne that is offered us, we refuse it out of strength rather than weakness. Our refusal will anger the sick for a time, but it will be nothing compared to the hatred for the one who ascends the throne. That will be hatred of those who have taken away the souls of men.

We can get along without our souls for a little while in life, but not for long.

The time often asked for us today, by so many forces in our culture, is much too long.

That is one reason, perhaps the greatest, why so many are so sick.

It will always be true, therefore, that the hope of the sick lies in destroying their idols and restoring their own souls. As for the well, the question is: how can they help? If they have goodwill and wisdom, too, let them at least stay off the mighty throne of God.

One final word. Such is the need and such the demand of men for gods and absolutes, that it will often be wise to descend firmly indeed but slowly from the throne. It is a pity that this must be. But the fact that there is one God and no more is for all of us, the well and the ill, the most difficult proposition in this world.

part two

TOWARD A PSYCHOLOGY OF HOPE

Chapter 1

On Wishing and Hoping

Here we begin our exploration of the possibility of a psychology of hope.

This first chapter will deal with the centrality of the act of wishing in any exploration of hope. As our other chapters move along they will slowly add those qualities to wishing that bring it closer and closer to the precise nature of hoping. They will add to our original wishes the elements of mutuality, of waiting, of imagining, and the taking of help. Let us call their sum the beginnings of a psychology of hope.

It is first proposed that wishing is not the cause of anxiety or mental illness; the cause lies rather in an inability to wish. This may be especially and widely true of our generations —where apathy, the sense of meaninglessness, and boredom seem to have reached an unusual stage of growth.

When we cannot wish we are sick.

When we cannot wish we cannot hope.

Others might and indeed will make different suggestions for a psychology of hope and wishing, and that is more than merely good. For diverse formulations, if not contradictory, will illuminate the very important fact, which we incline to forget, that a psychology, or any science for that matter, is always a partial and an approximating statement. This does not mean that it is not true; it does mean that it is a finite statement and not final. It is relative and not complete. And this should give us great freedom to make proposals.

My own exploration of a psychology of hope will focus principally on the firm and constant relationship between hope and wishing. I assume that wishing and wanting reality in any or all its forms is basic to hope, and that it is hard to think of anything more in need of emphasis and analysis among us. For many are inclined toward apathy, which is to have no wishes; or toward not knowing what their real wishes are, which is to be separated from oneself; or toward throwing the interior gift of wishing and hoping out into the atmosphere, which is to let others do the wishing for us. How many can answer the questions: what do I wish? what do I want now?

These are the three evils we can come up against so far as a life of wishing and hoping is concerned: either we do not wish at all, or we have wishes and do not even know what they are, or we let others do the wishing and hoping for us. Any or all of these conditions can move us toward hopelessness, since any or all of them strike at the heart of our humanity and identity.

I speak that strongly because wishing and wanting, and the energy involved in these operations, must surely come very close to defining what is best and most necessary to man as he stands most truly and at his best before man and God. *What makes him ill when he is mentally ill are all the things in and out of him that prevent him from wishing.* When these things rise to a certain pitch of the inhibition of wishing he begins to be without hope and to be sick. He is in prison. Only the triumph of wishing will bring him release.

Let us anticipate and see where our analysis of wishing will lead. We shall discover that human wishing is tightly and strongly related to hope and to many of the specific qualities and needs of hope as well. We will see that, like hope itself, really human wishing goes hand in hand with imagination. Third, we will see that, over against the pernicious quality of endlessness that marks so much of hopelessness, the ideal human wish is absolute and unconditional and completely opposed to endless search. Furthermore, ideal wishing will be founded, as we saw hope to be, on mutuality; it will have become *wishing with*. Finally, the gift of waiting will have been added to it, so that wishing will be able to wait as hope can wait. But despite these additions, it will remain the wishing of man; it will always be able to be summarized in the single, meaningful phrase: *I wish.*

I

When we cannot wish, we are sick.

Freud sensed this problem, and he sensed his failure to resolve it. He tried at times to bring the wishing faculty of the libido and the organizing faculty of the ego into closer association. He protested that the boundaries of the one and the other should not be too carefully demarcated. Now and then he warned his fellow doctors not to take the monster picture of the wishing libido with such high seriousness and fear. But how to make the ego itself a daring, energizing, wishing entity seemed difficult for him. He looked ever so carefully for the origin of anxiety, locating it for the most part in the wishing of the libido or the instinctual drive of sexuality; *it never quite occurred to him that he should subvert this whole system and turn it on its head, that it might be the failure to wish that produces anxiety.* He was in touch with one form of the unconscious, the negative, destructive and inhibiting world of repressed wishes for the inappropriate and unreal. He rightly placed the seat of anxiety in the ego, but did he place it there for a reason that was total enough? The self is indeed anxious because it feels threatened by its own instincts. But is it not far more anxious because it feels blocked thereby in its *own* capacity to wish, to love, to move on in its search and hunger for reality? Does it not then feel immobilized, unable to love? Is it not anxious where it is not free? [1]

We are not afraid of freedom. Much of the theorizing of the existential writers says that we are. But I do not see how this can be true. It is our desire for freedom that is afraid when it is not free, when it feels itself cut off from wishing. This is the prelude to all the degrees of hopelessness.

Wishing is so much a part of us, so central and so constant, that it would be a mistake to cite a ringingly dramatic example either of wishing or of its opposite. That would suggest that wishing and its opposites are an exceptional thing in man, and pose exceptional problems. Let us take a simple example, drawn from daily life.

We imagine an American of middle age on a difficult

weekend camping trip. He has consented to such a weekend, though actually he had a very strong wish to stay home. But he literally does not know he has this wish. We hypothesize that he has been taught in childhood that it is wrong to have wishes if they are not in entire agreement with the wishes of somebody else. Therefore he does not have independent wishes consciously, for he dare not. But not to know the wish causes it to be dammed up and to grow in intensity. The more it grows, the greater the strain of the weekend. To escape the bad image of himself as one who really wishes he submits further and further to the wishes of his friends, not to mention his submission to flies, mosquitoes, and bad cooking.

We have every reason to believe that this is a widespread condition in our culture: we are out of touch with our own thoughts, feelings, hopes, and we disguise the fact by many forms of activism. On the surface we have a bewildering display of energy and activity, but this is often a substitute for the real thing.[2] We are allowing the atmosphere to wish for us. Thus we have the inevitable triad of steps: a strong hope, its interdiction, a violent substitution. We surrender our identity to others. We submit.

It becomes increasingly difficult for men to recognize their own wishes and hopes as the bare, uncomplicated, uninvolved facts they are or ought to be. Apparently it was impossible for this man to admit that he hoped for a quiet weekend at home. This he would have *imagined* as an act of hostility, a destructive thrust, which would have sacrificed belonging and the love of mankind. He lives on a blackmailing image: if I am independent and I have my own hopes, I will not be loved. He has been taught that the two, independence and love, cannot go together. He cannot admit it, but he has decided that it is evil or dangerous to have thoughts or feelings or wishes of his own.

Our camping friend is, of course, doing the opposite of wishing. By the opposite of wishing I mean a state or condition of not wishing or of not having any wishes. I have said that this state is more prevalent than we think, and takes humdrum—though painful—forms.

Otto Fenichel, one of the brilliant theorists of psychoanalysis, indirectly covers much of wishing's opposite in his study of *boredom*. His work vividly reminds us that just as hope is present as a savior in all of us, so, too, there is some degree of hopelessness in all of us, not only in the sick.

In our context, boredom can be said to involve two things: the death of wishing; and an attempt to revive the wishing by getting the outside world to wish for us. The hyperactivity of the bored man can and does mask an interior sleep or death of wishing. The mask can be brilliant, efflorescent, magnificent, apparently involving every manner of wish, but it is a mask for all that.

Boredom does remind us, even without analysis, of its more painful brother, hopelessness. Fenichel cuts through with a few strokes to the reasons why boredom may not seem painful but is. Behind it all is the death of impulse (which I have termed the death of wishing):

> Thus we should expect instinctual urges to be unpleasurable and lack of impulses pleasurable. The problem that pleasurable impulses do nevertheless exist has been discussed. The corresponding problem of the existence of unpleasurable lack of impulses seems to be presented in the phenomenon of boredom.[3]

And he defines boredom in a way that suggests our own supposition of the death of wishing.

> A person who is "bored," in the strict sense of the word, is searching for an object, not in order to act upon it with his instinctual impulses, but rather to be helped by it to find an instinctual aim which he lacks . . .[4]

If we are to get close to the real nature of boredom, and to the larger thing called hopelessness, we must be aware of the presence of two things: "a need for activity and an inhibition of activity."[5] We must further calculate that the inhibition is internal, or that, if it was once external, it has now been internalized. For, apparently, neither all the activity in the world, nor the presence of the most satisfying objects, is capable of resolving this state. To be aware of this will prevent us from rushing too quickly into the exclusive position that if a human being has a goal to shoot at he will not be or become ill. He needs the goal indeed, but this clearly is not enough. He must be able to move toward it with a free, internal life; otherwise the presence of the goal or the object will only intensify the difficulty. Certainly we must create objects and situations of hope and self-fulfillment in our civilization, but what is even more necessary, if we wish to restore hope, is to find out what are the internal forces that would prevent movement toward them in the form of wishing and hoping, even if the goals were there. Nothing tends more toward hopelessness and the sense of impossibility than such internal situations.

It is bad enough when we have a relatively high consciousness of what we want and of our inability to bring ourselves really to want it. But the mentally ill are far from the ultimately manageable difficulties of that state of affairs. Some such division of our being, some such inability to will what we wish, characterizes the lives of all of us. But the hopelessness is deeper in the sick. Such has been the history of their pain in wishing that they repress the very wish itself or try to kill it in a deeper passivity. Still, we can learn from the conscious experience of all of us what the more hidden and more inhibiting experience of the sick must be. The saints have had it, not least but most sharply. The classical example is the long dialogue in the *Confessions* of St. Augustine, in which the saint torturously tries to make himself really wish the obvious.

> For the will orders that there should be a will—not a different will, but itself. But it is not entire in itself when it gives the order, and therefore its order is not obeyed. For if it were entire in itself, it would not give the order to will; the will would be there already. So it is not an absurdity partly to will and partly not to will; it is rather a sickness of the soul which is weighed down with habit so that it cannot rise up in its entirety, lifted aloft by truth. So the reason why there are two wills in us is because one of them is not entire, and one has what the other lacks.[6]

I am not using this example to suggest that all the sick have to do is to will and they will be healed. This is too common a doctrine among all those who do not really understand why the sick cannot will. Rather, I am using it in a passing way, to help create an initial sense of comradeship of the well with the sick. We all have trouble in really wishing and willing.

II

This is obviously a partial and brief picture of what we

mean by the failure or the blocking of the ability to wish and hope.

Over against such general situations the important thing is to elevate the status and the humanity of the acts of wishing and hoping. This should be the first step in the construction of a psychology of hope. If there is no interior motion in men, what can we do for them? What indeed can we do for ourselves? It is not that we require great strength from people, particularly from the sick. Let those who are strong have their strength and take care of themselves. But all that we want from the sick is wishes and hopes, or the rediscovery of them, or the rebuilding of them. All that we want is that they be finally able to answer the question: what do you want? If we find a traveler prostrate in the desert and ask him what he wants, he will say: water. This is the sign of life, that he has such a wish and can name it.

There is always some danger that our rejection of the form of wishing contained in the working of the absolutizing instinct may frighten people away from the right and the need they have to wish absolutely. And so, we must tackle this problem again, particularly at a moment when we have just finished an assault on the grandeur of this instinct.

The absolutizers of this world, certainly the absolutizers in the United States, have the special propagandistic talent of spreading the suggestion that they and only they can truly wish and do. It requires a good deal of analysis to show that they are not really wishing at all, that they are rigid and trapped, and marked with everything but the vitality they claim to have. But they keep trying to steal this final march, with the claim that they and they alone are the enthusiasts of our culture. At the moment they have a new toy, like children; they are white enthusiasts.

We must think with humor, but without yielding, of the curious position Ronald Knox felt himself caught in when he finished his book, *Enthusiasm*. I do not feel myself caught, as he did, but I must warn against the heavy-handed propaganda of the far right, of the men who are always posing as the sainted and simple-minded saviors of our political order.

Ronald Knox was bringing to a close the work of a lifetime in this book on the elite enthusiasts of *ultra-supernaturalism* and heroism and zeal and apostolic simplicity and burning schismatic fervor who have kept emerging to question the unity of Christian civilization. St. Paul himself had to warn the Corinthians that a preoccupation with certain burning charismatic gifts of the spirit would create an atmosphere alien to charity.

> With this danger in view, the apostle proceeds to a series of injunctions (chapter xiv) which will introduce, it may be hoped, some kind of discipline into the behaviour of the Corinthians at prayer. Speaking with tongues merely for the sake of theatrical effect is to be discouraged; it is childishness (verses 1-20). . . . There must be no speaking with tongues unless they can be interpreted (verses 26-28). The prophets are to speak one at a time, giving place to one another; women are not to prophesy in public at all. . . . Evidently it is the curb, not the spur, that is needed in first-century Corinth. Let these exuberances go unrepressed, and the state of the Church may anticipate, before long, the scenes enacted in eighteenth-century Paris; scenes which the older and staider element in Jansenism was powerless to control.[7]

And Knox went on with his splendid work on the enthusiasts, reviewing the life and spirit of the Donatists, the Montanists, the various enthusiasts of the Middle Ages—the Albigenses, the Cathari, the Waldensians; he moved through the Anabaptists on into the Reformation, seventeenth-century Protestantism, Jansenism, Quietism. But at the end of it all he found himself expressing a charming hesitation.

> How nearly we thought we could do without St. Francis, without St. Ignatius! Men will not live without vision; that moral we do well to carry away with us from contemplating, in so many strange forms, the record of the visionaries. If we are content with the humdrum, the second-best, the hand-over-hand, it will not be forgiven us. All through the writing of this book I have been haunted by a long-remembered echo of *La Princesse lointaine:*
>
> *Frère Trophime.* L'inertie est le seul vice, Maitre Erasme;
>
>   Et la seule vertu est . . .
> *Erasme.*   Quoi:
> *Frère Trophime.*   L'enthousiasme![8]

If enthusiasm is not the only final human virtue, perhaps some kind of wishing is. And we must all fight for this position and not yield it to the wrong people. I keep repeating that we must not surrender the gift of wishing absolutely and strongly to these absolutizers who are precisely incapable of any real human wishing.

There is a mistaken notion that Christianity, because it is zealous to keep the absolute out of most of our thinking and wishing, is opposed to wishing things intensely or at all. I reject this notion, totally. Unfortunately, it is not a dialectical, a purely intellectual question. Christianity has regularly been interpreted as a great source of inhibition and as an enemy to wishing and willing. If this interpretation were correct, we would have to acknowledge that Christianity itself is one of the prime sources of mental illness. But it is not true; only those who will always refuse to wish will, in order to legalize their position, invoke a counterfeit Christianity that calls their refusal health or virtue. If Christianity were such, it would be the perfect system for taking away hope, piously pronouncing that if we remained thus hopeless until death, it would intervene at that moment to reward in death the hope that was never allowed to function in life.

Christians themselves have given ground for these misinterpretations. This is not a part of our Christianity, however; it is a part of our sickness. It is this that makes us confuse the ascetical tradition within Christianity with an attack on willing and wishing, on creativity, on the development of talent, on joy and pleasure in doing, on independence and identity. These are different things, asceticism and the inability to wish strongly, each to be determined and judged by its fruits. A mark of health is the ability to judge that one thing is not another, even though it looks very much like the other.

What is the difference, we may ask, between wishing things intensely, absolutely, and wishing them as absolutes in the sense that religion wars on? The answer need not be obscure if it is sought in the concrete individual situation. When something is wished as an absolute, there is an enormous discharge of fantasy into it from the absolutizing instinct. This powerful spiritual and biological force has an objective that can be displaced in bizarre ways, as we have suggested. When it attacks an individual object it makes an unreality or a dream out of it. As it flows unreservedly into the object, the ironic result is an obliteration of the object's true outlines: the object is melted down, rejected and hated. The

final consequence is that the thing is really present neither
to consciousness nor to wishing. It is not only impossible to
wish it intensely and absolutely; it is impossible to wish it
at all.

This is true, not only for our contacts with ordinary
things, but sometimes with superbly beautiful things. Every
American tourist in Europe has had something of this experience. After perhaps years of anticipation, he goes to
Paris and the Louvre, to charming Southern France, the lovely Rhine, to the Italian lakes, the Parthenon, the Toledo of
El Greco, and here and there he must ward off feelings of
disappointment and contempt. Here and there, so preoccupied was he with the dream, that the reality was simply
not there for him. If he returns when the dream has exhausted itself, the things may be there in their reality, ready
for his enjoyment. Only then can he love them absolutely,
with all his strength, according to all the reality they possess,
according to all their identity. Things must be loved in their
reality, even though they are understood against the force
of the absolutizing instinct, which magnifies and deforms
rather than understands. Deluded by this instinct, human
beings fear that they will not be loved if they are really understood: and so they hide.

We can love others only if we put the absolute in the
right place. We must keep the absolute out of things, rather
like good, homely atheists. This comes close to the religious
teaching that we cannot love anything unless we love God
first. In this light, religion is the reverse of an inhibiting
reality. Rather, it makes clear thinking and clear, accurate
wishing possible.

A very common notion about Christianity is that it "de-
sexualizes" people, takes from them the gift of life, love,
wishing and affection. Actually Christianity is or should be
a complete validation and sanctification of the strength of
our wishes. Where the right tradition is tapped, in the right
kind of spiritual writing, we find God's special love for one
kind of man: the man of desires, *homo desideriorum*. He
wishes for God, but this allows him to wish strongly in
every moment of the way, according to the full reality of
everything he confronts. I wish with all my heart that someone would write a major book on the whole idea of Christian wishing. There is a great, a very great need to restore
this idea, this force. It is especially necessary for those who
are in charge of the spiritual education of Christians, par-

ticularly of seminarians and members of religious orders. There is very little doubt that many in such high places of responsibility fear to encourage individuality, strong interests, creativity; their fear is in the name of the love of God, but they will find to their cost that such tactics will lead to love neither of God nor of man. Man is all of one piece. You cannot prevent him from hoping in one order of things without preventing him in every other order.[9] It is obvious that our wishes need education and orientation, but they are not going to be educated by any assumption that it is wrong to wish and act at all. People are sufficiently fearful of energy and life without making it worse, without elevating the fear to the level of a principle and a virtue.

III

Christianity, when it is true to itself, proclaims the centrality of wishing and hoping. An equally decisive and positive statement can be made from the standpoint of the new mental sciences. I would like to attempt a brief defense of the preeminent status of wishing, using the psychoanalytic language of libido, sublimation, and fixation. We will find, while we are doing this, that we are also advancing the construction of a psychology of hope.

One of the most important elements of Freud's attempt to clarify the problem of the wishing of the ego itself was his theory of sublimation. And it is here that we have to be careful of the distinction between the absolute or rigid and the adaptive or flexible. For in actuality the word "sublimation" can be used with two different meanings, the one rigid and the other free.

To understand the concept let us first think of a body of instinctual drives which come under the common name of libido, whether we define the latter as sexuality or by the wider name of love. When we transfer this drive or drives from an inferior and inappropriate level to a superior and more acceptable area of action or object psychoanalytic theory calls the process "sublimation." Such an alteration of the direction of sexuality and love, says Freud, is responsible for all our advances in culture and civilization. That is true. But the crucial question is, how does this come to pass? For sublimation can take place in a sick and univocal way or in a free, adaptive and healthy way. In other words there are two kinds of sublimation.

In the one, the sick way, the drive of sexuality moves in a disguised manner onto a new and higher plane of operation and object. But it is still itself in every other way, and is still unconsciously attached to its original objects. There has been no real change. There has been no liberation. The higher object is only a disguise and a defense.

In the second and truly adaptive form of sublimation what happens is altogether different. Where it is successful, sublimation has consciously faced the problem of the attachment of the libido (or sexuality or love) to inappropriate or immature areas. It has released this energy and neutralized it, making it ready for shifts and flexible application in any new direction, whether that be appropriate sexuality, work, the life of the mind and spirit, or any adult activity. It is free, truly free, to meet new worlds on their own terms. *It is a free, generalized energy or love or capacity for wishing* that may be sexual, cultural, spiritual, friendly, interested, wishing, planning, according to all the needs and realities of human life.[10]

Where it is free and adaptive, it can be sexualized or desexualized according to the wishes and decisions of conscious human beings. Where it is fixated in sexuality, or rather in an inappropriate sexuality, it has become univocal in my sense of that word.

Let us conceive then of a single human energizing and wishing faculty that comes close to being man himself. It is constantly searching for objects and reality and may be said to take on the shape of whatever it contacts or has wishes for. It is not exclusively sexual, but is sexual where it should be sexual. It is pansexual, completely sexual, only where everything becomes for it a disguised form of *this* area of energizing. Being of itself free and generalized it can become interested in anything. Its whole vocation is to move forward into reality with interest and desire. Ideally it can enter into anything with full commitment, not withholding any of itself, yet does not feel trapped by the commitment because the commitment does not exhaust it potentiality. It antedates sexuality, honors sexuality where it meets it, but needs no neutralizing to become more than sexual.

We can sum things up briefly by saying that this energizing and this power for wishing thrives on commitment but moves toward sickness through fixation. Whatever in its fullness is the difference between the two, between commitment and fixation, it is certain, I think, that the one is filled with and possessed by hope and the other by hopelessness. For it seems to me that when we commit ourselves (that is, when we really wish something) two things happen:

1. Through this sense of contact with our own wishes we feel ourselves to be in contact with our own souls, whether this possession be called identity by the medical man or salvation by the theologian. For it is I who wish and nobody can do it for me, though we shall see that others can help. Thus, whatever "salvation" or the saving of the soul is, it is not a magical thing, achieved in some single strange act while the bells peal and the angels sing. It is a cumulative interior thing, most essential to which is the possession of my own soul through the possession of my own committing wishes. And lest there be any illusion that I am supporting a Wagnerian campaign to "get-in-there-and-wish," to the point of constant great things and exhaustion, I would like to make it clear that people may and should very often want to do nothing at all and that this is an excellent idea, as well as an excellent part of our humanity. Actually the most important thing is not that I should work or rest, important though both may be, but that the soul do either in a state that possesses itself and truly wishes to do either. This will be better understood the more we come to realize how separated the sick are from their own thoughts and wishes.

2. The second thing that characterizes commitment or real wishing, is some kind of conviction that something will come of it. A true wish never occurs in a state of despair. When I am in a state of despair, I do not wish. I ask, "What is the use?" When I wish or commit myself, I do not so much say that *I* will be able to get out of what I have put myself into —for that would not be wishing—as that *something* will come out of it. Thus when I commit myself to a book, I hope that I can finish it and that some good will come of it, not necessarily the good I planned, but something. Thus wishing is born out of and lives on hope.

On the other hand there is fixation. On the surface it is a fixed strong resolve or wish. But the feelings which, under analysis, are found attached to it betray it as something altogether different. The fixated wishes which plague the sick have the tones of situations in which human beings are trapped or stuck. Actually they do turn out to be trapped or mired in some past situation. They cannot escape or get free from it in order to move freely into the future and into new wishes. They are trying to work something out in the past but never quite succeed. The truth seems to be that even in relation to this situation of the past they cannot quite wish one way or the other, cannot quite carry off some act of wishing. The result, to leave the picture there for the moment, is an accumulating feeling of helplessness and hopelessness.

Thus, as I deeply associate the idea of hope with the ability to wish I also suggest as strong a relationship between some prevailing inability to wish or move and the state of hopelessness. If this is true, it is important that we go on with our study of human wishing.

Chapter 2

The Absolute Wish Versus The Willful Act

The ideal and healthy form of wishing is absolute and unconditional in several important senses.

To establish this is to establish the unfortunate qualities inherent in many distortions of ideal wishing. Grave harm has been wrought, for example, by teaching that a man must find the will of God, never his own, in all things.

Where we are within reality and there are ten reality choices, it is man's choice that is absolute, that makes the choice right. There is then no need to be on the perpetual alert to find the one haunting, threatening, objective good thing to do. God wants us to wish. In our wishes is His will.

Both the act of wishing and the willful act, which is at the heart of so much hysteria, are absolute, but in startlingly different ways.

We have already concluded that hopelessness usually involves a constriction of the imagination. To escape from hopelessness, it is necessary to imagine context and perspective and a way out, in other words to meet hopelessness with some enlargement of the imagination. We also maintained that the ways in which hopelessness handles the world are hopeless and that their principal feature is their endlessness. They could never reach a term or an ending. They could not rest.

The two qualities of really human wishing that we will examine in this chapter are meant to confront these two problems. For ideal wishing is not only imaginative; it is also unconditional and absolute; it is at the very opposite pole from every form of the endless. These two qualities of imagination and unconditionality form the first substance of our psychology of wishing.

This chapter will offer an initial thrust at a psychology of wishing. For the simple reason that any definition of the ideal wish—unconditional, free, spontaneous, rejecting all compulsion, self-possessed and full of autonomy—comes so close to the willful act, I will be especially interested in the relations between the act of wishing and the willful act.

Through all of this we will be on the track of clues to the healing of illness. The world used to think that mental illness was an illness of the mind, but now it is much more inclined to think that it is an illness in the faculty of wishing. When we are looking for the causes of illness we will do well to look for the pathology in the act of wishing.

Some feel, often vaguely, that if we only could eliminate wishing, we could also eliminate mental illness. This is a more sophisticated attempt at the truth than that which conceives mental illness to be an illness of the mind. But sophisticated or not, it is just as false. In fact, the truth, as I have proposed it, is the very reverse. When there is no wishing there is illness and hopelessness. Wishing, after all, is the opposite of apathy.

There is reason enough for the vague misunderstanding that the elimination of wishing will do away with mental illness. There are, clearly, wishes that are either sick or evil. But we have always known that. We have always known that certain types of wishes can be moral or medical monsters. What we had not known—and I think it is this that has created a good deal of our new misunderstandings about illness—what we had not known was *how much* wishing was going on in the human world, how omnipresent and operative the act of wishing was. If I may speak in some of the new popular tones of discovery and enlightenment, we have discovered that the villain lurks everywhere.

I

I take some of the simplest propositions of Freud as one of

the easiest ways to indicate the newly found universality of
the act of wishing.

According to Freud the whole order of human thought has
a wish behind it. The old epistemology had seen no difficulty
in declaring that a wish could follow any thought, but this
is not the same as to say, according to psychoanalytic epistemology, that you do not have a thought without a previous
wish. So Freud says that "nothing but a wish can set our
mental apparatus at work." [1]

What he has to say of dreams is, of course, more obvious.
A dream is a disguised form of a wish; it is a hallucinating
attempt to gratify a wish. "Our theory of dreams," he says
simply, "regards wishes originating in infancy as the indispensable motive force for the formation of dreams." [2]

And he has said the same thing of all symptoms in illness:
". . . the theory governing all psychoneurotic symptoms cul-
minates in a single proposition, which asserts that *they, too,
are to be regarded* as fulfillments of unconscious wishes." [3]

It is unnecessary to review our new knowledge of the symbol insofar as the latter is recognizable again and again as
a disguised and distorted expression of a wish. We are told,
for example, that "it is fair to say that there is no group of
ideas that is incapable of representing sexual facts and
wishes." [4]

And so it goes now with us, in many other ways. For
what is repression if it is not the repression of a wish? What
is omnipotence if it is not a powerful generalizing wish to be
everything and to be able to do everything? Or what is the
usual ambivalence in illness if it is not a steady, radical inability to cope with contrary wishes about the same thing?
In hallucination we hallucinate the existence of an object
that is not there in order to gratify a wish that is there. This
is true for the well and the sick. I expect and badly want a
certain letter. The result is that I can make the vaguest bit of
light or white look like that letter protruding from my mail-
box. It is only by self-knowledge and habituation to the way
and power of my wishes that I straighten or correct my
thoughts all during the day. At night, of course, in dreams I
succeed less. [5]

In most forms of mental illness we rather take for granted
the hidden or disguised presence of one of the many forms
of childhood or infantile wishing. The child wants the moon,
he keeps wanting it, and as he grows up he is in a constant
traumatic state because it is not there. Or perhaps the shoe

was on the other foot. Perhaps someone wished something of him, wished from him with a sense of demand for something that was not there. This demanding wish of another or others finally gets into the very inside of the character; everything and everyone the sick person meets is making or seems to be making a demanding wish on him. The result can be a constant inward rage and severe illness.

These are some of the forms, guises and disguises in which we have begun, in the last few generations, to see the act of wishing. Thus I would suggest that we ask a few questions.

Is it not true that the major feeling about the act of wishing is that it is dangerous?

Is it not true that we would generally tend to honor the German proverb: where there are no wishes there is peace?

Is there a general feeling about reality that it is not the object of all our wishes but is a check and a limit and an inhibiting force upon them?

Is it true that all in all we have a similar concept of the ego? Do we at all incline to think of the ego as itself a powerful, energizing, wishing force? Or is it not rather a final gate or filter where wishes must pass muster before they are allowed to go further? Does the ego have any wishes?

Are there, therefore, for this area of the act of wishing, certain puritanical notes to be found in the feeling and theorizing of Freud? And in our own?

Do we take the whole order of human wishing as a kind of problem and not as the very heart and essence of human nature?

And if we do not clarify our own feeling and thinking about wishing, where will that leave the mentally ill if all their trouble lies in this area and if they will often find that those who lead them are but a little less blind?

I am not talking merely of the half-hidden feelings and thoughts of many medical men, including Sigmund Freud. The matter touches everybody. Unfortunately it seems to have a special way of touching the religious mind. I do not say that it is clearly said in any particular proposition of religious thought, but it seems half accepted—without propositions—by the religious mind that wishing is not quite the best thing in the world and that having one's own wishes might possibly be the worst thing in the world. There is, for example, a fondness for the isolating of that one prayer of Christ in his agony: *Not my will but thine be done*. Seldom cited are such phrases as one that explains why he was put to death. *Quia voluit,* the Vulgate reads: because he wished it.

Many seem to feel that a truly religious and truly good person will not have any wishes on his own but will only seek the will of God (the supposition being that his own will cannot possibly be the will of God). I intend to examine the dangerous qualities of this kind of unqualified proposition. But before I do, let me remark how close, unless it is qualified, the proposition would bring us to the condition of many of the sick who have been told that it is wrong to have a wish or a thought of their own. The next step—if indeed it is not a still earlier step—is that it is wrong to have a soul of your own. And this again is the constant condition of the sick, that they do not feel they have or should have a soul of their own.

I may be exaggerating the misconceptions that lie behind the attitudes of many groups toward the act of wishing. But all in all I think the distortions important and clear enough to go ahead with our attempt at some clarifications of the whole question. One central question, of course, is this: to the degree that there is obfuscation, fear, or prejudice against wishing, what are some of the principal sources of these attitudes?

I propose again that the primary source of these attitudes is the resemblance and resulting confusion between the act of wishing, even in such ideal states of wishing as I shall describe, and some of its opposites or contraries. Chief among these opposites or contraries would be the willful act. Other contrary forms or qualities would be the egoistic act, the defiant act, the obstinate act, the omnipotent act, the mean act, and so forth. If the pure act of wishing has so many unfortunate resemblances it is certainly in need of explication and delineation. The ill are notoriously unable to distinguish one thing or one case or one situation from another. We need not pretend that we do not occasionally share some of these difficulties. We are in the midst of a case in point. What do we mean by wishing?

The first simple thing I have to say about a wish is that it is a tendency or a movement toward something; the movement or tendency includes the qualities of affirmation, acceptance, approval of the thing toward which I move. I call a thing a good for me and want it. There is a positive feeling for and imagining of the object. Others may define a wish otherwise, but if there is such a reality as I am now beginning to define, that is all I ask.

Actually, we are only beginning to approximate a correct way of talking about our subject, and are already in serious trouble if we do not go forward. For example, I have called wishing a tendency or a movement, and if I leave it at that I join the ranks of those who do not really think a wish is a wish. For there would be an implication that a wish is really a drive, a thing that happens in me but is not really mine or me. As I see it, the only kind of simple sentence that can describe a wish is what we used to call in school a completely transitive sentence: that is, there is no other way to describe a wish save by the two words: I wish. It is my act, my wishing. There is a temptation in the Freudian topography to reduce a wish to a drive with a number of impersonal qualities. But what I am talking about is the wish of a wishing person who is actually wishing. It may only be half a wish; it may not be a very strong wish; it may be conscious or unconscious, or partly both. But to the degree that it is a wish, it is a transitive, personal act. To the degree that a person really wishes, it is he that is acting; he is not being acted on by anything inside or outside of himself. He is wishing; we are thus in the presence of an absolute fact. An ideal wish is an absolute fact. It is not something rising out of the substratum of the self. It is my self. If it is half a wish it is half me. In itself it is an absolutely autonomous fact. It is a self acting on its own inward, wishing terms.

An ideal human wish, a wish that is effectively human and humanly effective, is imaginative and accompanied by a correspondingly full act of the imagination in relation to what it wishes. By imagination I do not mean fantasy, but that total set of forces in man which contributes to the formation of the full contextual image of an object.[6] The more there is the wish for a thing the more, the better, and the more widely do we incline to imagine or "image" it. And this is another test of really human wishing, that as it wishes it keeps working in conjunction with the realistic and contextual imagination to image forth its object. A good deal of the poetic energy of T. S. Eliot has been devoted to ironic descriptions of states of wishing and imagining in contemporary life that are flat, dead, non-reactive in either wishing or imagining. Here is the death of wishing in *The Wasteland:*

Unreal City.
Under the brown fog of a winter dawn,
A crowd flowed over London Bridge, so many,

I had not thought death had undone so many.[7]

I think we are in rat's alley
Where the dead men lost their bones, [8]

She turns and looks a moment in the glass,
Hardly aware of her departed lover;
Her brain allows one half-formed thought to pass;
"Well now that's done: and I'm glad it's over."
When lovely woman stoops to folly and
Paces about her room again, alone,
She smoothes her hair with automatic hand,
And puts a record on the gramophone.[9]

The two states of wishing and imagining seem always to accompany each other. Where there is no imagining there is no wishing: where there is no wishing there is no imagining. Imagining things rightly and fully is among the most human of gifts. Most of us, while not artists or poets, are better at it than we think. Indeed there comes a certain point of imagining under which we cannot go without beginning to be literally sick and mentally sick from literality. By literality I mean the rigid imagining of a fact in absolute isolation of its context or history or analogies. Let us summarize that the trouble with the ill is not too much imagination or imaging, but too little. Where there is too much fantasy, we may investigate whether the too much is not part of a secondary and substitutive process that is consequent upon a too little, a failure to image the real in any way save an absolute literal and non-contextual way. Here is a man riding in a car in Dallas, Texas. If I imagine for a moment more, I might get the image of a friend, a fine man who did not understand aggression unless it was really called for. This is the truth. Failing this and failing the imagination, I shall charge at him with my fantasy. I who have no imagination will rock the world with my fantasy and my twelve-dollar gun.

II

I will go a step further and suggest that the ideal wish, one that best lives up to the essence of wishing, would be a kind of absolute. I wish for something. There is nothing outside such an act that would justify it. It would be its own justification. Is this necessarily egoistic, or subjectivistic, or diabolical? I think not. What I want principally to say here is that such an act would be free of all fantasy of being for or against someone. It might very well be and ideally should be an imaginative act, but ideally, too, it should not be accompanied by the battle fantasies of *for* or *against*. Or it should try to wish objectively (that is, imaginatively) even in the very midst of battle fantasies. In an act of sheer conformity, on the other hand, I first find out, before I wish, what someone else wishes, and then I wish. Or in an act of pure defiance I indeed find out what another wishes, and then go directly counter. Or there is the provocative wish and act; in it I am not in the least interested in the object or the wish for it, but aim only at disturbing someone. All these acts are full of fantasy but empty of imagination. An ideal wish is at peace and not in battle; in this sense it is a self-justifying absolute that is neither for nor against any one.

Let me look a little more sharply at this absolute and self-contained quality of ideal wishing. It is a crucially important quality, but again if we do not amend the idea it will be almost a lie. For the contrary also seems a legitimate hypothesis, that all being is in relation; if wishing is no exception we should explore the possibility that every wish is either for or against someone; it is not, therefore, a self-contained absolute. What shall we say of this, and what does this do to our previous chain of thought?

My own position would be that this new hypothesis is true, but that the ways in which it holds true for the act of wishing on the one hand and for the willful act on the other are remarkably different.

What accounts for the possibility of an absolutely autonomous act of wishing that simply wishes a thing and is at peace with itself in doing so is some relationship of mutuality. Let us imagine that the individual has achieved a satisfactory relationship or set of relationships of friendship or love. Granted such a relationship, the individual does whatever he wishes so long as the range of action does not put him outside the relationship. In saying this I am only trying to find a way of explicating the sentence of St. Augustine: *Ama et fac quod vis:* Love and do what you will. How best to explain it I am not sure, but because it is important we must keep working, clinically and theologically, at the explication. (I shall devote the whole next chaper to it.) It is important for the sick because so many of them have the feeling that everything they set their hearts to is forbidden. What I am saying, on the contrary, is that, granted the right relationship, everything is permitted. Such a man, for example, possessed by the right relationship with God, will not sin. But for the rest, let me say it in an apparently shocking way, he will or may seek his own wish; he will do his own will, and not be possessed by the hostile fantasy that in so doing he may not be doing the will of God. The fact is that where such a relationship has been worked out the question simply will not occur. Neither, therefore, will the fantasy of hostility or conformity.

Let us keep thinking of the sick who are concerned about everything. They are concerned about whether to take a cup of coffee or a cup of tea. We say to ourselves that it does not matter. But are they in the internal presence of a psychic image who is saying to them that it does not matter which they wish, coffee or tea? Suppose they want a cup of coffee. Are they immediately in the presence, fantastically, of someone who thinks it should be tea? Or are they in the presence of someone who does not think it matters, who communicates freedom, and who therefore freely, according to the manner of a true adult, absents himself from such decisions? Ideally it is not a decision. It should be determined by a wish, spontaneous, loving, innocent and free. When I want coffee there is no need, in an ideal wish, to think of someone who wants tea. Ideally it should not arise as a question.

I think that we are in the middle of a question that is caught between the horns of nihilism and love. Either defiance (if you prefer tea and insist) or love (if you think it does not matter). But only in the latter eventuality am I allowed to wish with an absolute wish, with a wish that is correct for the sole reason that it is mine. Such a wish is the sign not of the solution of a conflict but of its absence. It is the sign of a relationship that makes absoluteness possible. Only within such terms can I really wish. I do not have to make a telephone call to find out if such and such is all right. I know that it is. I do not even think of the question. This is the ideal for wishing.

On the natural plane, therefore, the absolute situation I am describing could be described in this way: he who has a real friend need not consult him. On the religious plane it might be described in the form of a paradox: he who thinks constantly about God can forget about him. Even that severe religious writer Thomas à Kempis has the following to say:

Love feeleth no burden, thinketh nothing of labours, attempteth what is above its strength, pleadeth no excuse of impossibility; for it thinketh all things possible for itself, and all things lawful.[10]

The way some philosophers and theologians would put it, not too differently from the clinical psychologist studying human relations, is that there is a double movement of the human spirit, a movement toward God and a movement toward the world. The successful maintenance of the movement toward God is the very thing that makes possible the free, uninhibited movement of man into the world in every possible form save sin: in work, in the family, in politics, in science, in the literary imagination, in literally doing whatever one wishes. The key sentence here is: *For ye are gods*.

III

It is clear that the willful act is absolute in an altogether different sense and is in relationship in an altogether different way.

It is absolute indeed, or trying to be. One of its gods is to wish and to act without reason, or contrary to reason. It does not wish to act in relationship to reality and, therefore, is trying to act without imagination. I will something precisely because there is no sense to it. In this sense the willful act is full of will and nothing else. It has an objective but no object.

It is indeed in relationship, but in an altogether different way from the act of wishing. It is relation *contra*. It chooses a thing because it is against. Where the act of wishing establishes a firm relationship and can then be said to be free in it and to be free of it, the willful act remains preoccupied with the relationship and is always in its presence. It is always striking back, and it would never will anything unless it could anticipate accomplishing this objective. It would find no joy in life if it were not spiting someone. It is never simply in its own simple presence, never in the possession of its own soul or wishes. It is thoroughly without imagination, because, not interested in the object of its wishing for its own sake, it is full of endless fantasy, all of it hostile. In my sense of the word it may be said not to wish at all.[11]

Willfulness is, I think, essentially a mocker of reality and people. It is a universal human fact, and has myriad degrees of intensity. At its best it is harmless; it is possible, indeed, that we innoculate ourselves against a good deal of willfulness by basing most of our games on it, all the way from chess to football. If a man wants to go through tackle, we object and block him. It probably lies behind a good deal of the tactic of our two-party system. In the sixteenth century, the Jesuits had two distinguished lecturers following each other in a Spanish university. The second would always find out what the other had said, and then begin his own lecture with the words: *ego vero contra.*

So much for the willful at its best. At its worst it is diabolical, the spirit which completely mocks and negates reality. There is a brilliant description of it in Thomas Mann's portrayal of the last stages of Leverkuhn in *Dr. Faustus.* At its worst it has all the marks which tradition in the West has always associated with the devil.

Thus a man who is really *wishing* needs nothing but the object of his wish. For the *willful* act the object only happens to be there and is of no value save as an instrument for the satisfaction of his willful needs. A man who is truly wishing does not need an audience; he knows that he has a handful of friends who would approve if they were there. He is utterly unlike that character whom Camus calls the dandy:

> The dandy is, by occupation, always in opposition. He can only exist by defiance. Up to now man derived his coherence from his Creator. But from the moment that he consecrates his rupture with Him, he finds himself delivered over to the fleeting moment, to the passing days, and to wasted sensibility. Therefore he must take himself in hand. The dandy rallies his forces and creates a unity for himself by the very violence of his refusal. Profligate, like all people without a role in life, he is coherent as an actor. But an actor implies a public; the dandy can only play a part by setting himself up in opposition. He can only be sure of his own existence by finding it in the expression of other's faces. Other people are his mirror. A mirror that quickly becomes clouded, it is true, since human capacity for attention is limited. It must be ceaselessly stimulated, spurred on by provocation. The dandy, therefore, is always compelled to astonish. Singularity is his vocation, excess his way to perfection. Perpetually incomplete, always on the fringe of things, he compels others to create him, while denying their values. He plays at life

because he is unable to live it. He plays at it until
he dies, except for the moments when he is alone and
without a mirror. For the dandy, to be alone is not
to exist. The romantics talked so grandly about solitude
only because it was their real horror, the one thing
they could not bear.[12]

IV

There are a number of thoughts and questions which occur
to me after this brief look at two forms of relationship, the
relationship which produces the ideal, autonomous, independent and innocent wish and that which produces the
cantankerous thing called willfulness.

First of all I see that I have said: the relationship *which
produces* the autonomous act. And this is indeed what I propose, that it takes a relationship to produce autonomy in
wishing.

Therefore—and this is another way of saying the same
thing—there is nothing wrong with mirrors as such, or with
living in front of a mirror. It all depends on the nature of
the mirror. The ideal mirror should be creative. What I mean
by that can be partly explained by the nature of the psychiatric relationship between doctor and patient. Let us imagine that the patient says something to the mirror of the
doctor and the mirror responds, not passively with an exact
reproduction, but rather with a reflection of the fact plus
meaning, truth, symbol. And let us also imagine the reverse.
If the doctor looks into the eye of the patient he will first see
himself reflected back full of meaning, symbol and fantasy. But as *this* mirror of the patient's eye becomes more
active and creative, the doctor should be able to see that it
is progressively erasing fantasy and symbol and history and
too much "meaning"; it finally arrives at one of the goals of
a good mirror, which is the reporting of a pure fact. That is
to say—for one thing—the doctor becomes another human
being, not a monster or a god.

It is something of this order that an ideal realtionship does
to a wish. Ideally it will denude it or defuse it of everything
but itself. It will help it or allow it to emerge as exactly
what it is. What will it mean when I say that I want a cup of
coffee? Under the influence of a good relationship it will
mean exactly that and nothing more. It will not engulf the
wish in a situation that raises questions about it. It will

not suggest that it is a sign or symbol of anything else, whether of hostility or love. Certainly it will not create an aura of hostility around it. But even more important, it will not make it a sign or a condition of love. ("I approve of your taking coffee. I like coffee, too. It is a sign that you love me. I love you.") The freedom to take coffee may be created by a good relationship, but if it is an ideal wish it cannot itself create the relationship or be a condition for it. Such a wish must be unconditioned. It is created by the outside world but it is not conditioned by it. Therefore every real wish, no matter how small, is a truly creative act, introducing a brand new thing into the world.

Such a wish and such an act is a far cry from the wish and act of the romantic rebel. It is more involved in reality, in relationship, and in the imagination which imagines the real. But it is just as free, autonomous and unconditioned as any romantic wish would ever hope to be.

I believe that if a mechanism or a dynamism or a law or a principle has relevance in any part of the universe, it will have relevance, in some analogical way, in every other part. This would also hold true for ways of thinking. As a result a psychological truth—if we may use that phrase—should be able to meet a counterpart on the theological level of thought, and vice-versa. Let me suggest several theological questions which seem to call for the same kind of speculation as I have just outlined for the structure of the ideal wish.

First of all, there is the idea of creation. The sharpest difficulty we have with the religious idea of the absolute is that it seems not necessary and without a function. Modern man is quite well equipped with a scientific knowledge of the fact that things run by themselves and by virtue of their own inner laws. So why the need of an absolute to keep pushing them around from the outside, so to speak? But such a notion of the absolute is mechanical and not creative. A concept of Himself that would be a greater compliment to God is that he is more truly God to the degree that he communicates his own autonomy to everything. Even a little child yells with joy when it puts something together that is suddenly able to go under its own steam, without the child's pushing. His normal exultant reaction is: look at it go! Accordingly, even if it is not the fashion so to imagine, we can well imagine God exulting when man comes through with a wish of his own. And we can imagine him thinking: look at it go. Such a way of looking at God and things might get around to the notion that if things can take care of themselves then God is doubly necessary. What we would then be saying is that interiority and autonomy must come from the outside.

Another theological question that deserves this kind of consideration is grace. The generic meaning of grace is that of some help communicated from the outside, from God, to man. A still more precise meaning is that it is above all the demands and expectations of human nature, that it is given *gratis* by God, for no other reason than that he wishes to. He is not compelled by anything outside of his own freedom or outside of himself to give it. Some parts of the theological idea of grace must indeed be shocking to many people. There have been long wars among theologians concerning grace, most of them centering toward the triumphant proposition that not only can man not be saved without the grace of God but also that he cannot even be human without the grace of God. The theologians go even this far in insisting on the need of the outside for man.

Some of the concepts we have been discussing might serve to reduce the apparent rigidity of these ideas. Principal among them are two thoughts: the best and the most human part of man is the ability to wish, to say "I wish"; one of the most splendid qualities of the outside world, whether that world be things or God or a teacher or a parent or a doctor, is the ability to communicate help in such a way as to create in others the interior ability to really wish. Grace, therefore, should be understood as the act by which an absolutely outside and free reality communicates an absolutely interior and free existence. The theology of grace has talked mostly of the absolute act and wish of God; it should talk more, as should all of us, of that other absolute to which it is so deeply related, the absolute act and wish of man.

This relationship of mutuality, this creative relationship of the outside to the inside, occurs so centrally in so many of our discussions that I should now like to devote some pages to a consolidation of this theme.

Chapter 3

Mutuality Versus Alienation

A relationship of mutuality creates freedom and unconditionality in human wishing. Interior freedom is a gift (paradoxically, a gift from the outside) that people communicate to each other. Thus we give some explanation of the great Augustinian phrase, ama et fac quod vis.

We may relate ourselves to the world with hostility or with friendship. Here we analyze the gnostic imagination, the type of imagination that has always been alienated and has always seen the world as hostile. We take stock of the special ways in which the gnostic imagination operates on the American Scene.

This analysis is countered by an exploration of friendship and mutuality in human relationships. A real human relationship is creative. In it persons depend each on the other, and can therefore hope in the other, freely and without conditions.

A psychology of hope, if it is to be worthy of so beautiful a name, must search for what is most central to a psychology of hopelessness and must strike against it. In this chapter I again try to isolate the terrible phenomenon of the sense of endlessness and endless burden in the ill, and to strengthen the attack of hope against it. I look further for a sense of an ending and of absolute unconditionality in human wishing and action, for some point of feeling and action that is at rest and peace and does not have to go further than itself. And I continue to find it in the human or religious situation called mutuality.

Within this context, two positions we have taken in our analysis of hope begin to broaden and grow. The first position emphasized that the inside world of man depends on his outside world and that, to create interiority, he needs the outside world. This truth can now take more precisely human and concrete shapes and forms. For one thing, hope itself is a relationship to help. For another, freedom is a gift that is received from the outside. The second position is closely allied to the first. It comes down to this, that relationship is needed to produce freedom. Let us see what comes of this proposition.

However, before we turn to mutuality as the source of unconditionality and autonomy, let us look at its opposite. We already have some simple images of how the world looks or tastes when it seems to be with us and we with it. The simplest example of all is that, when I ask for air and when I breathe, the world responds. We and the world work together in the project of breathing, from the beginning of life to the end. How, on the other hand, does the world look and taste, how do we imagine it, when, as happens so often, some of the forms of mutuality collapse? How does the world look when it seems to be against us? At the very least, in such a situation, the world is no longer seen as bringing help. It does not seem on the side of hope. We do not, the world and ourselves, breathe together. This is a perception of the sick— and of the well.

We may profit at this point from turning our attention temporarily from the sick and asking instead a few questions about the well. How do we look at reality? With what kind of an imagination does American society at this moment look at reality? What and where are the strands of alienation and hostility that produce, in various degree, a hopeless relationship between ourselves and the world?

What I have termed the gnostic imagination has traditionally been the form of imagination that views the world as hostile. It is worth examination, especially in its current American forms. Then, armed with some vision of what the world looks like when seen with such eyes, we may be able to see more clearly the nature of mutuality.

I

Gnosticism is generally acknowledged to have been a syncretistic religion that emerged at almost the same time as Christianity. It borrowed elements from Judaism, Platonism, Zoroastrianism and Christianity itself. The parts fit together into a self-contained system of attitude and feeling toward the world, and, in varying forms, these attitudes and feelings continue to recur in civilization. Not only *was* there a specifically historical thing called the gnostic imagination, but, more important for our discussion, there always will be. There will always be a realistic imagination in man, but there will always be a gnostic imaginative tendency as well. This tendency will incline man to look on the world as alien and hopeless. The world, stars, things, people, are against me, the gnostic imagination urges us to say. My world is against me.

Man must be able to trust and distrust. The balance of the double vision is necessary to life itself. But the balance is crucial. And it is probable that today the balance has swung over to distrust of people and the world. This is one of the strongest features of gnosticism. It is not merely an ancient doctrine; it permeates our world, at this moment. It renders ours a hostile world where we and the ill are kin.

Let us pick a general image for both gnosticism and its imagination, an image and a fact that begins to reveal the significance of our gnostic theme. The fact and the image is one of alienation. For gnosticism God is alien to the world, and the world is an alien, a hostile alien to God and man. Let us think of that thing in the middle, that is to say, the world out there, as alien and an enemy. It cannot be trusted. This is a central image we may keep referring to as we pursue the subject of gnosticism.

If this particular image is sharp but not quite sharp enough, let me choose another in the same vein. A scholar of the gnostic, Hans Jonas, suggests a remarkable affinity between the central drives of the original historical gnosticism and some of our existential tastes of existence. This clue ultimately brought me to the conclusion of Albert Camus' *The Stranger* (of whose sharpness no one will doubt). The hero, Meursault, speaks ironically until his final sentence, in which he carries the gnostic image of the hostile, alien world to its ultimate conclusion:

Almost for the first time in many months I thought of my mother. And now, it seemed to me, I understood why at her life's end she had taken on a "fiance"; why she'd played at making a fresh start. There, too, in that Home where lives were flickering out, the dusk came as a mournful solace. With death so near, Mother must have felt like someone on the brink of freedom, ready to start life all over again. It was as if that great rush of anger had washed me clean, emptied me of hope, and, gazing up at the dark sky spangled with its signs and stars, for the first time, the first, I laid my heart open to the benign indifference of the universe. To feel it so like myself indeed, so brotherly, made me realize that I'd been happy, and that I was happy still. For all to be accomplished, for me to feel less lonely, all that remained to hope was that on the day of my execution there should be a huge crowd of spectators and that they should greet me with howls of execration.[1]

The novel shows us man in the relationship of Stranger to a strange universe, which reacts to him with howls of execration. This image of a man exulting because he has received the derision he expected is a gnostic parody of hope. That parody can be individual, as in the case of Meursault; it can also be cultural.

Let us contrast gnostic culture with two other cultures or ways of looking at the world that run in rough historical parallel with gnosticism: Greek civilization and Christianity.

Surely we can say of Greece, as we cannot say of gnosticism, that it never conceived of a radical gap between man and reality. The Greeks thought of themselves as a part of the cosmos, and they thought of the cosmos with reverence. The world was human. But the gnostic thought of the cosmos as alien, and he thought of it with contempt. True, the Greek perceived the vengeful in nature, laws that were destructive of the human. There were also blind, mechanical forces that were far from human in their ways, but even such Furies did not make the Greek give up; in the *Eumenides* Aeschylus masters these forces and turns them into gracious human spirits. They remain an expression of law and of cosmic law, but to some extent at least they are understood, humanized, and accepted. The terrible pain remains for man, but it does not come from something that is altogether a hostile stranger; Greece did not yet live in our hostile world:

And what exactly is the change that has taken place in the Furies, to explain this change of attitude in the play? Is it that they have given up their claim for a purely mechanical working of the Law that the Doer must suffer, and have accepted Athena's principle that not only the deed shall be considered, but everything that caused or surrounded the deed. They accept πειθοῦς σέβας, the sanctity of the spirit which persuades and hears Persuasion; that is, they will listen to Persuasion and will think again. They become no longer a mechan-

ical Law of Retribution which operates blindly; but a
law which thinks and feels and seeks real Justice.[2]

In Plato (in the *Sophist* and in the *Timaeus*) there is an even
more astonishing statement of the deep fundamental kinship
of man and the universe. For the great categories of human
knowledge (Being, The Same, The Other, Motion, and Rest)
are precisely the fundamental structures of the cosmos. It is
clear that this is no longer our way of imagining the world.

For the gnostic, not even the beginning of such a relationship could exist or develop. The thought would be unholy,
not because the cosmos is so sacred that it should be approached with naked feet and bowed head, but because it is
so evil that it should not be approached by the spirit of man
at all. It has been created by lesser gods than God (the
Archons or rulers). The universe is a vast prison, the earth its
innermost block, and the body (and even the soul) of man
its innermost cell. Gnosis and the gnostic religion endeavors
to bring two and only two pure realities together: God and an
innermost point in man that we can call the spirit.

Everything else between these two things is an obstacle to
the redemption of man and the unity of these two things.
Everything else is alien. And we must live the life of aliens
within the world. Man, therefore, is "lonely, unprotected, un-
comprehended, and uncomprehending." [3] The gnostic picture
of the world differs but little from that of the world as the
devil attacking man. Where the Greek imagination viewed the
world with reverence, the gnostics, to put it in a word, viewed
the world with contempt. Such an imagination, when particularly alive in a culture, paves the way for all the elements of
mental illness and hopelessness.

There is an equally large gap between gnostic imagining
and the new Christian taste of the world. There are so many
apparent pieties in the gnostic view of things, so much seeming virtue in its contempt of the world, that it is just that
much more important to realize how, in the moment of truth,
it became the great enemy of Christianity. The final opposition is total. But the superficial resemblance continues to deceive us. Christianity was fighting its way toward a clearer
and clearer dialectical awareness of the truth that human acts,
these simplest of all cosmic acts, became acts of God in the
Incarnation. It was not even a question of what taste things
had for the Divine Person, as though he were talking about
things outside of him to which he might respond in a gnostic

or a Greek way. God was not alienated from his acts. They were his own acts; he learned the alphabet; he ate, drank, used the earth properly to support his feet or else he would have fallen; he suffered and he, the Divine Person, died. The gnostic could respond by avoiding the issue, by declaring that this was only a seeming body. So the gnostic Simon Magus is apparently speaking of Christ when he says that "he appeared as a man, though he was not one, and was thought to have suffered in Judea, though he did not suffer." [4] We might justly assert that he was in fact speaking of himself.

We, too, have been fighting the same gnostic battle. We say of the gnostics, "who were they?" when the answer very often is *tu es iste vir*—thou art that man. The gnostic version of reality fills part of the soul and imagination of every man. It works in the soul of every Christian, and it still bothers many theologians. Mention the idea to many learned Christologists that Christ learned the alphabet and was helpless without his mother, and it is reasonably sure to produce an almost apologetic set of qualifications, and an explanation that Christ really had infused ideas of all kinds. He knew everything—he knew all about the atom bomb and understood the Gregorian calendar. Even if it is true, what is the reason for this reaction? In it we come very close to the position of Simon Magus: he learned the alphabet but he really did not; he had a mother, according to the final triumphant statement of the Council of Ephesus, but he really did not need her. We must not blaspheme by thinking that he really became man, that he actually could not physically go further, that he simply had to give up under these circumstances and die.

The evidence is strong that whenever reality is or looks too difficult there is a tendency to fly into some gnostic and private version of reality. And this is the inclination of psychosis: to decide that the human reality is not manageable and to build a new, interior world that can be managed. This kind of imagination begins to function where the forms of mutuality break down.

Another factor in the historical reality of the gnostic imagination was its extraordinary mixing of asceticism and freedom. If the world is evil then we should abstain from it; but if it is evil it is also true that its laws are evil, and have no power over us. Indeed, it would be a sin for us who are the children of God to observe them. Moreover, we who know, we gnostics, we the elite, we who alone have knowledge, must have these evil forms of knowledge, too. So the gnostic must experience all things, this being the only way to destroy what has emerged as the wicked law of a wicked God. We must hate reality but must experience what we hate. Psychoanalytic theory might call this a conspiracy between id and superego.

Such an imagination will always be competent to expel all evil from its own soul and find it in a projection onto the outside. It will be a master in inventing scapegoats. If, for example, there were not Jews to blame for everything, the gnostic imagination would invent them. It hardly fails of any of the forms of illness.

The historical idea admits of two and only two points of goodness or beauty or salvation: one is in man, a perfect spot, a perfect faculty, a secret gift, the place of an inner imagination; the second is a single and secret place in reality, which alone is good, divine, beautiful—a safe fortress if only you can get to it, whether you call it God, or beauty, or the Hebrides, or Atlantis, or Hawaii, or America. Everything else is ugly, evil, dangerous, alien. These two things take many forms. I am only suggesting a general structure for them.

From the beginning the gnostic imagination found itself in conflict with the Hebraic imagination, and this conflict continues. We see it in art. For example, though obviously a painting of a Hebraic-Christian fact, Dali's painting of the Sacrament of the Last Supper is at the farthest pole from the Hebraic imagination. The Hebraic imagination is full of reality. Dali's fantasy dissolves reality. It is occult, a dream. No one looks at Christ and Christ looks at no one. Christ is pagan. No man like this man was ever born on land or sea. The inner imagination has substituted its own inner reality for the outer. It has overcome what it could not trust. It has overcome the alien world. In this way it comes close to the art of Hollywood. And I remind myself that in his book *Love and the Western World* Denis de Rougemont has elaborated on this gnostic tendency not only in the western world but also in the western part of our own country.

This is one of the most recurring habits of the gnostic imagination—to be perpetually falling back on some absolutely central point in itself—deep, deep, deep within the spirit, where it can declare an isle of safety against an alien and dangerous world. Where there is no mutuality there must be retreat. The isle and the retreat can take many forms. One —and it is terribly immediate—is the film *Dr. Strangelove.* Its underlying theme is that not only the crazy among the military are crazy but that everybody else is crazy—everybody, that is, save the director. He possesses an imagination superbly released from all the instinctual laws that make a good joke—anything that occurs to his imagination goes. Here the imagination is its own law.

This is the divinely free imagination. Another form of the gnostic imagination is what we might call the innocent imagination. The world is mad, in fact it is mad, mad, mad, mad, mad. I alone am not. My imagination alone can be trusted; it is a spark that cannot be quenched. I walk innocent through a world of thieves, a world of evil, and I emerge beaten but triumphant. In the theater this was the basic assumption behind the technique and vision of such plays as Paul Green's *Johnny Johnson,* or Robert Sherwood's *Idiot's Delight.* Others have suggested that it is one of the basic attitudes toward the world of Huckleberry Finn. I think it is the offending quality in the direction of *Dr. Strangelove.* Surely it is the basic characteristic of the western, that the bad are bad and the good are good and the good guys always win. This is a pious thought, but like many pious thoughts it is not true.

I wish that all the books of the gnostic imagination were pleasant, interesting, or funny. There are a number of books which reveal the more horrible works of the more modern gnostics—all the way from the revolutionaries who alone possess the truth or are willing to crush the other nine-tenths of the world to get to it, as in *The Possessed* of Dostoevsky, to a Hitler who thought that if his bunker and his imagination must come down then the rest of the world should come down with it. Some of the good books on the subject of gnosticism in politics are Eric Voegelen's *The Science of Politics;* Henri de Lubac's *The Drama of Atheist Humanism;* Albert Camus' *The Rebel*—and that great novel, *The Possessed.* I had gone far afield in discussing the non-mutual image of the world but no more than some of these men. They tell us of the terrible streak of violence in this imagination.

I am not about to paint a terrible picture of the gnostic features of the American imagination. But there are several things in America's thinking about herself that I would like to mention in any discussion of gnosticism. First of all there is our concept of ourselves in space, and, secondly, there is our concept of ourselves in time.

Surely I am not straying from the truth if I suggest that America has conceived of herself in space as surrounded by an alien world; how often have we not thought that we are *the* point of goodness and safety in the world. And how often have we looked on others as alien, questionable, potentially evil. The outside world is a jungle. And there is our concept of melting down everybody into the beauty and the glory of the new melting pot, plus the rejection of cultural pluralism for this melting pot idea. People are asked to give up *their* dancing, to give up *their* music—for the melting pot. And what has often come out of it is tremendous sacrifice. In a situation of cultural pluralism nobody would be an alien. But in the melting pot concept everybody was and now—if he has let his music, his dance, his language, his mannerisms dissolve—now he is not. The melting pot demands that everyone become non-alien. And every generation that wins the fight tends to look on the next newcomer as an alien—and wants to keep him that way. We were alien. Now, thank God, another group has come along. They are the aliens. We are not—we belong. And so we are surrounded by an alien and a dangerous world which can only be trusted and depended upon if it is transmuted into our own likeness. We incline to consider difference as a threat. The trouble is that we further extend this way of imagining reality into our domestic life. We tend to fear the normal forms of regionalism and difference and to move toward conformity as a solution. This is ironic, that we try to overcome our alienation by extreme and distorted forms of mutuality.[5]

Of our image in time, R. W. B. Lewis has suggested in *The American Adam* that, just as we tend to see ours as the only point in space, so we are perpetually seeking an only point in time, an absolutely new and good and pure point. The gnostic inclines to isolate himself from every other point in time—from the past. And into this picture the spirituality of obsolescence fits with perfection. So, Lewis speaks of a radically new personality, the hero of the new adventure:

> an individual emancipated from history, happily bereft of ancestry, untouched and undefiled by the usual inheritances of family and race, an individual standing alone, self-reliant and self-propelled, ready to confront whatever awaited him with the aid of his own unique

and inherent resources. It was not surprising, in a Bible-reading generation, that the new hero (in praise or disapproval) was most easily identified with Adam before the Fall. Adam was the first, the archetypal man. His moral position was prior to experience, and in his very newness he was fundamentally innocent . . . of history.[6]

Thus nobody can blame anything on us. "And America since the age of Emerson," he feels, "has persistently been a one-generation culture," constantly trying to invent a view of a new world in the complete sense. No one answers for what occurs before his time in American society. As de Tocqueville said, "In America, society seems to live from hand to mouth, like an army in the field." [7]

One burden in this notion of the American Adam is that we must wake up every morning completely ready to create a new world. We can fall back on nothing. We must question everything. The result is that we find ourselves in the astonishingly ironic position of living in a completely moralistic world. We must question everything, asking whether it is right or wrong. Mothers must rear children with moralistic anxiety in every detail: is this right? wrong? It is not that we have simply and freely decided that nine-tenths of what we do in our culture is *this,* and not *that!* No, we must start all over again and question everything. But the final irony is that instead of giving us freedom this endless questioning creates a totally and hopelessly moralistic world in which we have to question everything in order to get a good night's sleep.

God helps those who help themselves. What does this American catch-phrase, which appeals to the gnostic part of our souls, mean?

I am terribly afraid it, too, involves the concept of reality as a jungle. God helps those who help themselves, and God help you if you don't help yourself—nobody else will. You are living in a jungle and must take measures to defend yourself.

Let other nations locate and define their own gnostic elements, and the areas where *their* bonds of mutuality with the world break down. I have been sketching a few strands of the American version of this problem.

II

By mutuality, on the other hand, I mean an interacting relationship, an interacting contribution that occurs between man and the world, or between person and person, or between man and God, from which something new and free is born. I assume that the problem of mutuality *is* critically important to us in our generation. We have enough evidence, clinical and social, for the suspicion that it is so. The breakdown of many forms of relationship, and of the hope it invariably creates, is probably a source of the waves of mental illness and anxiety that flourish among us. We become increasingly aware of this.

There is scarcely a scientist who will not insist, at least in the order of clinical and therapeutic practice, that some critical point of cure and hope for mental sickness involves the achievement of a relationship with the world: between doctor and patient, between the well and the sick, between society and the alienated individual. It is a kind of miraculous but not magical point to reach.[8] It is not reached without travail and preparation.

To put the matter as simply as possible: The patient begins to feel, after the travail of work and of grace, that the doctor is on his side. Until that moment the doctor has been a judge, a punisher, hostile, a threatening giant, an enemy with whom to contend. He is the law in all its objectivity and exteriority. He is the symbol of all the exterior and interior giants before whom we seem helpless. He is omnipotent with an omnipotence that forbids interior growth, action and equality. The agonies of the sick before such images are incalculable and without hope. But now the moment of revelation and of grace has come. It is as though the soul relives on a small scale the whole history and development of the race through the Old and New Testaments, through the law to love. The first insights into the possibility of mutuality are remarkable in their effects. This transfiguration is the object of all the hopes of the sick and the well. Now that one point of reality is transformed, the whole of reality is transformed with it. The doctor, who was the enemy, is now seen in his actual role of a helper: as a result half of the pain vanishes, because the pain had been a construct of hopelessness. The patient had felt the constant need to be alert; but now he enters a new and creative passivity, that acts almost without acting, because it now wishes *with* and not *against,* and is felt to be wished *with* by another. To be wished *with* by a true friend, or by a few, who are in touch with the depth of real feeling and wishing in the soul, and who help a man to discover and contact his own soul, is a possession without price. Now there is real hope, no matter what happens in the world outside such relationships. For the final object of all our hope is love.

Now, too, we are in a position to "create" our own souls and foster their growth, and to have them created and fostered by another. Real love communicates a self-identity and autonomy that is no longer in basic conflict with real mutuality. It takes two real self-identities to make a relationship, and it takes such a relationship to make two real persons. In mutuality, each of the parties helps the other to become himself. Even if we limit ourselves to that much and no more, it is already clear that such a unity is creative.

Real mutuality also communicates freedom. If we remember that mutuality includes a profound wishing together, we may understand how this is so. In real friendship or love, the mutual situation seems to rise in a completely liberating way above the necessity of defining itself by any precise wish that says in effect, either wish this or there is no friendship or love: Take a trip with me today, or have a drink with me now; do as I wish, or there is no bond. Such either/or situations have two effects: 1) They determine the nature of mutuality, not from within, but from some precise, objective, and limiting fact on the outside. Wishing and wishing together become completely externalized, and what becomes divinized here is not love, but some petty external fact, all-consuming and threatening. 2) This fact, whatever it is, establishes itself as a dominating, tyrannical, demanding condition. It makes mutuality conditional at its heart: if you take this trip with me, I will love you. All mental illness has this deep sense of conditional love.

Not only does this reduce friendship, love and mutuality to the external and the conditional; very often they become plain, outright blackmail. This kind of relationship, if sufficiently extended, produces some degree of mental illness. It also makes creativity impossible. Creativity, we have noted, may mean many things; but it invariably means, among these many things, that what is brought into the world is completely new, unconditioned and in contact with the depths of personal thought and feeling. In all these senses, it is felt to be free.

It should be clear that real mutuality, real love, does what it wishes and allows others to do what they wish. (*Ama et fac quod vis.*) It seeks a moment that will be internalized, unconditioned, and totally new, therefore creative. Before we reject such a human hope out of hand, as absurd, irrational and dangerous, let us consider this ambition with great care.

I propose that (in this critical question of locating the heart of true mutuality) the ideal situation at which Christianity aims is totally removed from the situations that tend in our day, and in any day, to produce mental illness in a civilization.

In mental illness, the striking, recurrent phenomenon is that of the wish that seems to be wrong, forbidden, judged, condemned. This holds true even for two wishes that form a pair of contraries—one of which should certainly turn out to be all right. Mental illness discovers that not only is it forbidden to go for a walk, but so also it is forbidden not to go for a walk. The prohibition and the inhibition have become progressively universal. Most agonizing and most destructive of all, the exterior human figures and situations which originally did the forbidding are now incorporated and literally become psychological parts of the self, so that the self denies, destroys, and inhibits the self. The oppressive system, obviously and essentially noncreative, has been incorporated as an actual, living entity. There is no mutuality between the real self and this incorporated self, and the more the latter prevails, the less freedom there is.

We have seen that in Christianity the terms of our human situations are totally different. In terms of illness, everything is forbidden. In terms of Christianity everything is permitted. The only condition is that we observe the limits of good and evil. But this is not a condition as we have used the word condition. Evil is essentially wishing for some form of nonbeing and the nonhuman; it is best understood as a refusal to wish the human. Therefore, we can express the freedom of Christianity in another simple form: if the human personality is inserted into reality, if its choices are reality-choices, then it does not make any difference what it chooses. It is free, and absolutely free. Let us be as simple as can be in our examples. It does not matter before God or man whether we walk or ride, whether we take coffee or tea, whether we decide to be a doctor, lawyer, priest, butcher, baker, or candlestick maker, whether, if both are possible, I rest now or work, whether I continue this sentence or end it here. This is surely part of what is meant by the freedom of the children of God, who are no longer servants or slaves asking the master of the house if this or that is all right, but are rather children of a Father who communicates family rights and does not question.[9] It is we who raise the question.

This is the most extraordinary and most fruitful form of mutuality in the world. Granted our presence to reality and to love, God wishes us to choose, in the knowledge that it is all right to choose and that choosing and wishing make the choice all right. This is not subjectivity or solipsism because every choice of love is related to reality and is the choice of a reality. On the other hand, neither is it magic— which would be the case if there were only one choice among thousands which would be the best, and God help us if we do not find it. The theological supposition that there is one right way is the ultimate source of all externalism.[10]

This kind of "magic" has the effect and intention of absolving us from wishing and thinking, and from all the operations of a truly interior life. It supposes that there is some one precise, magical thing or person or event in the world outside us that will happily come along to do the wishing for us. It allows us to project our identity, our capacity for thinking and feeling and wishing, outside ourselves, and so we are left haunted by that sense of a lack of identity characteristic of all our illnesses.

There are other ghosts to haunt and afflict us. If we insist upon inserting "morality" into the wrong places, if we insist that there is one right answer for everything, if we require that the object do all the wishing, without the mutuality of our own wishing, there are ghastly consequences. First of all, the process never works; *it introduces an endless and exhausting search into life*. Pure externalism involves endlessness. Secondly, no matter what we do within such terms as these, there is a sense of failure and of guilt and of being judged by some anonymous object with which, no matter what we do, we cannot make contact. For this magical object we seek, this one right thing, is really nonexistent; but it exercises a strange and absolute tyranny over everything we do. Because we are not free and because we lack Christian interiority, we are oppressed by an anonymous and ruthless sense of law. The strange myths of the novels of Franz Kafka are full of this sense of constant and anonymous judgment upon ourselves from which we have no recourse, for the guilt cannot be located, and the judge is anonymous, and the judgment without reason. How can such a psychology or theology produce anything but hopelessness?

Clearly there is no mutuality in such situations. The object does all the work. As often as it does so, it becomes tyrannous and unfruitful for us. But if we are honest we will recognize in ourselves a secret and powerful wish to conspire with such totally objectified and tyrannous situations, to abandon our own wishing, to give up the burden of our own souls. The Grand Inquisitor of Dostoevski was half right. God wishes us to be free, with the freedom of mutuality between subject and object, between ourselves and the world, between ourselves and Him. But half of us rejects this freedom, this mutuality. It is too much trouble.

This is only part of the truth, however. There is also in every man and woman a deep, absorbing desire for identity and for the salvation of which identity is an analogue. This desire is an actual, vital, driving force whose strength we simply cannot calculate. Where it is frustrated it produces the only agony that really matters. If man cannot in this sense create, he feels lost and lost to himself. He is not in touch, he is out of touch with himself. Rather than being absorbed by biologically dangerous wishes (as we read in the system of Freud) he now refuses to wish, or takes the cosmic stance of wishing *against*, because of the failure of his search for mutuality. I agree, therefore, with Dr. Leslie Farber that the probable basis of hysteria is some form of refusal to wish or of wishing *against*. These hysterical roots he summarizes under the name of *willfulness*.[11] We have seen that it is a good word to distinguish the whole world of the willful, the irrational, and the solipsistic from the creative world that I have tried to summarize under the idea of wishing. And we can repeat the words of the angel of God when he said to Daniel: "The Lord hath loved thee because thou art a man of desires."[12]

No two sets of terms can be more unlike than the terms of illness and the terms of Christianity. In saying this, I have no slightest intention of criticizing the sick or of excluding them from Christianity. Indeed, it seems necessary that all of us, in our spiritual history, should pass through this way of law into the life of Christian liberty. But how shall we progress if we do not sense that the terms of the stages differ?

To mental illness, all is forbidden and nothing is right. Its final logic is checkmate, the failure of mutuality, and hopelessness. It often involves a struggle to the bitter death between two inner parts of the soul—that which seeks identity, mutuality, freedom, and that which is the very spirit of denial and negation. But to Christianity, once the decision is really made, everything is permitted, anything may be wished, there is no more bowing to every wind from the outside world, there is possession of one's soul, and the possibility of restoring the old idea of the soul as a garden. There is definiteness and rest.

All this is the fruit of mutuality.

We are apparently in the midst of a great anthropological age, wherein man advances toward new heights of creativity, knowledge, mastery and self-actualization. Perhaps he does not so much fear the power of the atom as he fears his own power for acting and for wishing. He does not feel that it is altogether right to wish so much and so greatly. Therefore he stands guilty, not in fact, but in fantasy. He feels that he lives in opposition to the old gods, and therefore does what he does without a sense of mutuality, and with the taste of the forbidden. A superficial theology would be tempted to say that these feelings and fantasies are correct, that man dare not aspire to be God. But why not, why not wish greatly and go forward boldly, if God wills it so? Christianity alone, with this sense of absolute freedom within reality, can take away this anxiety. Within what other terms can man be creative in peace? How can he get through this daring and difficult period successfully without this sense of mutuality? without this profound assurance that it is all right to grow up and all right to be man? without the confidence that it is God's will as well as his own?

Chapter 4

Hope and Waiting

The ability to wait is central to hope, and must therefore have an essential place in human wishing. If hope directs itself toward good things that belong to the future and that

are only difficult to achieve, then it must know how to wait.
The kind of wishing that can wait is the mark of growing
maturity.

Two kinds of waiting must be carefully distinguished. One
waits because there is nothing else to do. The other, which
goes with hope, is positive and creative. It waits because
it knows what it wishes and wants.

This quality of waiting is central in the psychology of
Freud, and represents the most characteristic difference be-
tween the primary and secondary processes in his system. It
is also a basic element, for this system, in the explanation
of the origins of human thought.

If hope means a number of things, it certainly means the
ability to wait. It means this by substance and by definition.
For by definition it means that we wish a difficult future good
or that we are in trouble and cannot yet see the way out. It
means that we decide to wait.

The decision to wait is one of the great human acts. It
includes, surely, the acceptance of darkness, sometimes its
defiance. It includes enlarging one's perspective beyond a
present moment, without quite seeing the reason for doing
so. Fortitude and endurance are there, to an extent, beyond
the merely rational. Waiting is sometimes an absolute, which
chooses to wait without seeing a reason for waiting. It does
not ignobly accept such pseudo-reasons as "don't worry,"
"don't fret," "don't be silly," "listen to better judgment," "a
Christian knows there is no reason for stress." It simply
chooses to wait, and in so doing it gives the future the only
chance it has to emerge. It is, therefore, the most fundamental
act, not the least act, of the imagination.

The combination of two qualities, decisive wishing and acting on the one hand, and the ability, on the other, to wait,
is almost the secular definition of maturity; but they are also
analogies for the central structure of a healthy theological
atmosphere. In either case, we are talking about the ability
to wish and the ability to endure frustration.

Pure religion and pure Christianity, therefore, call both
for the power to wish and act and the equal power of ascetical waiting.

It is important that we have a correct understanding of
this crucial word *waiting.*

There is a strong bond, almost to the point of identity,

between waiting and hoping. When waiting is a true power, when it is neither apathy nor despair nor panic nor willfulness, it is ready to spring if a possibility appears or an exit opens. At times, in full control, it is simply enjoying the luxury of choosing among alternatives—shall I go swimming or go to the opera?—allowing itself the sweet taste, without hurry, of being in command of itself and its world. At other times, full of pain, nearly overwhelmed by impossibility, it may choose, for no reason at all, to live rather than to die. That is, it may simply choose, nothing left, itself. It may choose to wait. This is the greatest victory of all for the sick, one without which everything else is impossible. To choose, in the moment of the impossible, to live and not to die, may very well be for the mentally ill that extraordinary moment where the difference between wishing and willfulness breaks down at last, to their relief. They have defied reason, many of them, all their lives; they have suffered through endless, compulsive periods of a willfulness that was beyond their control. Now let them be willful enough to wait beyond all reason and to defeat illness by its own weapons.

The waiting we are talking about is positive and creative; it makes real wishing possible. When properly understood and exercised it means the ability to remain fixed upon a goal, to cope with obstacles, to make detours when an immediate path is blocked, to be willing to take all the intermediate means that are essential to the attaining of the goal. It also means the ability to handle other wishes so that they do not impede the realization of the central wish.

To be able to wait, therefore, also includes the ability to handle hopelessness. It will not panic, like a child, at any and every appearance of the hopeless.

We may further say that positive waiting is not altogether passive. It is, rather, active, in the sense that it does not yield. It confronts hopelessness, acknowledges it, grants it its rights and proper domain, but does not yield to its assault. There is a good and central point to be searched for in mental illness, that being asked to yield it does not.

The sick person, when he does not yield, need not know what it is he does not yield to. In fact, for a time he does not and cannot know. This is the extraordinary quality of this moment, to fight with an unknown enemy and not to yield, though the fight may take a lifetime. What is important is that we grant this man the right to fight against an unknown enemy and not burden him with the nonsense of various abstractions. We must honor his darkness and not burden him with our interpretations, because every interpretation is at that moment a burden and a demand, of the very kind that has made him ill to begin with.[1] Interpretations can come later, but not at this moment when any interpretation or moralistic help is a mockery and an attack. Many people cannot respect this moment because they respect only their own views and preachments.[2] Many confuse this moment of absolute waiting with despair. The confusion is wrong— and harmful. What is involved here is an act of waiting and not yielding, no different, save in degree, from all the moments in life where we do well or badly at waiting. But there is a point and a hump which, if waited through and got over, will make conversation and discussion possible.

One of the qualities of waiting is that it accepts the need and reality of all intermediate worlds. One of these worlds is the world of the means that are necessary if we are to get to the world of ends. To be able to accept this conditionality is to be able to wait.

If I want to get somewhere I must take all the intermediate steps. We have all had the kind of dream in which, say, we skip intermediate stations on a railroad to arrive quickly and angelically at our journey's end. The unconscious, which is the place of the dreamer in us, cannot wait. It can indeed wish, but it cannot wait or act intermediately.

If that part of us which cannot wait acts in this way with regard to space and the leaping of intermediate spaces, its action with regard to time is somewhat the same.

The hoping part of man waits for a given moment and a given time. There is an extraordinary sense of real time and real timing in real hope, and the ability to wait through all the intervening moments. The uneducated part of man, the negative unconscious, does not know how to wait for the appointed moment and pretends that time is for lesser mortals than itself. This part of us, really the child's part, is imperious and eternal, using the language of eternity to conceal the fact that it cannot wait or hope. Let us listen to Freud himself on this pretention to timelessness.

As early as 1897 he had declared that "disregard of the characteristic of time is no doubt an essential distinction between activity in the preconscious and unconscious." There are allusions to this extraordinary desire for timelessness in *The Interpretation of Dreams,* in *The Psychopathology of*

Everyday Life, in *Beyond the Pleasure Principle,* and in Lecture XXXI of the *New Introductory Lectures.* In his essay on *The Unconscious* in 1915, he remarks that:

> The processes of the system [it uses] are timeless; they are not ordered temporally, are not altered by the passage of time; they have no reference to time at all. . . .
>
> The unconscious processes pay just as little regard to *reality.* They are subject to the pleasure principle; their fate depends on how strong they are and whether they fulfill the demands of the pleasure-unpleasure regulation.[3]

As I understand it, then—and this understanding can be further spelled out in the language of Freud—the human unconscious is not yet educated to the idea or reality of time. Whatever wish occurs to it belongs to what we may call an eternal present; this may be interpreted, as you will, according to a brilliant romanticism or according to the homelier way of a child; if I have a wish there is only the present and no future. The wish must be gratified now, or else. There is no time. If, therefore, the object is not present now—right now —the alternative is not hope but despair.

It is not sufficiently understood how much hope, considered in terms of this sense of time and this capacity for waiting, enters into the fundamental structures of psychoanalytic theory, especially the psychoanalytic understanding of the very genesis of human thought. Thought, so interpreted, is a construction that has learned to do without the immediate presence of objects and to substitute interior facsimiles of and for it. It has learned to save the energy which is ordinarily spent on objects, to make it wait, and to *think* of things by means of this waiting energy. Thus it begins to be clear that a form of waiting—and, we might add, of hoping—enters into the very nature of human thought.

II

The most crucial issue into which the whole specifically human ability to wait enters is that of the decisive difference between what Freud chose to call the primary and the secondary mental functions. It is in the medical discussion of these two processes that we will see the emergence of the ideal relation between wishing and waiting.

This is not a technical book, and I therefore regret that, because of the importance of the question, I must in a moment enter into a short technical discussion of what Freud meant by these terms. In a book that defends the primacy of wishing this happens to be essential. I maintain again that wishing is under a cloud and it is only these two emphases on its relation to mutuality and to waiting that will give wishing its place in the sun.

For what else are we doing and have we been doing but *examining* the nature of wishing? And that is what Freud's great distinction between the primary and the secondary processes was doing; it was *examining* wishing. This is itself the complete difference between these two stages of life. The primary process is pure wishing; the secondary process is a life of *examined wishes,* but wishes for all that. Between the two moments, the primary and the secondary, there has been enough of a gap to make the difference between an animal and a man. Only a man can wait this much and only a man can decide, in hope, that this act of waiting and the momentary renunciation it involves may turn out to be worthwhile.

Ernest Jones says unhesitatingly that the exploration by Freud of this distinction between the primary and the secondary processes, together with the related distinction between the "pleasure-principle" and the "reality-principle," represents Freud's chief claim to fame and transcends in importance his discovery of the unconscious.

What is the problem?

According to Freud we must recognize a primary element in us that is the home of wishes and "that is unable to do anything but wish." [4] This is the part of us that is timeless and eternal, so to speak, not seeing that everything has a time, but clamoring, instead, for a present where all is fulfilled; it sees no contradictions in wishes; it always chooses the line of least resistance. It cannot wait, cannot tolerate frustration, "is unable to do anything but wish"; [5] it must at all costs discharge and release its excitations.

In the language we have been using we can further say of it that its goal is the immediate; it has no perspective; it lives on the literal, and has no imagination. Because it cannot imagine, it cannot wait and cannot hope. It is as instinctive in withdrawing from frustration and in flying from the displeasing as it is in moving toward the immediate good. So far as the unconscious is in an equation with this primary system of action and reaction, "there is no negation, no doubt, and no degree of certainty; everything is absolute."

It should be clear that the primary processes can have either one of two histories:

1. They can follow an isolated history, remaining by themselves and not growing into the examining, appraising, exploring, and structuring shapes of the secondary processes. So far as our subject is concerned they then become or remain the place where all things are simultaneously and hopelessly hoped for. Their place becomes the place of a hopelessness that cannot appraise, relate or wait.

Clearly, too, these processes, if left to themselves, are omnipotent. And since omnipotence is a satisfactory state, they tend to avoid contact with other processes or with the testing of reality. The "hopes" of these elements and drives are so large that we can do nothing more accurate than associate the tonal quality of all of them with the boundless or unlimited. It is understandable, then, that if they do not keep moving into the fuller identity of the secondary processes these omnipotent forces will treat every limited human thing with contempt. And to the degree that man is under the influence of these forces he will be unable to be quiet and will always be in motion; he will not be able to put down roots in any definite place, nor will he be able to be satisfied with one wife. He will never wait. He will be a cynic.

2. We must not suppose, on the other hand, that the adult man, all primary processes and omnipotence put aside, now stops wishing. Rather, we must understand that he has learned to wish more firmly and no longer allows his wishes to be shaken by every wind of another wish. Only a man who really knows how to wish knows how to wait. Why else would he wait? [6]

There are, indeed, other kinds of waiting that must be distinguished from the waiting of real hope.

There is the waiting that has forgotten its own face, has forgotten what it wishes, and is just waiting. It is no different from apathy; it is related to deadness of feeling and thought. This seems to be the kind of waiting Samuel Beckett was talking about in *Waiting for Godot*, a waiting that is always fearful it will forget the very last fragment of an interest and a wish it once had:

> *Estragon:* (*having tried in vain to work it out.*) I'm tired! (*Pause.*) Let's go.

Vladimir: We can't.
Estragon: Why not?
Vladimir: We're waiting for Godot.
Estragon: Ah! (*Pause. Despairing.*) What'll we do, what'll we do!
Vladimir: There's nothing we can do.
Estragon: But I can't go on like this!
Estragon: Is that all there is?
Vladimir: There are radishes and turnips.
Estragon: Are there no carrots?
Vladimir: No. Anyway you overdo it with your carrots.
Estragon: Then give me a radish (*Vladimir fumbles in his pockets, finds nothing but turnips, finally brings out a radish and hands it to Estragon who examines it, sniffs it.*) It's black![7]

This deadly, brilliant talk continues in the middle of lives brought to a dead point by people who like pink more than black radishes, have "tried everything," are looking for "an occupation" or "a relaxation," and whose strongest vow is: "let us persevere in what we have resolved, before we forget."

This is a pure form of waiting that has no quality, is dank, is not human and is, in some strange way, without hope and also without hopelessness. It is a no-man's-land untouched by the questions of hope or hopelessness. It is a world somewhere between the well and the ill, a world we are liable to opt for.

This waiting comes near to the common forms of illness which afflict many of the well in our generation. It is a dull, neutral, inhuman waiting that tries to hide itself under talk like the above. It is not quite hopelessness. It is a kind of secularization of real hopelessness, not even allowing our hopelessness to climb to the level of something really significant and human. Thus, a few lines later, Vladimir remarks, "This is becoming really insignificant," and the retort of Estragon is, "Not enough." [8]

III

I think that for exploration's sake we must make the decision that this is where we are in our generation, in a midway world between hope and hopelessness, not quite able to catch up with the life or the rhythms of either. We make fun of people who hope and we put people in hospitals who do not hope. And in between are very many men. We used to wait for one or the other, for hope or hopelessness, to descend upon us. Now one of my hypotheses is that of a new culture in between hope and hopelessness.

This situation does not work out in favor of the ill, because a civilization that is rooted in these midway assumptions is going to be alarmed by any fraction that breaks the rule by moving too decisively toward hopelessness. Such a move will rock a whole society if its metaphysical and theological and humanistic assumptions rule out the possibility or value of strong moves toward hope or despair.

Another assumption behind the kind of non-human waiting we have just been describing, over against the waiting that characterizes hope, is the interdiction or death of the imagination. This waiting does not involve an act of the imagination which keeps reality open and keeps declaring that not all the facts are in. Nor is it able to create a perspective for a fact. It waits because wishing is dead and there is nothing else to do but wait.

This waiting comes from a lack of attention and wishing. Beckett has another character say: "I don't remember having met anyone yesterday. But tomorrow I won't remember having met anyone today." And another says: "You're sure you saw me, you won't come and tell me that you never saw me!"[9]

Our other kind of waiting, the waiting of hope, has made up its mind and wishes so strongly that it will wait for what it wants.

And it will not forget.

It is this positive ability to wait that insures the relationship of our wishes to reality, preventing them from being the expression of hallucination or omnipotence. Thus waiting makes real wishing possible and real wishing makes waiting possible.

Which takes the primacy and comes first, the wishing or the waiting, I do not know, nor do I think it necessary to find out.

Leaving these two principal elements in a psychology of hope, wishing and waiting, firmly if mysteriously related, let us turn now to the reality they both seek or wait for. What are some of the elements and structures in reality that might relate more sharply than others to hope? In asking this question and in trying to answer it, we will explore the possibility of a metaphysics of hope.

part three

TOWARD A METAPHYSICS OF HOPE

Prologue on

HOPE AND REALITY

At this point we begin our exploration into the possibility of a metaphysics of hope. Can we begin to assemble into one picture those aspects of reality which are healing and which correspond to the needs of hope?

There will be three main areas of study in these final chapters. First, it will be proposed that reality—that is, existence itself, which is the great object of philosophy—is also the great object of hope and is curative in all its wide forms. A mastery of fantasy and a restoration of different contacts with reality, with what we will call "the bare fact," is the great need of the sick and the well. Then we shall talk, in a further chapter, of the centrality of the human reality as healer. Next in importance will be the proposition that reality is non-conflictual; it does not of itself involve conflict and hopelessness. The final chapter will illuminate the role of the realistic imagination in the healing of illness.

It will be suggested that the student of philosophy might very well study the processes of mental illness, and the relationships of healing to existence, if he wishes to become a better philosopher of existence.

The title *A Metaphysics of Hope,* which I use for this final section, seems to me an altogether good and valid phrase. I wish I had invented it. However, it has been used, and used well, several times before.

Gabriel Marcel opens his book *Homo Viator*[1] with a well-known essay, "An Introduction to a Metaphysics of Hope." I have not been slow to use several of his central concepts about hope, and am sure that this book has profited from them.

Another and still more fascinating writer who uses this phrase and explores its meaning is Norman O. Brown, professor of classics at Wesleyan University, in his *Life Against Death: The Psychoanalytic Meaning of History*. Undoubtedly *Life Against Death* has shocked some people, but I believe that the substance of the book, while open to misunderstandings, is solid and important, and should be studied by serious students of theology or psychology. Though we may not agree in detail, there are two directions in which my own studies and his travel together: he strikes out in the direction of life, as I do of wishing; and we share a distrust of every theory which supports essential conflict anywhere, in reality or in man. Since we shall come to this problem later, I shall at this point only cite a single sentence from Brown's book: "Dialectics rather than dualism is the metaphysic of hope rather than despair."[2] I shall discuss the meaning of that sentence in Chapter Four of this section.

I

My own reason for using the phrase *a metaphysics of hope* seems more general than the reasons of either Gabriel Marcel or Norman Brown. I cannot put this reason more simply than by saying that metaphysics has always been more deeply engaged than any other science of man in getting at existence as existence and reality as reality. What hope is trying to get at more than anything else, especially amid the hopelessness of mental illness, is the healing power of existence and reality. Metaphysics and hope, therefore, have the same object.

The difficulty with most forms of the study of metaphysics is that they are, professedly, dedicated to an exploration of existence and its most final structures but do not have enough to do with reality, with the very reality they profess to study. Too many courses in metaphysics make contact with existence with indecent haste and then weave an enormous structure of speculation around this slight and nominalistic contact. The taste of existence is lost almost as soon as it is gained. The first act of metaphysics, it seems to me, should be to make a solid and prolonged contact with existence itself, and the student should be taught to practice a constant return to this contact all along the line of his speculation. Otherwise he is only playing a game with logical counters and is bringing philosophy into further disrepute. This is one very good reason why philosophy is not respected in our civilization.

It was for such reasons that Plato would not allow a young man to study philosophy. We need not be as strict as he was about the matter, but we should at least insist that a reasonably substantial place, over a few propaedeutic years, be given to this first act of metaphysics, that is to say, to the actual taste of existence. This can be done in many solid ways: it can be done through an extended taste of the work of the realistic imagination in literature and the arts; it can be done by a serious study of the difference between sophistry and truth, as the distinction between the two was forcefully and beautifully carved out by Socrates and as it has been elaborated in many forms in the history of the West; it can be done in many significant ways through the study of reality and illusion in politics, or through the exploration of the ideal of objectivity in science. My own work in the past has led me to believe that it can be done in an exceptionally human way through the study of the literary imagination as an instrument for the exploration of reality. And I now propose that the student of metaphysics, the student, if you will, of reality, would be greatly aided by a study of the processes of mental illness. I shall make some occasional suggestions in that direction through this whole section.

We must leave it to the clinical worker and theorists to work out the fact in detail. But the fact is that reality is healing for those who are without hope, and it is the separation from reality that causes despair.[3]

It is all the forms of separation that cause all the degrees of hopelessness. It is all the degrees of contact that give us the degrees of hope.

The first chapter in this section, therefore, will try to come to grips with the meaning for the sick of these two words: *existence* and *reality*.

The second chapter will move a step further into the content of these words; it will ask questions and make some statements about the human reality as the hope and the healer of the sick. If they hope for anything, short of God, they hope to be human.

II

To these central thoughts about reality I would like to make a critically important addition. Reality, and the human reality, is indeed the great healer, and it *is* our hope that we be able to reach and keep in touch with that healing point. But the other half of the hope of man, especially of modern man, is that he should himself be able to make some contribution to the nature of reality, especially to the immediate reality in which he lives. Otherwise he remains passive before a huge set of completed objects and situations and giant mechanisms with which he has had nothing to do; he tends to feel helpless and hopeless before them. He is told by many voices that:

Business is business, with its own laws and he cannot do anything about it.

Politics are politics, an objective life he must accept.

War is war, with its own terrible laws, and who will question them?

All are completed; all are gigantic. They are parahuman, beyond all help or hope. Thus, because of the heavy weight and threat of the outer, objective world, human beings are greatly helped in their hope by an understanding of existence which would give them *their* share in the making of *their* world. We have seen that it is possible to create a psychology of hope within which this human contribution is possible, within which the wishes of man can be both realistic and autonomous. We should therefore ask parallel questions about metaphysics. Can man shape reality as well as be shaped by it? Is it possible to make a subjective contribution without the net effect being seen as any the less objective? Can imagination shape the world as well as be shaped by it?

When we turn to our first question, the shaping of man and of hope by reality, let us keep these other questions in mind. For man *must* also have an internal life at any cost, and an internal life which makes a contribution to the external world.

There are, of course, exaggerating ways of describing this problem of the place of reality and the place of man's imagination in the shaping of our world. But usually the exaggerations have a reason. Today, for example, the object, the objective world, the organization, is in such a state of dominance that the human person is more than usually compelled to find a place for his own imagining and creating.

One protest against this imbalance is the protest of the modern artist. In so many cases he would choose "the discrepant" rather than work which even comes near to representing an object. "We refuse, as emphatically as Byzantium refused," says André Malraux, "to be ruled by appearance." [4]

The fantasy life of the mentally ill is the most extreme, yet understandable, attempt of man to restore the balance between the subject and the object.

Actually there is no such thing in man's life as a pure "object" or a pure "fact" to which he has not contributed. And *this* rockbottom "fact" can be the basis for his continuing hope that he *must* have a place in the world or be ill.

Man is made not only to have a place but to *make* places, to make worlds, not out of whole cloth, not in terms of an isolated and therefore sterile imagination, but in terms of an imagination that is in a constant and creative relationship with the world. It is on this state of mutuality that even the simplest facts depend, and out of this relationship they emerge. Here is the way Marion Milner puts it in her book *On Not Being Able to Paint*:

> Certainly seeing with one's own eyes, whether in painting or in living, seeing the truth of people and events and things needed an imagination; for the truth was never presented whole to one's senses at any particular moment, direct sensory evidence was always fragmentary and had to be combined into a whole by the creative imagination. Even the perception of a chair or a carrot was an imaginary act, one had to create imaginatively, out of one's past experience of walking around things or holding them in one hand, the unseen other side of the chair or the carrot. And how much more did one have to create the inside of things. And when the solid object was a living person, what great feats of imagination even the most unimaginative person achieves in recognizing them, not only as solid bodies with things inside, bones and nerves and blood and so on, but also as having their past and their future inside, memories and hopes and ideas.[5]

While this is indeed putting in a strong claim for the creative action of man in his partnership with the world in the making of the world, it is still not the most adventuresome of the contemporary claims in that direction. There are other discussions that go even further and are bolder. Whether technological culture is a proof of these happy claims or an incredibly ironic commentary on them is a good question. It is certainly clear that in many ways they satirize and destroy the hope that nature itself, and the very act of human thought, establishes in man: the hope that he can participate in the making of his own world.

Is this one of his great forms of hopelessness, that man must today stand passive, inert and apathetic before so many of the giant forms of our day? Does he therefore again differ only in degree from the ill who gaze with terror at their giant forms?

We shall study some of the possible forms of an active, creative and composing human reality in the third and fourth chapters of this section. In particular we shall study the ways in which this activity has no trouble in wedding with passivity and the ways in which man longs to be both independent and dependent. If these opposites are always at war, denying and cancelling each other out, the human condition is hopeless and death is the only principle. If we can have both, if *this* possibility is rooted in the very nature of reality, then there is hope.

Chapter 1

The Science of the Bare Fact

It is the wide forms of existence and reality itself that are curative and healing, for the sick and the well. This chapter will look at some of the meanings of the statement that "the truth will set you free."

There is nothing the sick find more difficult than to enter the presence of the bare facts in which they are to be involved. These facts have, for them, become surrounded and distorted by shadows and fantasies; the present moment is with difficulty seen as the present and not the past. There are symbolic displacements of all kinds. Yet those of the well who are tempted to think it is easy to come into the presence of a fact might remember the penetrating dictum of a wise poet and critic: the highest test of a civilization is its sense of fact.

A fact, or a truth, or a reality, is a kind of absolute which, if acknowledged, eliminates those endless and hopeless displacements that never work except to fatigue the spirit of man.

The new medical science of the mind might aptly call itself the science of the bare fact. "The truth will set you free," says St. John (8:32), and this could be interpreted for the sick as saying, "the bare facts will set you free," if only you can locate them. This takes time and is not an easy process for anyone, much less for the ill who have a thick undergrowth of shadows to march through. But we all have shadows, residues of the past, contaminated areas, where present facts are confused with past shadows.

The truth is that we are all sick to a degree, though that is nothing to disturb us. For all this means is that we are never in complete and undistorted touch with things as they are. Time and life itself are meant to purify our vision. Time and life itself do a pretty good job analyzing most of us: and that analysis means a progressive march out of shadows into truth. One example of such a march is our broken but steady movement out of the omnipotent self-image of the child into the finite but real self-image of the adult. We never perfectly accomplish the task but we do move along the line. And the important thing is the discovery that this is a stronger and more effective, a more powerful way, rather than a weaker one. For reality and limitation are charged with power, whereas the child is not. Our best hope and our best help is in the truth. It involves only an apparent sacrifice. When we give up omnipotence we only give up fantasy. We give up only false hopes which, when frustrated, as they must be, produce only anger or despair.

The medical aim is to put us in the presence of what we might call psychological facts and in the presence of the real external world of facts. How both these processes liberate is a long story and difficult to explain. A few examples are necessary so that we will not be talking in a vacuum.

I

The subject and psychological fact: A man may be angry on a given occasion yet not consciously know it. But some area of his personality knows it; otherwise it would not resort to so many defenses against a "fact" it has decided is too difficult because of its power, or too dangerous because of its consequences, to handle. Methods of avoiding this knowledge are endless, as is the energy progressively required for all indirect solution of a psychic problem. The angry man tells himself he loves rather than that he is angry. He avoids anger. He concocts love. He gives more money to the object of his anger than he ordinarily would. He seeks out his company more often, thus losing valuable time and multiplying frustration for himself. More and more energy is being spent in beating back and keeping the emotion out of consciousness. Most unfortunate of all, he turns the anger back on himself, since it must go somewhere.

The reintroduction into consciousness of the first anger —the original simple fact—reduces the endless derivative problems to one problem to be handled. It takes us from the presence of a potential infinite of energy and fantasy into the presence of a recognizable finite fact. It probably increases rather than depletes energy because the very introduction into consciousness is a triumph: consciousness will look only at things it can handle. What makes this reintroduction possible in many severe cases is the presence of a man (the doctor or his equivalent) who is not afraid of his own anger and is not repressing it. What was once impossible, an unendurable fact, now becomes a fact admissible to consciousness. A hundred other specious "facts" and expenditures of energy become thereby unnecessary.

The psychological fact is now endurable to the extent that it can be introduced into consciousness, because it is no longer the terrible fantasy it once was, but is now the actual fact it really is. It has lost its original horrendous proportions and is no longer magnified. Its first reintroduction will no doubt be frightening, but this is a limited fear that is far from the exaggeration of the impossible. This reduction of a fact to its proper factuality is usually achieved in the presence of another human being who is himself able to tolerate anger and hostility more than the sick person. Therefore the new science involves an interpersonal achievement, in which the physician's personality is involved in the medical situation. His whole attitude must be the reverse of the scandal-taker (the magnifier of facts) and his whole trade must bear in mind the maxim: woe to him by whom scandal cometh.

In this example we can now begin to reckon with a third

liberating form of emergence into the presence of psychological facts. If the anger has now emerged in a pure and direct form, it no longer exists in those hidden regions of the personality where it can spread out and contaminate every other feeling with its own presence. A neurotic love had become a disguise for anger, so that the anger had contaminated real love. But now a host of positive feelings, love above all, can afford to come out of hiding and express themselves. The process is slowly restoring the power of love by breaking down its inhibiting identification with hatred. And if love is being restored, so is hope; for our greatest hope and wish is to be able to love.

II

The Object: If this process of locating and defusing such feelings is continued far enough, the sick person begins at last to be in the presence of real objects, of reality, of things as they are. (He need no longer use all his energies in fighting back even the hint of a genuinely human feeling.)

To enter the presence of objects is an extraordinary experience. The mentally ill experience them as though they had never been there before; as though for the first time there is nothing wrong; as though there are no questions. Indeed, there are no questions if things are thus in place. The mind is at rest. It senses a relationship of mutuality with objects, as though they were made for it and it for them. The sense of hostility is now gone, or manageable, and with it most of the exhausting, endless movement of the mind. Not for nothing did Dante see so close an equation between the emotion of anger and that endless rationalistic attack upon things that can never stop its thinking assault.[1]

These are rare moments, for the well or the sick, these pure, untroubled moments of quiet contact with objects.[2] In them the ghosts and shadows seem gone and dead, as indeed for the time they are. The mind acts without fixations and can therefore be fixed on what is really before it. There is no sense of effort or conflict, not because the will is dead but because it is completely concentrated, without inhibition, on the task or the thing or the person. Nor does this involve any artificiality of "working" at relationships because this is seen to be unnecessary, or, better still, is not even considered.

Such relaxed and unclouded presence to things or people or work may be our best understanding of the healthy positive nature of what the psychologists call dependence. We incline on the whole to give this word and situation a pejorative, demeaning force. But here we recognize that no such connotations are involved. The object is there and I am there, and the two are inseparable. It seems impossible to think of the one without the other. Neither is demeaning the other; there is no quarrel, and no exploitation. Even more important, with the shadows gone or reduced in their power, there is no longer any sense that there is a barrier between the subject and the object, as though this feeling of some intermediate barrier were an external reflection of the internal inhibitions we have been talking about. Nor is there any longer any sense of hostile space between it and me, that cannot be crossed and is an unbridgeable gap. There is no sense of loneliness. We use many words to describe this phenomenon: interest, contact, spontaneous reaction. There is no need to force feelings; indeed, it is somewhat doubtful that the emotional life is involved in the frequent sense of that phrase "emotional life." Erikson's word *mutuality* continues to be a good descriptive word.[3] We must remember, however, that between the mutuality of the child and mother and this new mutuality there must intervene a painful separating-out of the self into self-identity before it can reconquer mutuality on the higher plane. Men and women have to pay a price for each new level of innocence.

III

Fantasy and reality: The methods of life the ill are inclined to use are, unfortunately, characterized by sterility in proportion to the degree that they distance themselves from reality and fact. And because this distance from the real never manages to bring life to the stage of satisfaction, it is inevitable that these methods grow in intensity and move toward the total or the absolute. Before the close of this chapter we will see how this works in two different instruments of illness: in its creation of fantasy life and in its adoption of what we shall call negative identities.

There is a tendency in the sick toward a wide and sterile split between dream and fact. They increasingly attach their hopes to fantasy rather than to reality. This is because reality, for one reason or another, has not worked for them; or because they have been unable to cope with it; or because a disgusting image of reality has been communicated to them. To the extent that we can satisfy any of their real needs, or hopes, or tastes, we remove the source of these intensely autistic drives. This fantasy life, these omnipotent dreams, are attempts to cope with life. Superficially, they resemble the nature and the processes of hope. In fact, they are a brilliant and exuberant counterfeit of hope. But on examination they prove to be the very reverse of hope. They are based on a hidden despair of coping with the human reality, or they are based on the bad taste of this reality that has been communicated to them. Secondly, they are a form of "hope" that proposes the impossible rather than the possible. Thirdly, they consistently adopt methods that have a built-in certainty of never achieving their object.

When there is real hope, there is no need of this counterfeit. Where there is contact with the reality of our own humanity or that of the outside world, there is no need of this autistic fantasy life. But this is really an equation we speak of, this hope and this contact, because hope hopes for contact. This contact, when really present, is its own answer, and it needs neither excessive intellectualizing nor fantasy to justify itself. It is satisfying and it is pleasurable. This pleasure and satisfaction is not sought for its own sake, but it arises whenever there is contact. It is a form of what Heidegger calls "being in the world," and it simply means being in one's self and being in reality.

Such contact is not puritanical in the sense that it would forbid fantasy and condemn us to a life of reality. Every human being wishes to dream, to have ideals, to hope for things beyond what he has. *But reality is a better producer of dreams and visions than nonreality*. Satisfactory fantasy has to feed on reality and must keep returning to it. The further it would soar, the deeper it must plunge into facts.[4]

I have elsewhere suggested one example of how true fantasy and vision can relate themselves to reality.[5] Let me repeat it briefly here:

In a section of *The Brothers Karamazov*, Dostoevsky explores the passage into the exact structure of a fact by what I call the realistic imagination as opposed to the "fantastic" imagination. Thibion, the monk whom Aloysha loved and who had been the father of his soul, is dead. Contrary to the Orthodox tradition that would attest the presence of sanctity, his body is already decaying. Now the air is filled with fantasy, with lies and nonsense, and Aloysha's imagination (together with Dostoevsky's) must travel through it all, give shape to it, and find a way. The friends of the monk are aggrieved: he can't do this to us! The enemies of the monk are filled with the immemorial: "I told you so." "I saw him talk to the ladies." "I saw him bring sweets into his cell." Others are interested only as journalists, in the superficial accounts of what is going on, with no interest in the meaning or quality of the news, demanding the equivalent of a half-hour television report. It is as though Aloysha, like Dante in the *Purgatorio,* passes among the ghosts of the seven capital sins before he can enlighten his mind to see the true nature and dimensions of a simple fact. And he reaches it: the simple fact is that he whom I loved is dead. That is all that is there. There is nothing else. But this limited fact, isolated now from lies and autistic fantasy and wishful thinking, becomes, somehow or other, a great depth, creative and productive of what we have differentiated as true fantasy and vision. At this stage, therefore, the achieved fantasy is no fantasy at all, but a sense of vision, a reach of the imagination, a sense of contact with the fullness of being, that is effected by a perfect contact with some part of the human reality. This is the epilogue that the novelist adds to the imagination of Aloysha, and it is true. Facts, truly constructed along human lines, have it in them to generate these epilogues and this quality of vision. We are faced with a restriction that is no restriction at all.

Those who doubt the importance of this sense of fact, and who think it simply a new invention of the positivists, or a new trend of antipoetic puritanism, should heed one of our own major contemporary poets and critics when he says, without any suggestion of being extreme, that "the sense of fact is something very slow to develop, and its complete development means perhaps the very pinnacle of civilization." [6] This is surely an unusual remark, but I think it attests the meaning of much that I am saying in this book. It seems to me critically important, not only for the evolution of a civilization but for understanding the processes that heal the sick. Of course, it must be understood rightly, without the pejorative connotations that a "plain, simple fact" often has. Dante devoted the entire *Divine Comedy* to the contemplation of a few simple facts. For the sake of the sick, I contend only that these elaborations should not abandon the original facts.

IV

There is no reason for limiting our present consideration of "presence to facts" to some narrowly sentimental thoughts on the idea of presence to beauty in the external world. What is more important, since we are talking about illness, is the wider generalization that presence to any form of truth can be liberating. Far from being a purely sentimental consideration, therefore, this includes real presence to evil and guilt. Let me elaborate on these as examples of a greater range of truth or fact:

Evil: We all wish at times to do evil. And we can. These facts can be frightening. But there is nothing wrong, contrary to the whole ethic of the strong man, with fearing evil. To deny its possibility in us would lead to more evils than it would prevent. The line from Scripture is itself a beautiful one: *qui potuit transgredi et non fecit:* who was able to sin and did not. A frequent neurotic solution is to deny the possibility and to try to live in a world which is without these serious implications. This is one of the things we mean by a compromise neurotic solution based on denial. It would be more sensible to recognize the kind of world, internal and external, in which we live, and to avoid real dangers by effective means, rather than by the childish way of denial. This would be a reasonable combination of attack and retreat.[7] It is *attack* because it recognizes the problem, and it is prudent *retreat* into a point of security, the world of the good. It reminds me of the sage metaphysical advice recently given by a taxi-driver: "My father always taught me never to run away from a fight—but to walk away from it. If you run you might break a leg." This suggests a more correct picture of what happens in therapy (granted the common sense of the doctor) than the distorted notion that the mentally ill are asked to flood themselves with the whole potential of the unconscious, sexual or otherwise. This is precisely what the unconscious of the sick has often been doing, in desperate attempts to work out problems that no longer exist. The frequent effect of most good therapy should be double: to recognize the problem, and *to stop working it out*.

But the point we are making is that a reasonable facing of evil can liberate us from evil.

Moreover, it is by keeping a rational and balanced sense

of the presence of evil or its possibility in us, neither denying it nor being overwhelmed by it, that we help to
liberate ourselves in our dealings with evil in other people. If
with reasonable exactitude we recognize what we are or can
be, we will know that *we* can be at fault and that others
can be right. If on the other hand our basic image of ourselves is that of evil or if we solve the problem by the other
extreme method of denying the problem, then we may be
totally incapable of finding evil in other people. *We* will always be wrong, always in a condition of neurotic submission, never asserting ourselves, never daring to wish or hope.
We will be slaves. We will be angrier than ever at ourselves
and inevitably will take it out on those faultless people. If
we want to love others we must accept the evil in them, or
at least their limitations. One analyst told me that a great
turning point in his own analysis occurred on the day *his*
analyst calmly responded to a question that he did not have
the slightest idea of the answer. This experience broke in
him the neurotic childhood need to be perfect, omniscient,
omnipotent, that had been fostered by the corresponding
image of the analyst.

This seems to be the fundamental difficulty that adults
have when they are required by some circumstance to handle
a situation of obedience. Undoubtedly the reality-situation
contains part of the difficulty, but the greater problem is
the shadows from childhood that creep back into an adult
situation. The situation, let us say, is that of a religious
who has subjected himself to a vow of obedience or a soldier
who is subject to strict discipline. The facts, if they were
not complicated by shadows, would be simple. Where there
are many factors and many people involved in an important situation, someone must decide the course of action.
There is nothing demeaning in the subject position for anyone, and all agree in the abstract that it is a necessity of
nature which robs no one of his maturity, soul, identity or
worth. But the shadows can intervene to contaminate the
facts. Emotions are reactivated here from the childhood situation in which the obedient one is the helpless child and the
commander a giant. The sense of helplessness, passivity, and
worthlessness returns, not in fact but in fantasy. Such dependence reintroduces the sense of evil into the soul. The
bare fact is obscured by the neurosis. The subject, asked to
accept a necessary situation of adult obedience, becomes
in his own eyes a weak and worthless child. But no man can

endure too much of this identity, and the results are predictable—all because evil and helplessness have been read into a situation where in fact they have no place.

Things are much worse, of course, and the chances for such reactivation much greater, if the one in authority has not somewhere along the line become conscious of his own childhood impulses and mastered them. If he is a neurotic and dependent character he is sure to repeat his childhood experiences and treat others as he was treated: under the guise of adult experience, he will treat his subjects like children. He will consider himself the only adult in the group and will act accordingly. He will call spontaneity and independence disobedience, thus intensifying the potential for this ambivalence in his subjects. He will be afraid of freedom and call it evil. All this is a defense, but it does import more of the sense—not the reality—of evil into the atmosphere.

Religious obedience requires persons more mature than usual to accomplish its ends and to avoid its potential risks. Once more, our great hope is the increase of the number of adults in human society. Only adults finally can obey and only adults command. Both parties have to act maturely, especially if there is great risk that the sacred name of religion be tarnished. Above all, we must choose superiors who will regard it as the first necessity of a religious situation that the men or women around them grow up and come fully alive. To the extent that they do not, they take away hope, and energy with it.

In these situations obedience, freedom and evil are seen, not as three distinct things with their own boundaries but as mutually confusing and destructive; obedience is an attack on autonomy, autonomy is an attack on obedience, and both are sensed as deeply evil. Each is a fact but no one of these relations is a fact, except as it is distorted by some shadow from the past. Actually both parties are making a great fuss about what we can call by the highly technical word "nothing." Both should eliminate from their business transaction a devil who does not belong within its terms. But the observer to any such situation would be mistaken to underestimate the potential of fear and pain in the sense of evil thus evoked. It can create unbearable fear and aggressiveness, until one or both learns to retreat graciously away from a painful position that literally has no relevance. We return to the notion of mutuality, which would, in this case, be two wills wishing the same thing, whether from the position of dependence or that of command. When two people wish for the same thing, then the one does not "submit," nor the other "exploit."

It is often only fantasy that thinks of opposition of wills before the event. Such fantasy, in terms of which so many people must work, is expressed in the classical psychiatric joke of the man whose car had broken down, and who found himself trudging with his own thoughts toward a farmhouse a mile away, to ask for a jack. The image of the hypothetical farmer and his anticipated refusal grew in his mind as he walked. When he knocked at last on the farmhouse door he heard himself yell out: "You can keep your goddam jack!"

Guilt: In the case of evil we see, for one thing, that it is important to face it as a fact, but that there is also such a thing as giving it too much attention. It gets into places where it does not belong, and this deprives us of the liberating presence of persons, situations and things. Both these possibilities are true of the feeling of guilt.

The feeling of guilt is so universal and important a factor in mental illness that we cannot explore it fully here.

If I were writing as a moral theologian of sin and guilt, I would have to include a careful set of theological chapters on these two *facts*. For they *are* facts, and we are all sinners, every day, and we are all guilty. But we are dealing with mental illness, where the more important thing is not guilt but how to handle it, whether the guilt be fact or fantasy.

The mentally ill do not know how to handle guilt and they need help to cope with it from every resource, natural and supernatural. It is nothing to play with and the sick tend to play with it too much. Guilty or not guilty is beside the point; they think they must play with guilt, which is an ineffective tactic. Certainly, guilt cannot be denied, but it must be kept in its place. This is one of the abiding hopes of every human being, that he can keep guilt in its place. Even real guilt must be kept in its place and must be the right kind of guilt. Above all, it must be creative and not destructive. No man has the right, no matter how guilty, to strike at himself destructively. Real guilt should be liberating and creative; it should strive to restore things to place, to restore the good, to rejoice in the release from evil. A proper sense of guilt creates energy, restores personal relationships with man and God, gives peace. Inappropriate guilt, which is destructive and which makes matters worse than before, is not true guilt, but another form of evil. This must be said vigorously for the sake of the sick, because so often they feel an obligation to be self-destructive.

It may seem incredible that human beings come to feel an obligation to negation: self-destructiveness, sickness, evil, anxiety. Let the reader consult his own experience, which is milder than that of a very ill person, and the truth of this should be clearer. We all feel unworthy, at times, of being good or positive or creative in our actions. At intervals, or for an hour in a day, we give up hope in our own self-image. There is an element in us (what the scientist would call the irrational superego) which suggests that we are in substance destructive or evil, that, therefore, we have no right to peace or positive action. Most of the mentally ill are preoccupied by this negative, weak, worthless, evil image of the self. The image is accompanied by a corresponding ethic (in reverse, if you will) of action. It would deny the patient the right to ordinary wishes and impulses, to positive and constructive actions, to the usual aggressive instincts of a human being. It refuses the right to hope, to wish, to have goals, to take help.

This image will evoke such specific illnesses, neuroses, or perversions as will confirm the image. Everything we do to eliminate the cause and to create an opposing image of the self will to that extent eliminate the source of endless forms of illness.

There is the succinct comment of Agostino Gemelli:

. . . if they [psychotherapists] keep in mind their experiences with disordered patients who are incapable of healthy love of self, and, therefore, of normal love for neighbor, they will conclude that the plan to follow in treating neurotics is precisely, and first of all, to teach them to have a proper estimate of their own personal importance, a feeling for their own personal success.[8]

V

Negative Identity: It is central, and instructive, that those of the sick who have not yet fully yielded are inclined to hold on to any kind of actuality, so long as it is actual, rather than make the final break with reality. They, and we with them, will hold on to anything rather than yield entirely to the substitute life. They will hold on to bad parents and bad friends rather than none at all. They will hold on to unpleasant feelings, and even to hate itself, rather than to nothing at all in the feelings. An unpleasant fact is better than no fact at all, and anything is better than having *no* interior life and no self. This is why it is no help for the pious to say to the sick that they must have done with negative feelings; this, at such a moment, might be ridiculous and a participation in the beginning of an act of self-annihilation.

Some inward life that is existent is necessary, even if it is a dubious one. Do not, in the name of reason, remove it too quickly from the ill, because the hell of no feeling at all and no identity at all may be on the other side. Where we do not know what we are doing, we should let these people be with their strange grasps on existence. We might better look to ourselves with a question or two.

It is not necessary to create a brief for negative thoughts or negative identities to recognize that even these negative things, where there is nothing better or nothing promising to take their place, can come to represent existence itself and can create horror at the thought of their disappearance.

We can say two things about this phenomenon of negative identity.

Negative identity represents a hold on reality. And a human being will hold on to any scrap and the last scrap of reality.

But these negative situations give such unsatisfactory grips on reality that it seems necessary to absolutize them, to blow fantasy into them until they have become larger than life. Thus they, too, partake of the sterile nature of a fantasy that is isolated from reality.

Erik Erikson has the following to say about this double drive in such negative situations, the drive to grasp reality in their terms and the inevitable drive, a consequence of their sterility, toward totalizing or absolutizing them. His first step is to define a negative identity as

an identity perversely based on all those identifications and roles which, at critical stages of development, had been presented to the individual as most undesirable or dangerous, and yet also as most real. For example, a mother whose first-born son died and who (because of complicated guilt feelings) has never been able to attach to her later surviving children the same amount of religious devotion that she bestows on the memory of her dead child may well arouse in one of her sons the conviction that to be sick or dead is a better assurance of being recognized than to be healthy and about.[9]

These choices of negative identity are based on failures of those positive identities which we shall soon be discussing, and they have a temptation toward totalism rooted in them. Erikson has given a few brief examples of this totalizing movement:

"I would rather be quite insecure than a little secure. . . ."

". . . at least in the gutter I'm a genius."

And his conclusion is that "Where the human being despairs of an essential wholeness, he restructures himself and the world by taking refuge in totalism." [10]

If I may interpret this in my own language, there is an increasing need to intensify the negative situation to the very degree that it fails to create those reality-satisfactions which are rooted in actual situations.

This is in fact the very definition of one central aspect of all neurotic and psychotic needs, that they are never actually satisfied, being out of contact with reality-situations, and must therefore lead toward absolute forms of themselves.

But it also remains true that the threat of the disappearance of even these negative images may represent annihilation, or a complete separation from reality.

There is something of the same feeling of separation in grief and mourning, in every act of renunciation, and in all the acts of growing up. Unless we combine all of these processes of separation with equally powerful feelings and goals of unity and attachment to actuality, it is impossible to endure life. That is to say, it is impossible to endure too much separation from reality. There is a degree of separation beyond which men cannot go without desperation.

This should be the key to our understanding of the further burden of desperation added to the life of the mentally ill by their social and psychological isolation from the communities of the well (as often as the latter build more and more of their "ideal" and self-enclosed cities).

For reality is the very atmosphere of men. They must breathe it or perish. To the degree that they *are* or *feel* isolated from it, they are in trouble. In the case of the sick it is certain that ordinary things and events more often represent and symbolize deeper forms of separation than with ordinary people.

It is surely necessary to be separated out from many

things in life and to become individuated, but it is just as necessary that we create a metaphysics where individuation does not mean separation and excommunication. This is why I have myself gone to such great pains to eliminate any note of conflict between the absolute unconditionality and freedom of human acts on the one hand and absolute mutuality on the other. The other polarity would be found in the very frequent double-bind: "grow up and God help you if you do." In this polarity the issue of conflict is created by some dependent and aggressive human being.

I repeat that it is amazing what people will cling to in the name of existence. For they must hold to touch or contact at all costs. To live without it is impossible. Among the saddest and most powerful lines ever written by Albert Camus are the following, in which he seems to suggest that even hell would be better than to lose contact with reality.

> It appears that great minds are sometimes less horrified by suffering than by the fact that it does not endure. In default of inexhaustible happiness, eternal suffering would at least give us a destiny. But we do not even have that consolation, and our worst agonies come to an end one day. One morning, after many dark nights of despair, an irrepressible longing to live will announce to us the fact that all is finished and that suffering has no more meaning than happiness.[11]

The sad thing is that this remarkable man could not have hoped in existence as strongly as he clearly wished for it.

Chapter 2

The Human Reality

The human reality is a source of hope and a fount of healing for the mentally ill. On that statement our metaphysics of hope must build.

The sick deeply fear that they are not human. They interpret an endless variety of problems and distresses as nonhuman. They are therefore possessed by a sense of being ex-

communicated from the human community. This is their psychological variant of theological damnation.

And here we second the analysis of the Lutheran theologian, Martti Siirala, who has given us a distinguished account of the various "ideal" but destructive concepts of human society that have been formed by the well against the sick. These concepts are rigid, narrow in their concept of the human, exclusive, and "damning." They injure the well and shatter the ill.

To have the image of oneself as human is the beginning of hope. The sick, then, are in a hurry. They are in a hurry to be human.

The ill are helped and healed in so far as they find the reality that is inside or outside themselves. This must be their basic metaphysics. It is not theirs alone, however. It is the metaphysics of every man.

Now let us go a step further and ask about the relationship of the sick to the human reality. It takes us that much closer to the metaphysical problem of the ill. They feel they are not human but that at any cost they must be. And so, indeed, must every man.

Thus we come to the human as the chief source of all their hopes. For the mentally ill it is a distant and arduous future good, that they enter some day as citizens of the city of man. It is a precious good that needs help in the attaining. The human reality, like reality itself, is our food, our air, our atmosphere, without which we die. If we reach it, we can go further. Without it, there is nothing.

What is the human?: We know, better than we think, what it is. It is both a determined and an open idea. It is completely open, but it must always be human. When two men land on the moon they will know what the human is from the light in each other's eyes. The sick know it from its absence, because they have been exiled or feel exiled from it. (And we, the poor and foolish well, think we have it.) I recall for the reader that Harry Stack Sullivan explained the high restlessness and urgency of the sick, their inability to wait, by their passionate haste to be human.[1] The alternative was the feeling of difference, shutoffness, separation, excommunication, a feeling of what we might call damnation.

The possession of our humanity is clearly something that human beings will go to any length to preserve. It causes the deepest fear and disorganization when it is lost. It involves self-love in the best sense of that phrase, and can cause overwhelming anxiety when it is seriously threatened.

On the theological level this reality and the threat to it have been traditionally discussed in terms of "the salvation of the soul." There has, of course, been the implication that it is all an invention of religion, priests and inventors of superstition, who found such terrors to their purpose. But now it becomes clear, from the revelations and analyses of illness by the new mental sciences, that it needed no theologian to invent them; they were so actual and so altogether valid and well-founded. I do not say that the mental illnesses are the same thing in actuality as threats to the soul in the moral order. There is very little doubt that a human being can have all the sensitivity, in the psychological order, that belongs to the terrible image of the loss of the soul, and yet be quite all right, and saved in the eyes of God. But the psychological reverberations of the loss of human identity can have a terrible resemblance to what Christianity has described over the centuries as the loss of the soul. As long as we remember that it is *not* the loss of the soul, and that it may mean its gain, we will be helped by this concept to understand what illness involves. It *is* a kind of feeling of damnation.

When people are mentally ill they excommunicate themselves or are excommunicated by human society as much as, if not more than, by those forms of excommunication in the middle ages which give us so much offense (in the very act of our taking an excommunicating step further). We know how powerful and terrible a weapon it was to cast some one out of the Church. In the present case, let us imagine the mentally ill as living the life of excommunicates from our humanity, from the human race. There is a good deal of clinical evidence of the hopelessness produced by this interior state of affairs.[2]

Such is our enormous drive toward contact with the human reality that if we are not in touch at all we are in hell. For the sake of the sick, therefore, we must be concerned to *enlarge* the concept of the human so that it can include everything in them.

I

What, then, shall human identity include?

It has taken and will continue to take a vast act of the imagination to answer that question. And it will take the rest of history to answer it. That is how inclusive the term should be. Obviously we must restrict ourselves to a few strokes of description here.

First of all I want to turn the usual question around. Here is the usual question: You know that you are a human being, but can you forget that generalizing question and ask who you, John Smith, as an individual, really are? This is the desperate modern question.

My question will rather be: You, John Smith, know painfully and fairly exactly what you are as John Smith; you are rather overwhelmed by such an identity. Nothing could be clearer than the answer. But has the thought and the reality of John Smith deprived you of the sense of your humanity? This means exactly what it says, no more, no less. It does not mean that "I believe in myself," with a belief which, interpreted in the Horatio Alger sense, means that I make a blind thrust of the will to say that even if I hate myself I believe in myself. It simply means that, no matter what the inner and outer reality into which history has thrust me, I see myself in the light of some final saving grace of being human. (I, John Smith, am a human being.) This acceptance eliminates the need of these blind and violent thrusts of the will. Hitler would not have had to fall back on those violent thrusts if he had possessed the taste of his own humanity. He knew very well he was Hitler but did not think he was human.

This human identity is not a concept in abstraction; it is not an idea or a category or a class in which we place ourselves. It is not a label or a game. It is a sense of contact with my own existence: *my own* thoughts and feelings and wishes, my internal and external reality. It may be an unpleasant contact at times. At times it may be a contact with myself as a sinner. But at least it is contact, and it is myself identifying myself, with at least this fundamental "grip." It leads to such phrases as "ill-favoured but my own."

Anyone who takes this grip from us is our enemy. This is the land that Christ designated when he said: "The kingdom of God is within you." This self-identity is the great gift of God. It is not merely the gift of existence, but the gift of a sensed and possessed existence, the calm, fundamentally comfortable possession of the good and the bad in us, of the good certainly—but of the bad in a certain extraordinary sense, too. This is where such a thing as forgiveness enters the picture, for I develop internally God's gift of forgiving myself and thus of possessing the whole of me, without getting involved in some process of self-destruction.

There is a sentimentalism in the air which has told us that our identity is really to be found in what we should call the "true self." The implication is that this might better be called the "beautiful self." (We shall shortly examine the same sentimental concept of the human community.) According to this way of looking at things, we have only found ourselves, and established contact with ourselves and our identities, when we are in touch with our healthy and beautiful wishes and thoughts. On the surface this is an attractive doctrine with which I am tempted to agree. But I do not. For contact with the self means contact, in increasing directness, with *whatever* is there. Of course self-knowledge is difficult and painful. But I think that all the talk in our culture about self-knowledge, and especially the knowledge of the non-romantic elements in our humanity, moves too far in the direction of the pain of it all, and not nearly enough in the direction of the happiness that can come from it. Compared to this knowing, the not knowing, the loss of contact—even the loss of contact with the destructive elements in us—is like an agony compared to a pleasure. This true, sweet self is a dream that forbids membership in our humanity to anything else but itself. It makes contact with more and more of the human self impossible. It constantly proclaims that a good person would never have this thought or that feeling. It assures us that a good man or a good woman would never feel anger or despair, or think of suicide. It makes impossible that recognition which is the prelude to acceptance and mastery of these things. This is the ideal self, out of contact with the self, which excludes every sick element from its holy membership. It knows neither Jew nor gentile, nor black, nor any strong feeling about anything. It is simply beautiful.

The human terms of existence are the conditions with which artists, economists, politicians, doctors and the rest of us have always had to deal.

They begin with the human body, with all its needs. There is birth, growth, and death, the line in time that the thing must take for there is no other. There are what the theologians call the roots of the seven capital sins: the reactions of envy, lust, greed, anger, apathy, reactions which are as certain in certain situations as the visibility of the sun and the moon. There is the whole mystery of the inner life of man.

Then there are *other things,* the objects of the external human world. They have a density, thickness and factuality of their own which must be handled or the cost is great pain. If we try to *go through* them, their own substance resists and we are hurt. We must learn to enter into the proper spatial relationship with them. We cannot penetrate heavier objects. No gnostic assertion of our omnipotence or of their non-existence can cope with them. They are as real as we. The same is true of people, with whom psychic rather than spatial relationships are involved.

For there are *other people,* who are equipped with the same powerful interior forces as we; if we are naive enough to deny that this is so, it is usually because there is no acknowledgment of these human forces in ourselves, or because we are demanding that other people be God. This demanding force is powerful and can lead to trouble, for obviously it must result in frustration and anger, not to mention hopelessness. To go through people is a mad project. It is a demand without hope of realization. Physical space and its laws are quite clear to every human being who is not seriously ill, but the laws of "psychic space" between people are neither known nor respected with as much universality or wisdom. Men and women need psychic space in which to grow and move. They must recognize other people operating within this space, whose equal needs cannot be ignored.

We have taken it too much for granted that anyone with sense can and must, for very life's sake, understand the laws of physical objects in physical space—but that it requires a higher and a later wisdom to understand the laws of persons operating in human psychic space. A number of philosophers have dared to suggest the very reverse of this priority: that the knowledge of things human and personal is the primary model for every other form of knowledge. They had said this to counter a certain kind of positivistic mentality, but were themselves interpreted as mystics who could not produce evidence for their whimsy. Now the tide is turning. The clinically competent people are beginning to supply us with new and positive evidence for the priority of the knowledge of the human over the knowledge of objects. Here is an example of this priority, drawn from certain schizophrenic situations: [3]

We have seen that there is good reason to think that

schizophrenic children are afraid, to the point of terror, of open, undefined spaces. But if we "articulate" (if we give lines and connections to the same area), if we communicate definiteness to it and give its parts some quality of differentiated functions, there is a notable relaxation of fear. The same emotional problem is apparently true in the problem of time for these children. There is a relaxation of fear if order and function are given to the parts of the day.

But more important for these children, as they deal with these agonies, is the discovery of the healing power of a reorientation in their personal relations, especially with the mother figure. If the child and the parent are able to rework their relations *in human and psychic space* more successfully, the reorientation in physical space and time seems to follow as the night the day. We can hardly doubt that the first hope of the child, dim of course, and indefinable to himself, must be that he can act, react, and interact in a satisfying way with his mother. Every other hope in space and time probably has its prototype and its first taste of possibility at this precise point. It is a reasonable conjecture that if the child is given this first good taste of the human he will be willing to make his first renunciations of that fascination for the gnostic imagination which is so powerful a part of our makeup. He will be well on the way into the human world, and will have made his first conclusions that it is *all right,* in every way, to be human.

This is another example of the degree to which we receive our humanity from the outside.

For how can the child possibly know that it is all right to possess this sudden gift of a difficult humanity if it is not told that it is all right in a maternal language that is far more powerful than a language of words. Consider what it is suddenly asked to accept, without any developed interior resources: the body—a very difficult body to handle—helplessness—a life surrounded by an order of giants—interior threats from its own powerful feelings and frustrations. After all, some reputable, adult philosophers and artists have not been able to accept or love a single inch of this human reality. The child manages this philosophical task by a received love, by grace of which he is able to say to himself with growing clarity that it must be all right to be what he is. I use this phrase *by grace of which* with deliberation, because the psychic discoveries of the new sciences have a remarkable affinity, in the natural order, with that traditional idea of grace in Christian theology which holds that the salvation of the soul is impossible without the grace or help of God. This idea is not an affront to our humanity, our resources, our autonomy. If we would think of it as the communication of inwardness and identity and autonomy from the outside, we might have considerably less resentment of the outside world. Fortunately for the child, he is neither philosopher nor theologian enough to theorize about the radical improprieties of grace, or his momentary lack of autonomy. He grasps spontaneously at the grace, and if *we* had not, we would not have lived to write or read this book. Unless he had been a child no one would have lived long enough to be a philosopher and to argue the issues of life and death.

Thus the child is for the first time confirmed and assured by his humanity. He learns to accept it and not reject it.

But he may have to learn again, as the ill person most certainly must. Let us imagine an ill man undergoing the learning process with one of the many forms a doctor may take.

For the first time in his life the sick person finds himself, with fair consistency, in the presence of someone who confirms his humanity and his identity as it is, someone who refuses to steal it from him or destroy it. The doctor *can* take it away, he is offered every opportunity by the patient to take it, he is sometimes trapped into doing so; but in substance he does not, he refuses. That is why a measure of the materials in any analysis are certainly "fictitious," not in the sense that they are fraudulent but because they are continued assaults upon the self, in order to test the gnosticism of another human being, the doctor. If that other is heroic and does not yield, if he refuses to confirm the sick in the fantasies of their "inhumanity," if he honors the sick against their own will, a point is reached where the sick person is willing to enter upon a new set of terms with the other. In the simplest possible language, he is willing to get better. It is the dawn of trust. He takes back his own humanity and identity, which he had been trying by every means to surrender. He becomes a friend and not a slave.

In another terminology, a devil has been cast out. That devil had been appropriated from the exterior world (from someone or some group that could not tolerate the things of man) and then internalized. On the surface, it is a polite and a holy devil, full of refinement and demanding a non-human form of goodness. Underneath, however, it is a beast, full of hate and resentment of man. It rages against our humanity. I am not asking for a literal interpretation of the devil, but if the idea of the devil is only a metaphor here, it is an accurate metaphor. What happens in healing the sick is very much like an exorcism. This is not to condemn the sick, for their relief at getting rid of this burden is enormous— and, after all, it is other people who are internalized. We are all devils, unwilling to be exorcized.

I would point out to the medical men that there is a Christian legend of the wicked angels who fell from heaven because they were given an anticipatory vision of the humanity of Christ and refused to adore it. It occurs to me that the medical men are daily asked to watch an analogous situation as they observe the gnostic part in all of us refusing even elementary acceptance of our own humanity.

II

The question is, what is this acceptance of our humanity? Since it is not an easy concept, we ought to try to say something further about it. If it *were* an easy concept we could settle for the first beatnik formula that might come to mind. There are dozens of facile representations of it in the air, but few of them face up to the difficult nature of this extraordinary and liberating reality.

First of all, acceptance is not an ideal word for the kind of emotional and spiritual state it is trying to describe. In ordinary speech it connotes putting up with a fundamentally bad situation, or making the best of a bad job. Furthermore, it seems to represent for many, and even for some theologians, the idea of "permissiveness," in all the unfortunate senses of that word. It may seem that I have myself so used the word in developing the idea of the *all-rightness* of the human. It is the agonizing question of the sick themselves: is it really all right to be human? is it really all right to have this or that human feeling in the concrete? What do we really mean by acceptance of these things? What is the difference between acceptance of the human and that permissiveness about which people rightly become concerned? How does it differ from the forms of the nonhuman which frighten the sick? How, finally, does it differ from evil? These are some of the questions that arise when we refer to that acceptance of humanity which means joy in it and the grasping of identity through it.

In answering such questions, the speculative and rational intelligence must be guided by the findings, insights and certainties of the intuitive intelligence. One certainty of the intuitive intelligence in this case, one insight of our high common sense and experience, is that acceptance of our human nature can be creative and curative of the very problems that are accepted. Human envy (for instance) will not be healed in whole or in part unless the envious one first enters into this drive with honesty, directness, and acceptance. Lest this point be minimized or etherialized, let us add that we mean more than mere *recognition* of the presence of envy. We mean a deep form of acceptance that goes beyond recognition, an entrance into the fact that takes hold of the fact, but not with the grip of evil. There is no progress in health or virtue without it. The third step, after recognition and acceptance, is indeed mastery—self-control—and the freedom that is the companion of these things. But we do not understand acceptance if we do not see it as the foundation and prelude for mastery.

Acceptance is more important than mastery itself. Mastery of envy is impossible without acceptance. Unfortunately this crucial step in the movement into the human has not been sufficiently studied and analyzed by students of theology. On the whole it seems to be far better understood by the mental sciences, though they in turn have often met the sad fate of being misunderstood when they talk about it. Perhaps I would not be discussing it here if I did not realize that it is impossible for the sick to survive without being given acceptance as a gift. It is often the extremities of our humanity that compel us to think more truly as men.

The acceptance of our humanity must be a central feature of the healing process (as its rejection is the cause of our sickness). This acceptance will be identical with that act of the imagination which always remains open and is always extending the bounds of the human. But this imaginative act needs the support of the new sciences.

A fundamental and dangerous feature of mental illness is the rejection of their humanity either by the sick themselves or by the form of human society that we have been calling the "ideal" society. While the first form of rejection, of themselves by themselves, constitutes the very essence of the illness, it seems necessary to give priority to removing the second and external rejection, the rejection of the sick by the human community.

There must be a creative action from without that will slowly succeed in internalizing itself in the sick. Thus we need a double transformation: a psychic transformation of the sick person, and a psychic transformation in the surrounding society, so that both can move toward a new goal and a new healing.

III

Here, then, we come most clearly to the alternatives I have mentioned in the introduction to this book: Shall we build a wall, real or metaphorical, around the sick, or shall we build a city of man that is wide enough, in its understanding of the idea of the human, to contain the idea and fact of illness. Which alternative requires imagination should be easy to decide.

Let us try to understand some of the meanings of the first alternative, the decision to build two cities, the city of the well and the city of the ill. What are some of the implications of *this* decision?

One motive for building any city is security. But in this case what a security! The white Christian, intent on his property, builds walls around the Negro; the well man, fearful unto death of his peace, builds walls around the sick.

We all need security, safety, reassurance; some of us find it in realistic ways and others find it in various forms of illusion. Some of us to a great extent, all of us to some extent, incline to think that everything is all right with us if only something is wrong with others. We need the external projection of our inhumanity in others to convince ourselves that it is we alone who are human. We return again to the excessive gap between the sick and the well. Now we are in a better position to see that there can be a wish behind this gap. The well can need the sick. Until they hear this often enough to understand, there will be no breakdown of the wall between our humanity and their alleged inhumanity. The fact that the sick serve a purpose and a need is one factor that keeps them sick. They serve the needs of the well.

The size and strength of this wall, as we shall see, is largely dictated in two ways: by healthy or rigid concepts and ideals of humanity and the human; by a healthy or a rigid concept of an ideal human society. Let me quote the distinguished Finnish thinker, Dr. Martti Siirala:

> We in our modern society tend to build upon a myth of an ideal society, consisting of selected and approved individuals—of 'normal' human beings, with average intelligence, average bodily health and with a sufficient degree of psychic maturity. These selected and privileged individuals have—it is true—the obligation on their shoulders, in the name of humanity, to take care of the others who do not belong to this class of the *'true' society*. This kind of care does not, however, acknowledge the sick as belonging to the body, *unless* they recover. One might say that sick people do not belong (according to the dogma we enact in our shared life—without, it is true, ever becoming aware of this doctrine by practice) to the true society. The prevalence of this idea among us is obvious if we think how we speak of the sick man's *return* to society, as if he had not been in his society while sick—especially if he has been in a hospital. Racial discrimination is not in any way an isolated phenomenon among us! It is as if we thought that human defects and illness do not belong to our 'proper life' and that individuals who had by accident succumbed to the fate of being ill (or dying!) were not actual, proper members of society—unless they recovered—unless they could be made healthy again.[4]

It is not too easy to explain why this "ideal" society has found it so necessary, apparently at any cost, to retain these barriers. There are, of course, simple psychological explanations. For example, there is the need to project the fears we have of our partial problems upon the complete problems of the sick, so that our partial problems are negated or denied by this maneuver, and the world is thus transformed, so far as emotional problems are concerned, into a "we" and a "they." This virginal approach to reality by the well—they would be the virgins, untouched by original sin—is quite understandable, but it does the well no good; it only places them on a virginal pedestal which is too demanding *on themselves*. They forbid themselves to be at all sick. Again it may be that any mental trouble reminds the well of possible acts of violence toward themselves; but this is also a defense. For what then is really feared is not the external violence which they imagine may come from the sick, but *the internal violence and hostility which is in their own hearts, of which this illness in others is an unconscious reminder.*

But even this seems insufficient to explain the special taint of mental illness among civilized people.

It seems clear that it is no moral taint that causes the reaction, as those who shout loudly of guilt would seem to suggest. For there is nothing that "good Christians" love to boast about more than their kindness to sinners and their willingness to forgive *any* guilt in the name of God. In this one instance, however, it seems impossible to call forth any Christian feeling. We love sinners, but we do not love the mentally ill.

It is my own theory (perhaps over-simple) that the ill remind us, by identification, of the possibility of the loss of our own identity, which is to say, of the loss of our humanity. We allow ourselves, in fantasy, to be reminded by them of the horror of the non-human. None of us can tolerate not being in some way or other human. Not to be human involves that terrible separation of the self from the self, that *psychological* damnation and loss which I have been unable to analyze nearly enough, to analyze it in such a way as to distinguish it from the moral implications of ontological damnation and loss.

What is happening here, in this frightened retreat to a rigidly "true" and ideal society, is an intensification of the situation that originally produced the illness. This whole process must be reversed, so that the idea of the human and the idea of human society and identity begin in a healing way to cover more ground and to be less rigid. Thus the human, instead of contracting itself increasingly into a stultifying notion, will enlarge itself as a saving grace from the outside. It can and must come from the outside, but it must not remain on the outside. If it does, it will do no good. At the most it would then be kind, but patronizingly so, preserving its own identity, from the outside, at any cost, as defense of the true society. Only if the human communicates itself on the inside of people who had never before suspected that they were human, will they be able to rise again. If the outside stays on the outside, it is wasting its time, and is condemning itself to its own illnesses.

IV

The usual form of citizenship created by these exclusive cities of man is that of the ideal or the beautiful self we have earlier described. But the form of citizenship created by the technological cities of exclusion is that of *the useful self*.

Only the useful part of the human self gets into the kind of community we will describe by the name of formal or mechanical organization.

This kind of monster among us is worth looking at in our present context. It will have an especially ironic way of imitating the real city of the human because it, too, will have a great desire to include the mentally ill. Let us prepare ourselves for irony.

Organization, in the formal and mechanical sense of that word, may very well be the final enemy that both Christianity and the new sciences of man will find themselves analyzing and fighting in a perfect act of collaboration. But we will not understand it until we understand how it limits the search of the soul for itself and for human identity.

By mechanical organization I mean a completely pre-planned, purely rational and logical pattern of work or life which is dictated and controlled from the top, without any participating decision by the subordinates, and which uses only some minimal and precise talent of the human beings involved (or caught) in the pattern. Surely this kind of organization is present in our culture and we can safely argue that it has much to do with the incipient presence of mental illness in millions of people. For it does not allow anything but a small fraction of human identity to emerge. It also breeds passivity, submissiveness and dependence. In fact, it often requires these qualities of human beings, in order to insure its own well-being and success. The more mature the people involved, the more painful and self-limiting will be their confrontation with such systems.

The following example may seem to be an exaggeration and a parody of the truth, but the reader should remember that the situation it describes is broadly true, though in less extreme forms, for thousands of more "normal" situations. I quote from the book *Personality and Organization* by Christopher Argyris, Research Project Director of Yale University's Labor and Management Center:

It is not difficult to see why some students of organization suggest that immature and even mentally retarded individuals would probably make excellent employees. There is little documented experience to support such a hypothesis. One reason for this lack of information is probably the 'touchiness' of the subject. Examples of what might be obtained if a systematic study is made may be found in a recent work by Brennan. He cites the Utica Mill, which made arrangments during 1917 with the Rams Institution for Mentally Defective Girls to employ twenty-four girls whose mental ages ranged from six to ten years. The girls were such excellent workers that their employment continued after the war emergency ended. In fact the company added forty additional mentally defective girls in another of their plants. The managers praised the subnormal girls highly.[5]

And we read the following from the research by Brennan:

In several important reports, they said that 'when business conditions required a reduction of the working staff,' the hostel girls were never 'laid off' in disproportion to the normal girls, that they were more punctual, more regular in their habits, and did not indulge in as much 'gossip and levity.' They received the same rate of pay, and they had been employed successfully at almost every process carried out in the workshops.[6]

There is one thing to be noted with alarm about even so brief a segment of a report as this. It is affectionate and grateful! But there are different kinds of affection and gratitude toward those who are retarded or sick. A true doctor will love the person and hate the illness, which he wishes to eliminate. But here we see employers who favor the illness itself and are grateful for it, because its docility and deadness serve their purpose and the purpose of the mechanical system. If the workers were more mature and were in search of a wider, truer, more active identity, that would cause trouble.

It is possible to conclude from the total argument and materials of Argyris that mechanical organizations deal with the normal worker very much as they do with the mentally retarded. Much, very much of their tactics, even in the new fad of human relations, is meant to keep the employee happy in an unhappy job. The measures taken to produce "happiness" usually have nothing to do with the job situation itself, but for the most part are rewards, or accessories, which intend to keep a worker *satisfied with his dissatisfaction* and with his failure to find himself ("playgrounds, baseball teams, cafeterias, bonuses, company papers, and suggestion schemes").

A vicious circle is slowly set up between the top and the bottom of such situations. Where passivity and subordination are demanded of him at the very center of his life, the employee responds with a planned apathy as his only defense. "He may say (unconsciously) in effect, 'to hell with it; I am not going to permit myself to get involved. Why should I pressure myself to leave or to stay? Why should all this mean so much to me? I'll do just enough to get by. I'll block up my need for self-actualization until I get out of work. Then I will live!' " [7]

In addition to the usual charges that workers are lazy and lack goodwill, those on top respond with every measure save the kind that will nurture responsibility, autonomy, and, I would add, the good taste of the human self. They create "communications programs, benefits, suggestion programs, better working conditions, cafeterias, clean locker rooms, uniforms." [8] The communications programs try to make the worker feel that he is part of the company, supply him with information about plans and costs, and tell him that *his* work is important.

According to the logic of my own structure of hope, hopelessness, and false hope, I would classify all these measures under our third category, as measures intended to convince the human soul that it does not suffer from hopelessness when it really does. It is much better to let hopelessness break into full consciousness—as it did with one worker who reacted to the communications program we have just described by saying: "It hurts to know that four bolts are important. What a hell of a life!" [9]

There are those who will answer that this is a cynical violation of American team spirit, that this man should find his salvation in contributing to the new cosmic idea of the *team*, no matter how small that contribution be. Once again this is a clever counterfeit of the Gospel statement of the value even of the widow's mite, so long as it is contributed with love. It omits the essential Christian point that this was all the widow had to give and that God, therefore, was more than satisfied with the mite. These men and women

have more to give, but this "more" (which God has made)
does not serve the purpose of the mechanical organization,
the team, or the modern assembly line. It is absolutely necessary to keep religious ideas out of this whole discussion,
except to say that true religion must be an enemy to the
hopelessness that is born of assembly line concepts of the
human reality. The conventional response to this, of course,
is that it is not a "practical" reaction. From the viewpoint
of the mechanical organization, it is not practical that mature human beings, still capable of hope, should work for it.
The eternal hope of all such men and women is the possession of their own souls, and their own humanity.

Perhaps this has been our greatest contemporary cross:
that our humanity is indeed wonderful, but not much of it
has been found useful in the latest cities of man. What,
therefore, would a human organization and a human technology be?

Chapter 3

Reality Is Not Conflictual

*There would be little reason for hope and much reason for
hopelessness if reality were constructed on basically conflictual lines, in such a way, that is, that if one absolutely
necessary human goal were reached another would have to
be lost. Then we could not have any good thing without
tragedy or without illness.*

*It is not true that one human value is at war with an-
other. All the great human contraries are meant to be at
peace and to support each other. In this case the central
example we have chosen is that of the fruitful relations between dependence and independence in human beings. It is
necessary that a man have both. If he is dependent, which
he realistically is, it must be in such a way that he does not
sacrifice his autonomy. He cannot be autonomous without
being dependent.*

*Here both theology and the new mental sciences are in
agreement. In his very act of being master of the world God*

communicates his autonomy and freedom to men. He has not created an either/or world. He has not created a world where we must absolutize either of two contraries.

I would like to give a brief account of the subject of this present chapter and its relation to the final chapter of the book.

1. In the present chapter I propose that our next addition to a metaphysics of hope should be what may be called an organic or structural or integrated view of reality. For the sake of hope itself we will hope to discover, and I believe we will, that there is no basic conflict between any of the basic, permanent elements of the human reality. An organic view of things will make basic conflict impossible.

If the basic things that man *must* have at any cost are in conflict, if having any one of them necessarily means denying or killing off another, then we have real reason for a generalized hopelessness about life.

This is especially true of such powerful and all-pervasive contraries as passivity and activity, dependence and independence, relationship and autonomy, love and hate. If each member of these and many other pairs does not have its own rights and cannot stand on its own two feet as a kind of absolute, if one cannot make a positive contribution to the other, if each must always be in mortal conflict with the other, then there is no way out. If, for example, a human being cannot act independently without reality itself declaring him hostile or the enemy of that dependence that he actually needs; if, finally, this dilemma becomes somehow true of every act, where is the possibility of innocence or the sense in hope? The human reality itself would be the enemy of peace and the source of despair.

Actually, the human reality, like reality itself, is structured and organic; it nowhere submits to the dominance of one single form and always allows the rights of many elements. The *contrary* pairs I have mentioned, and others like them, are merely a way of giving an especially sharp point to our position that many *different* elements may enter into one picture and that difference need not—must not—lead to a life of negativism. Freud habitually thought in terms of twos. That may be a sign of his tendency to see things in conflict. Twos may make a special point, but any theory of integration must go beyond this sacred number. It is necessary to eat, to sleep, to eliminate, to drink, to walk, to bathe, to look, to listen, to talk, to breathe, to dress, to love, to hate, to work, to rest, to enjoy, to discuss, and thousands of other things in any sane view of the human reality. There is no conflict in the fact of a number of elements being present in man or in a number of things calling to be done. There they can be, all clamoring for fulfillment; but they must all learn to hope and learn to wait for the time of their fulfillment.

The elements of pairs and the elements of life are *not* in conflict. There are indeed thousands of conflicting wishes and possibilities in the heart, but that is not the same as saying that there is conflict at the heart of reality, and that there is no exit from this basic split.

I shall take the pair of dependence and independence as a model of two difficult human things to put together, and will try simultaneously to keep them separate and put them together in an organic way.

2. In the next and final chapter we will study what the consequences are when we abandon this structuring and organic task or when we are driven out of it by others. The chief consequence is a kind of despair over the temporary hopelessness of this fundamental task of living a human life and a recourse, as an absolute, to some single part of the human reality; in a word the part is made the whole; we will for the last time be faced with a despair that tries to hide under a brilliant false hope.

It may seem a pity to plan to end a book on hope that way, letting false hope explode again at the last. But let us trust the publicity we will give it. A neurosis lives on darkness, as does this absolutizing instinct that makes a whole out of a part. Let us hope it will go out not with a bang, but, like every neurosis revealed, with a whimper.

I

Since the beginning of time, the human mind and feelings have been dealing with pairs of opposites and the possible conflict between them. In some cases it means that men are trying to put difficult things together; in other cases we sense that battle lines are being drawn.

Among the Greeks it was the Pythagoreans who (long before Freud!) saw everything in pairs but moved to a theory of constant harmony between them. Thus they saw reality as containing:

The odd	and even
The limited	and unlimited
The better	and worse
The one	and many
The right	and left
The masculine	and feminine
The light	and dark
The good	and bad
The square	and oblong

These are the fundamental oppositions in the constitution of reality, oppositions brought together by a principle of "harmony," uniting the manifold and making the discordant agree.

The gnostics, a few centuries later, saw no slightest possiblity of reconciliation between their opposites, between the members of *their* pairs. Here are their two eternal principles, eternally embattled:

Light	Darkness
A world of splendor and of light without darkness	A world of darkness, utterly full of evil
A world of mildness without rebellion	Full of devouring fire
A world of righteousness without turbulence	Full of falsehood and deceit
A world of eternal life without decay and death	Turbulence without steadfastness
A world of goodness without evil	Death without eternal life[1]

And that equation which we have already seen, between this second world of darkness-hostility and the world in which we live, is generally valid.

Karl Menninger has put together the following chart of a number of the oppositions that have been invented by different peoples or individuals to describe the structure of the world as they see it:

life	death	
good	evil	(Mani)
love	hate	

Eros	Neikos	(Empedocles)
Eros	Thanatos	(Freud)
libido	mortido	(Federn)
forces of light	forces of darkness	(Zoroaster; later the Essenes, *et alii*
Yang	Yin	(ancient China)
assimilation	accommodation	(Piaget)
synthesis	disintegration	(Spencer)
diastole	systole	(Harvey, Goethe)
anabolism	katabolism	
constructiveness	destructiveness[2]	

Thus, at any rate, it is clear that the habits of structuring the universe and man in terms of opposites and relating them in terms of harmony or war is perennial. And now, in our time, the problem of integrating psychological opposites may very well turn out to be the key question of contemporary psychology.

I have already suggested some of the consequences if we cannot keep both members of the basic opposites and keep them together. First, if we cannot, then a life of repression and denial must become not an occasional need but the very definition of man. If I am or wish to be active, I must crush the passive. To be at all dependent is to strike at that autonomy which is the deepest desire of contemporary man. Second, to grant place to one of the pair will be to take away all hope from the other essential wish and to make it despair. Finally, to adopt such an either/or policy would strike at the very possibility of an innocent wish on the part of man. For whatever he does, whichever member of these pairs he chooses, will be striking in hostility against its colleague. It will not be chosen as an innocent and separable absolute, for its own sake.

I turn now to one of these pairs, dependence and independence.

II

The qualities of dependence and independence are both essential to every life history. There is no living without both of them. They must be present in the same human subject and they can be present as a double relation to the same object. Life is a complicated and difficult process, but perhaps nowhere more complicated than in its demand that we work out *this* problem in a mature way.

The task has created extraordinary difficulties for the American character. The American has special difficulties in handling the human quality of dependence. Such difficulties in accepting so absolute a fact can easily move in the direction of illness. On the other hand the drive toward independence and autonomy is just as absolute. The parent or the educator who blinds himself to this second drive is asking for trouble and always gets it, sometimes in savage form.

It is hard to realize how often a human being, young or old, becomes involved in situations, small or great, that center on the need to unify dependence and independence. Let me take a small matter first, and then a large one, though we must remember that the emotional impact of the small matter may be as intense as that of the "larger."

Dr. Bettelheim, in his *Dialogues with Mothers,* gives the following illustration of a growing child's conflict.[3] He has been struck unfairly by a playmate and, though he certainly has the wish, he cannot decide whether to strike back. As the situation resolves itself, the conflict was not really caused by the fear of the other youngster but by a deep uncertainty as to what his mother would think of such an action. Indeed, if *this* conflict were resolved there might very well be less need to strike back because this need is not quite the whole point of his trouble. Actually, he has an even greater fear— the fear of losing somebody very important to him. It simply will not do to say that he ought to break away from the apron strings, or from the silver cord, for that time has not yet come. Moreover we delude ourselves about apron strings. For there must always be apron strings or dependence of some kind, not a mother's surely, but dependence nevertheless, and for the strongest man. Even the strongest man cannot give up his need of a sense of support *somewhere* for his actions, though in some cases it will have to be the support of God alone and a good conscience.

A larger experience that comes to my mind, because of my own work and circumstances in life, is that of a good number of people who are drawn to the Catholic Church by the conclusion (I am not arguing the point) that it is the way of salvation. They run into the natural problem, many of them, that there they are, North Europeans or Anglo-Saxons in apparent danger of giving up their identity by entering what looks like an Irish-Italian environment. The desire to save the soul by belonging to the Church runs head on into the corresponding feeling of losing half of one's native soul. A rightful dependence is in conflict with a rightful need of independence and identity. And here it is the individual who is right; it is the group that must correct these subtle and sometimes not so subtle identifications between a universal religion and its own national qualities. This is a grave obligation on the conscience of the group, and it is not enough to say that it is up to the individual to work out the problem. For a universal religion must be able to confirm every valid act of identity or independence in this world *through the very situation of belonging to it*. As often as it can do this, it is indicating that the human act of depending on it is a creative act of dependence that creates truly independent persons and helps them to be more themselves than ever before. It must be able to resolve and not cause this perennial human conflict.

Each generation has its special problems about the double need of autonomy and belonging. We certainly have our own in the accumulating power of our collective styles of living and our frequent failure to shape them into human forms. We fear that many of these styles are stealing away the half of our souls, as indeed many of them are. Certainly they cause many symptoms in the bodies of men as often as they do not take into account the spirits of men. There is a heresy abroad which I will label the heresy of objectification, because it would claim that our social and economic forms of life have been fixed and have eternal laws behind them that guide their development and shape, and that the mature, well-adjusted man will have the sense to accept them. They are therefore equated with "reality" and divine law. This kind of thinking skips the question of whether such forms and styles of life were initially moulded by mature, well-adjusted people and whether they continue to be moulded in their development by flexible and mature people.

Such thinking is based on a primitive dichotomy which images an "individual" who must be "socialized" and a society (with its own laws) that must socialize. We ought, instead, to recognize that mature individuals, equipped with human qualities, should make and continue to make really human societies and human situations. Socialization, and increasing socialization at that, is necessary but it will never be a separate process with its own laws. We must return to the better picture of independent men forming such social relationships of dependence as will preserve and not destroy their humanity.

It is the secret fear of most people that they cannot have both dependence and independence, just as it is their secret hope that they can. Fortunately they not only can but must. But such a homely truth is not much preached in our land. We are forbidden to have precisely what nature demands most. We are often forced by our culture to deny dependence, passivity, the wish and ability to receive.

We do not seem able to rest. We have the greatest difficulty in being passive, in doing nothing. We are afraid of the gentler emotions. We misinterpret the wishes we have in these directions, and the wishes to receive and to be loved, as though these thoughts and wishes were wrong and had to be suppressed like the plague. As though, according to our culture and according to all the textbooks in psychology, there came a point when we are supposed to be grown up and not have such thoughts; as though at some magic moment when we reach the initiated age of twenty-one, we are no longer beings who have been created and have received all; as though we must no longer use help of any kind (which I have described as half of the definition of hope).

Not long ago I was in New England and walked through some of its old graveyards. They bring back history and the love of our best past, but they also remind us, with their tombstones, of a kind of curse we are under, that we must always remember these heroic souls who never thought a thought but one of duty and work and obligations fulfilled. These things are only the half of life. The other half is some form of rest. Indeed there is a sense in which it is true that everything in life, even activity, is rest and a form of dependence.

Even as Bettelheim's child in conflict, any human being can be very assertive at the right time and place if he has a relationship with God that helps him to see this assertiveness, plus the energy and interiority that go with it, as coming from and approved by God. In such an act we are resting and passive as well as energizing and declaring our identity. Thus we combine dependence and independence, in the same act, tightly intertwined, so that they are not separated after the fashion of the awkward and eternal dichotomy we have pictured above. Interweaving such opposites is important for the resolution of unnecessary conflicts and helps to prevent endless debate or confusion between the horns of unreal dilemmas. It eliminates the need of flying off to one corner of reality for dependence and to another for inde-

pendence; of seeking the neurotic solutions of submission
and defiance. But I repeat that the prerequisite for weaving
such opposites into a single act and feeling is the increasingly
close relationship with man or God that also creates psychic
space. Our picture of God is particularly false when we think
of Him as annihilating us if we rest in Him and when we do
not believe that independent action according to our own
lights might be exactly what He wants. We are really frightened by this fact and by any form of passivity. Therefore
activity itself, and finally overactivity, are sought only to
deny or to destroy a natural fact and need that cannot possibly be destroyed. There are many men and women in hospitals for the mentally ill today who, whether they know it
or not, are simply telling civilization, and also themselves,
that they will go no further, and that, whether the world likes
it or not, they intend to take a moratorium. But surely
it would be better for our culture to provide more realistic
and acceptable forms of moratorium.

III

Let us first look at dependence, and later at independence,
as separable absolutes, each having their separate, innocent
worth.

Dependence can become so deeply entangled in fantasy
that it loses its identity and cannot be seen for the simple
thing it is. What is it? It is a desire to deal with the other half
of our nature, to rest, to go no further, to observe the limitations of nature. Actually, human beings can both glory in
existence and regret having been born, because the plain fact
of the matter is that the latter involves trouble. Whoever says
he does not have this thought occasionally is not speaking
truly. It is inconceivable to me that there should be anything
wrong with this thought or wish as part of our total
thoughts and wishes. It is an ordinary part of the reaction
of anyone in trouble and is always accompanied by the
corresponding wish to live. It is part of the total drive toward passivity. It should be recognized without fear or scan-
dal-taking. The wish to be dead will harm no one, not even
the wisher.

How does this simple wish for passivity become entangled
in fantasy and interpretation, so that it loses its identity of
bare and unobjectionable fact? To answer the question fully
we would have to know the history of the individual in-

volved and the culture surrounding him. If dependence and relationship and need are denied, if they are regarded as a demeaning weakness, if choosing them is associated with hostility and defiance of the community, all these fantasies and associations do not change the truth that this half of our nature is basically innocent fact.

The same is true of the corresponding drive toward independence, autonomy and self-assertion. This, too, is a fact without which we cannot live. We must contact ourselves, our own thoughts, feelings, goals. We are not only related, we are also separated out from each other. This point of being separated-out must be achieved; to the degree that it is not achieved in reasonable substance human beings pay the price with some degree of sickness. It is a strong drive, with many obstacles in the way. Young people therefore usually need a good deal of help in achieving a decent measure of all the things it involves: inward autonomy and mastery, self-respect, originality and creativity, contact with their own thoughts and wishes. Only real adults, who themselves have achieved these goals, will be willing or able to give the help that is needed. Those who maintain the mastery, domination and exploitation of others, will not themselves be free enough or autonomous enough to help.

Though they give the opposite impression, these tyrants are really too frightened by the claim of nature to the ordinary substance of autonomy. If we looked into their souls we would see that actually such dominators need their subjects and are therefore subject to them. They are frightened by freedom and spread their own fear. Certainly it is all right to have such fears and needs, but we must recognize them and master them, so that we learn to leave people alone to the degree demanded by nature, to stop exploiting them, to help them find themselves. Only adults will help others become autonomous adults.

The most helpful thing we can all do is to see that this idea of autonomy is kept uncontaminated and to see to it that we have less and less to do with contaminating it ourselves by calling it the enemy of friendship or dependence. This is the special obligation of parents, teachers, and anybody in authority over others. They all have the power to corrupt or contaminate this essential right and need of the human soul. We can all corrupt it by calling it hostility and treating it as such. We can call it disobedience, thus equating and identifying things that need have no relationship whatsoever.

Thus we poison a good thing, with the inevitable result that
the growing child incorporates these confusions and these
contaminations, and often becomes inhibited in his essential
drive toward independence, in a profoundly manichaean
way. He may be forced, for his own interior safety, to choose
the path of total dependence; to become "a good boy"; but
the rage that is inevitable to such a solution, to this frustration of his elementary identity, is still there; usually it is
turned against the self and has a good deal to do with the
spread of the phenomenon of depression in the United States.
For the root of depression seems to be a defeated attempt at
self-assertion that is now turned against the self.

Here is a possible key to the folly of telling the mentally ill
to use their will-power and all will be well. It should be clear
from the above that the actuality and very idea of the independent will can be contaminated and blocked; frequently it
is the use of the will that is seen as wrong, or as forbidden,
or dangerous, or threatening to the self and others.

A good deal of clinical analysis indicates that the most pervasive fear in illness is that of the loss of love and the fear
of a separation that goes beyond the tolerable. An either/or
attitude seems to develop toward independence and dependence. The sick person seems to decide that if he is independent this must mean the sacrifice of dependence, and vice
versa. These two great human realities are seen as cancelling
each other out; they are not seen in a mutually fostering
relation. But there should be a creative mutuality between
them, so that both can be comfortably present in the same
human person. This is our great hope: to venture without
cutting ourselves off from human society; to join human society without destroying our own identity, without annihilating ourselves.

IV

The ordinary man will better understand the sick if he acknowledges the difficulties he himself has in balancing these
two parts of his life. Everybody hesitates to take a new and
independent position, even when truth and integrity call for
it, if it means arousing the hostility of the crowd or even
losing a friendship. If we can imagine the helpless situation
of the first years of life, when children can be blackmailed
by the implication that a move toward independence will
make them unloved, we can come closer to understanding the

mentally ill: being themselves comes to represent a threat to their very existence. Thus they accept an image of themselves as part of someone else, without ontological autonomy. Not only are they given an unhappy image of the meaning of independence; equally unhappy connotations will attach to the image of dependence, love, and relationship, because, after all, these things have involved a form of security that is destructive of their very selves. So both ideas develop the shadow of some form of death and helplessness about them.

One hope of the sick lies in the principle that what has become true for them in fantasy is not true in fact. Here, for example, both dependence and independence are seen as deadly and destructive, while as a matter of fact both are life-giving and creative. They are seen as an either/or whereas in fact they are a both/and; we can and must have both. What are needed are new experiences in a new setting which bears this out.

Dr. Thomas French gives a very simple example of what we mean here. A man who has been weakened by this unnecessary and destructive conflict between dependence and independence moves progressively toward a point where he realizes that a new and frightening self-assertiveness has the approval and support of the doctor. *But this is a situation where independence is beginning to put him in more rather than less touch with somebody else.* So that the conflict is evaporating.[4]

We also need more studies in the other half of the truth: that just as autonomy can produce contact, so contact or relationship or realistic dependence can be the necessary ground for independence and autonomy. Religion in particular needs more careful analysis in this direction than it usually gets.

For mere religion starts with a handicap. Its position has become suspect, partly because of accusations to the effect that religion, and religious dependence, involve a neurosis of submission; that this dependence is in fact destructive and not creative. This is not true, but not enough work has been done to dispel so general an impression. The case was put most strongly by Nietzsche, and we have not yet confronted his charges with sufficient analytical vigor. They were not mild:

From the very beginning, the Christian faith is a sacri-

fice, sacrifice of all freedom, all pride, all self-assurance
of the mind; at the same time it is servitude, self-mock-
ing and self-mutilation . . .

To shatter the strong, to infect great hopes, to cast
suspicion on the enjoyment of beauty, to break down
everything autonomous, manly, victorious, dominating,
all the instincts natural to the highest and best turned
out type of mankind, and bend it over into uncertainty, distress of conscience, and self-destruction—to
reverse every bit of love for the earth and things earthly
and control of the earth into hatred of things earthly
and of the earth: *this* was the self-assumed task of the
Church.[5]

This is an indictment indeed, and a very savage one. But it
is only half of Nietzsche, and many people stop reading
Beyond Good and Evil where these citations stop. There
were more sides to Nietzsche, more sides to his view of
reality than this. He had a wonderful sense of humor. For a
man apparently devoted to power, he could not endure any
disrespect in the treatment of the weakness of old age. There
was one form of power he could not tolerate and that was
any irrational form created by a group for its own interest
against individuals. The one thing he was striking at (not always accurately in his choice of villains) was what he called
"herd-morality" and what we now call conformism. If one
had continued turning even these pages, he would have discovered a great laudation of the creative qualities of real
obedience and discipline. He, the alleged arch-theorist of will
and power, was the arch-enemy of any form of willfulness,
in life or art.

The position of Nietzsche is not as extreme or as unilateral
as appears at first glance. On its part religion cannot afford
to seem unilateral and extreme in favor of dependence and
submission.

Within this integration the hopeful man will have a double
hope: 1) He will know that the act of becoming himself
does not necessarily mean he must leave all help and relationship behind; 2) he will know just as surely that the dependent act of taking help from God or man need not
mean the destruction of his very identity.

Epilogue on

The Imagination

This book ends where it began, with emphasis on the nature of the realistic and human imagination and its role as the enemy of human illness. It is not too much but too little imagination that causes illness.

Here imagination means nothing esoteric. It is the sum total of all the forces and faculties in man that are brought to bear upon our concrete world to form proper images of it.

The first task of such an imagination, if it is to be healing, is to find a way through fantasy and lies into fact and existence.

The second task of such an imagination is to create perspectives for the facts it has found. It will refuse to leave facts as scattered absolutes, to preoccupy and frighten human beings. Like hope itself, it will always suppose that there is a fact and a possibility that is not yet in. The imagination will always be the enemy of the absolutizing instinct and the ally of hope.

It would be good if this book should end where it began, with a last and now more elaborate word on the vocation of the imagination within the great task of helping and healing the mentally ill.

There is one central thing to be said with all the clarity we may command at this stage in the structure of our argument. It is that, so far as we can see, mental illness again and again possesses just those structures that can be healingly countered by the ideal structures of the imagination.

This is especially true of the tendency of illness to make a whole out of a part in any human situation. We have been appealing for a metaphysics of the organic. In a moment we will look at the ways in which the sick decompose these hard-won structures; they turn away in hopelessness from the task of integration; then they pick up one of the pieces and absolutize it—make it the whole. Erik Erikson has called the process totalism.

But what about the imagination, the realistic imagination?

I propose that here it has a double healing task: I have already sketched the first. What the imagination does in its way (as the new mental sciences do in theirs) is to make a bold and difficult passage through darkness or fantasy or lies of all kinds, in order to build or discover a reality. In tragedy what is built or discovered is the finiteness of man—the abso-

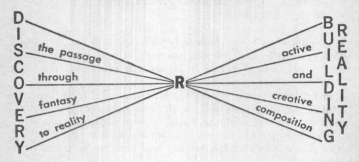

lute fact of it—after passage through the dreams of a Macbeth or a Lear. Or imagination discovers the existence and reality of time, or of other people, or of death, or of any fact in the surrounding darkness. In this, its first task, the imagination conquers fantasy.

But now comes the second major task of the imagination. It must not leave the discovered fact an isolated absolute, but must give it a perspective and landscape, a local habitation and a name. There must be no such thing as a pure fragment, a pure fact, untouched by the composing, enlarging spirit of man. It is the fragments, left to themselves and grown into wholes, that make not only the sick but all of us ill.

To the degree that our images of things and of life are left in fragments we cannot cope. The consequence of not being able to cope is hopelessness. We must therefore investigate this second function of the imagination as an instrument of coping and hoping.

Let us take the fact of death as our example.

Part of the vocation of the imagination should be to create true images of birth, life and death. It must deal with and help us imagine all the central points of the human odyssey. But, in our culture, there is nothing we are imagining, or can imagine, less successfully than death. Therefore we cannot cope with it.

The first failure comes from not finding or facing the fact. The first task of the imagination is to find and face the fact, penetrating through fantasy, lies, distortion, into the fact. There are several well-known studies of this failure, among them Evelyn Waugh's *The Loved One* and Jessica Mitford's *The American Way of Death*. An example of the kind of work that has the intention of reality is the second volume of Emile Mâle's *History of Christian Art*.[1] It is an absorbing review of the idea of death during the fourteenth century, the century of the plague. It leaves no doubt about the fact that death is real. Nor does Ingmar Bergman in *The Seventh Seal*.

What follows for the imagination if it does not have the elementary gift of dealing *directly* with the image and fact of death? It will then deal with it indirectly, that is to say, in bizarre ways. For what is there must come out. According to Geoffrey Gorer, the British anthropologist, the image of death will and must break out in underground ways if it is not directly confronted by the imagination. Gorer calls this underground handling by the imagination *the pornography of death*.[2] Its usual formula is violence. The violent and sadistic imagination, therefore, rather than indicating strength and masculinity, signifies the evasion of a fact. The imagination must be a coping, not an evading, instrument.

If the imagination is to cope with things, if in this case it is to cope with death, it must be able to form a total image of the reality, carrying all separate images of death to their proper conclusions, integrating them into total situations. It is images left in isolation that frighten human beings. A literary critic like Coleridge and a scientist like Freud would heartily agree about the differences in the nature of primary and secondary thinking or imagining. Most of our contemporary images of death, where we form *any* image of it, represent the work of the primary imagination. They are isolated images of disgust, or fear of isolation and separation, or the fear of complete passivity and helplessness.

In the period of decadent romanticism described by Mario Praz in *The Romantic Agony* sweet, sickening disgust with death fills the imagination.[3] As for isolation, we can conclude with the body of psychiatric theory that men are only afraid of death when it means separation from the community.

The image of death as passivity and helplessness may well be the great American fear. The American has not yet been helped by our artists to handle images of passivity. He has only demeaning and corrupt images of the passive, of not being able, like Horatio Alger, to do all things. And such are his images of waiting, or doing nothing, or being dependent. The American is not equipped, therefore, with an imagination, with a set of images, which would tell him that it is all right to lie down in good time and die, dependently leaving it to God to raise him up again. Therefore, he must, like Sammy, run.

As a mother would tell a child that it is all right to be human, so the high images of a culture should be able to tell us that it can be all right to be passive, and to die. Then we could cope (because the imagination had coped) and would have hope.

The artist in our time has not yet entered on this public task. That is not entirely his fault. But meantime all of us are the sicker for it. Even psychiatry is only beginning to discover the imagination, and is only now beginning to stop writing intellectually vulgar books about it.

The mental sciences must learn to take the imagination as an ally. They must recognize that they may not lose but will surely not win unless sufficient and sufficiently powerful images enter our culture to help human beings deal with the scattered elements of things and the different parts of life. Here then is work enough for generations, the work of building really human and composed images of the great points of life and death, so that we can live and die like men. And as a beginning of the work we should ask ourselves the questions: what is our image of birth? what is our image of death? what is our image of a man or a woman? what is our image of old age? what is our image of God? what is our image of love and anger? What, in other words, are our images? For our images are not formed by the eye alone, but by the heart and mind and wishing.

Recognition of our own fragmented state and fears, and of the fragmented state of the national imagination, may help us to look at the plight of the sick with better grace and more understanding. For the sick are again ourselves, writ out in larger letters. Let us in that spirit look at the way they make a whole out of a part.

I

It begins in childhood, this making a part into the totality, and illness will be an imitation of this beginning.

We can calculate that every moment of an infant's self is a new and different self, and every thought or image represents, at that moment, the whole of reality. Everything is an absolute. The picture can be put this way:

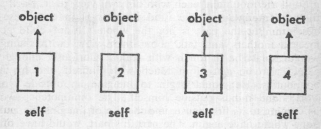

In each case we have an absolute self with an absolute view of the world, each self and each world fixed in isolation. In our sense of the word there is no imagining going on at all. If each image is an absolute, the infant cannot guess that there is a world and a perspective outside of the specific image. We can also say, therefore, that there is no hope, no transcendence, in such knowledge. Nevertheless we do not call this knowledge illness, because it is according to the nature of things and will move on to other stages. The child grows.

Let us look a little more closely at the way in which a child is educated toward a wider perspective of thought and feeling. And here I follow the analysis of the brilliant French psychologist Jean Piaget.[4]

We have good reason to think that when a very young child looks at an object—say a house—from different angles, the different views represent so many different objects, so many houses. Each view is self-contained and absolute. The different views are not yet coordinated as aspects of the same thing. We have equally good reason to think that it is by a "socializing" process, by a slow confrontation with the equally valid views of others, that he is able to conceive of the substantial and continuous existence of objects that are best defined by the sum total of the different views of many persons. The part is not the whole. Thus we coordinate "the relationships into a coherent ensemble which can support the deduction of real permanence . . . immediate experience is the ensemble of subjective impressions, successively registered and not yet coordinated into a system of relationships which encloses the subject in an objective world."

Let us again imagine (as he cannot) that a very young child, standing at a certain point on the ground, is looking at a mountain and that there are six other children scattered around the mountain, each with his own view of it. Each says that the mountain is *this,* and the *this* is in each case an absolute. But the part is *not* the whole. If our child could meet the others and talk about their views with them, he would at last be in touch with reality. Curiously enough he would also be getting in touch with himself and his own boundaries. He would begin to imagine an outside world, worlds and minds outside himself. The omnipotence would be coming to its first pause, and the life of imagination and of hope would have begun. The part, his part, would have found a perspective.

Thus everyone needs time to realize that what he saw was a correct but limited view of the complete situation. (Piaget calls it a "false absolute.") This is only one of the ways in which life dissuades us from absolutizing and preoccupying forms of thought and feeling. It is more than saying that I see things one way and others see them differently. The truth comes closer to this: that I adopt another's point of view as part of my own, a phenomenon which we have also studied under the idea of mutuality.

Children and the mentally ill are as yet deficient in this ability to keep many relative views together in one picture. Education or re-education, as the case may be, is called for.

Thus it is necessary for the human being to move progressively from a solipsistic world, where he uses only his own mind, to a world where he puts on the minds of others in an increasingly public act of thinking and imagining. If this is so, it is clear that thinking is more than a speculative process that occurs within the isolated intelligence; it in fact involves many acts of trust and faith; it is much more a process of putting on other minds than our conventional wisdom suggests. This also goes far toward explaining the process of religious faith itself because, whether or not we accept the process in the concrete, it is nothing more than putting on still another mind, this time the mind of God, with which to see reality.

Nevertheless, we must not give up the position that this works both ways. We have a point of view. So does the child have *his* point of view, and it behooves others to put it on.

Though we have not yet hit off the exact nature of the solip-sistic imagination of the ill, nevertheless we can say in ad-vance about them that they, too, after all, have *a* point of view, and it would behoove the well to take it into account.

Here, then, we can add a few ironic statements about the limitations of those who are "well."

II

The well very frequently forget that the sick person has a real point of view that should fit into *their* picture even though this view may, temporarily, be quite single, absolute, preoccupying, and therefore frightening. Most of us have been fortunate enough to have had the experience of being with persons who believed us to be right or in real need. Many of the sick have never experienced this recognition of their need, or of their point of view. The trouble is that this view or need of the sick, dammed up, builds an insistent pressure in the face of which the well feel panicky, helpless. This re-action makes the sick feel even more guilty about under-standable wishes that are not understood: for here they are in the presence of still another person whom they seem to be destroying. If the well could only learn to be less frightened and helpless, if they could only learn to listen, they might be amazed at the results of hearing another point of view, even if it is a sick one. *There* is an act which really requires imagination, to listen to the point of view, to put on the mind, of those we think mad!

Let us look at some of the ways in which the sick incline to absolutize their viewpoint. If the well would only examine their own lesser problems in this way, they would come closer to understanding many of those states of consciousness of the sick which drive them to make a whole out of a part.

The normal man is often startled and shocked by discover-ing some strong negative feeling toward someone he loves. Or it may be a "shocking feeling" toward God or the sacred. But he quickly recovers because he realizes that this is only a single, temporary part of all his attitudes. The recovery is possible because he is in touch with his total self and his total feelings. And thus he can move rather quickly out of the presence of the giants and the monsters. *The sick person,* on the other hand, *may very well have the same total pattern of feelings, but he does not have the same contact with them.* He is too preoccupied with the single and usually destructive element in the picture. It is very much like the preoccupation of a child. The part has indeed become the whole. But if the child can be educated out of it, so can the sick be re-educated. And their re-education must be in the direction of the restoration of the pattern of a more total set of human feelings. They must be helped to imagine themselves a little better and more broadly. What drives men to hopelessness is part of their feelings seen and interpreted as all of their feelings.

They must be helped out of the temptation of negative identity, the temptation to conclude that the ten percent of the personality which is difficult to accept is actually become, through preoccupation, the whole of the personality.

When we will look at the nature of the act of repression we will see that it is ironic; its intention is to get rid of a part of man that is negative or destructive or unpleasant; but, as a consequence of this mechanism, the part takes over and becomes the whole.

In illness the nature of repression is such that what is repressed remains operative and tends to become an absolute. We do not make a thing die by saying, as children do: go away, you are dead. Where the repression is too severe, it becomes freewheeling. That is, an affect is no longer attached to the situation which originally provoked it; having gone underground, it can circulate freely. It is an axiom that such repression, instead of preventing expression, tends toward universality of expression. (It now assumes an absoluteness of range as well as intensity.) The nuclei of consciousness in the first diagram are not really so independent. A unified substratum of the self can never, in reality, be abolished by any fantasy. The repression can course along its whole gamut, passionately seeking a totalistic domination of the imagination. Thus, we have the following situation:

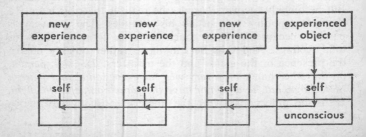

The experience that is thrust down into the unconsc̲
courses in the dark through the whole range of the self, a̲
constantly inserts its presence whether that presence is relevant or not. The part has conquered.

Once this underground finds its proper place in consciousness it looses its power. For every neurosis loves the darkness and grows fat and powerful on it. In the darkness it
becomes preoccupying, omnipotent, absolute, and threatens to
take over the whole of the personality. A neurosis hates the
light, for the light would reveal its proper size and place.
Therefore, it fights tenaciously against being exposed. Its tactic
is an attempt to take over completely by hiding its own
identity.

The character of a neurosis, therefore, is that it is hidden
but still operative, and universally operative. This is extremely important for the light it will throw on certain "moral"
questions and concerns that have come to surround the situation of analysis and therapy. If any or all of the fundamental
drives of the sick are not only present but in action, operating
in indirect ways, then it is right to bring them to direct expression and control. It is not at all a question of needlessly
rousing dormant things; it is a matter of the necessary
illumination of thoroughly operative things.

III

Preoccupation that makes a whole of a part is one of the
great human problems. The part of life, the thing that has
just happened or is about to happen, becomes, not the thing
that has just happened, or the thing that is about to happen,
but the whole of life. It threatens the closure of perspective,
the closure of the imagination, the end of hope, and, let us
say, suicide. In the concrete, it is not an abstract part that
has become the whole; it is a human fact or incident, perhaps
a mere word or gesture, that has a transcendent, an unlimited
impact upon the actual nerve ends of a man or a woman.
This, usually, as we all know, is what we actually mean
when we say that the part becomes the whole. A death, the
loss of a child, the rebuff of a man by a woman or a woman
by a man, a failure in a small thing, two weeks of humidity
in a dead place, a thousand little things turned inward on a
self that does not love itself, this is what human beings
really mean, when darkness comes, by the part becoming the
whole. This is what, as humans, we are fighting for, perspective

and a grip on life—fighting, all of us, that the part should not become the whole. It is not enough to say: do not do it; have sense. For nations and whole peoples do it: they talk about national honor and plunge us into war. The imagination collapses and cannot work; it is absorbed in passion by a single fact. The preoccupation grows and the anger with it. The fear grows that the anger might destroy the world, as it might. For now it can. Now the thought, the part, can do what it thinks; it *can* destroy the world. The part might destroy the whole, the part might destroy the world.

We begin to long for a return to a world where we were only a part, so far as consequences go, and, like the man poised immobilized in the hospital, we long for a world where an action might not destroy the world. These new sensations and anxieties are at times intolerable. At any rate they help us to understand the world of many of the ill, and they give us a taste of their fears and fantasies. For the first time we share the fears of the sick, and we, too, are flooded with the fantasy of destroying the world. Indeed, the fantasy of the sick has become the possibility of the well.

But let us go back to the problem and the moment of pre-occupation in which the part, the single event or the single word or the single destructive wish, has become the whole of consciousness and life.[5] And let us suppose that in illness this state of affairs abides. What is there to do?

This is obviously a large question. For one thing the answer would involve an appeal to the whole achievement of the new sciences of the mind and to whatever instruments they have developed for the restoration of perspective. I shall pay a final word of honor to these instruments in a moment, when I try to describe the critical difference between these creative procedures and the destructive procedures called brainwashing.

Granted the enormous range of what the whole answer to our question might be, I should like to make but one broad suggestion as we near the end of all these discussions on the nature and sources of hope.

It is a suggestion that would come close in character to a procedure we saw used by Harry Stack Sullivan. You will remember that he would ask a patient who was caught in a moment of despairing totalism: When did it happen? And the answer created a calmer context in time for this awful event or wish that was being described. The preoccupying whole was thus pushed back into its proper place. This is the important thing, to put parts back in place.

What comes to my mind is the healing power of the spatial equivalent of this temporal achievement of Sullivan. When we think that this incident or wish or moment of darkness is everything, so powerful is its impact; when its boundaries have become the boundaries of the world; when the perspective is dead and hope or a way out goes with it; then it is good to remember that we live in a real city of the really human and that there are others in the same boat. At our moment, their moment can be total, too. But this is blessedly impossible. For we all possess but a part of the pain of man. We, too, will discover the other parts of the truth if, like the child, we walk around the mountain and meet the other children. Perhaps it is impossible to really despair *with* someone. Perhaps it must be a private act.

IV

The process of "brainwashing" will be our final example of all those destructive situations in which the part is torn out of its place and made into a whole.

Brainwashing is the scientific elaboration of a process which goes on to some degree in all of us. Its central technique is to explore every element of what might be called "negative" identity in a human being and to bring this negative identity to a point of complete preoccupation and guilt in the consciousness. By negative identity we mean all those elements in our character which fall short of the positive ideal and identity we have set for ourselves, all those things in ourselves we neither approve nor like. What happens is that a hypothetical ten percent of a total self is deliberately and diabolically made to invade consciousness, not to heal by revealing the proper proportions of the negative, but to destroy by projecting the self as totally and absolutely negative, bad, false to itself.

The part is made the whole. The ten percent becomes an absolute. This is the method. It is deliberate, calculated, spiritual murder. The only way out of it is a new birth under new leaders who will give these washed and now submissive victims a new self in a bright new world. If you give them your soul, they will make it rise again.

The new radiant self places itself totally on the outside of itself, without reservations. For it cannot stand the human. It is ready for complete exploitation and for the kind of submission that is rooted in a complete inability to live with oneself. The victim, unable to endure this hell of the self, has rushed to the state for forgiveness. He confesses all his sins, leaving nothing out, and he dedicates his whole self, nothing held back, to a new life.

The displacement of the self that is created by such techniques is now complete and is called rebirth, resurrection. It gives a new hope, but this new hope is profoundly ambivalent for it really does not exclude its opposite, hopelessness, and is in fact a crooked name for the absolute hopelessness which the whole technique is intended to create.

The significance of the brainwashing process for part of the argument of this book—namely, that the difference between the ill and the well is one of degree—will be lost to us if we do not realize that the Chinese who brainwashed Americans in Korea—and, indeed, people in their own land —were dealing with good and relatively normal people. They were men of considerable virtue, but with the usual percentage—ten percent, say—of ideals not realized or vocations not perfectly lived. It was this ten percent that was fashioned into one hundred percent, the completely brainwashed men. They were tricked into an absolute image of the negative in themselves that was unrelieved by other points of view of the self.

The temptation to hate man and to hate ourselves is very great. It takes imagination not to be preoccupied with that which we cannot like in man.

But the absolutizing imagination cannot endure the taste and the smell of the ten percent. It is really an interiorized critic that becomes part of the sick man and demands a perfection that is inhuman, without boundaries. It expects everything, criticizes everything, *and counterfeits true hope because it insists that no task is hopeless.* The more it is allowed to grow, the less it is pleased with anything. Thus it gives a man the constant feeling of being checkmated, no matter what move he makes. And thus, in the very act of telling him that nothing is hopeless, it takes away the hope that any action will satisfy it. It is demanding, it is a dictator and a bully. And it thrives on keeping itself hidden. It tries to reduce the self to a hopeless and submissive state. In other words, what we are up against here is an internalized form of brainwashing. We brainwash ourselves.

Against such an imagination the antidote is a human imagination that can circle around the mountain of the until it sees all that is there. Such an imagination easily taken in by the fascination of the hopeless. It will condemn itself too quickly.

It will leave the judgment to God.

It is precisely not foreclosing judgment on ourselves but leaving final judgment to God that requires imagination and hope.

If the last word were ours, we would indeed be badly off. It is imagination and hope, even when they look at our worst, that leave room for another and a better word. The very ability to turn away from this judgment on himself is the best thing in man, transcending in quality and importance all the things he is tempted to judge.

It is the victory we need in our own time, to turn away from being our own executioners.

Supplement

In the following pages I present a supplement on the absolutizing and on the human imagination. It is my strong hope that the extracts will buttress and illuminate more than one point made in the body of this book.

I have collected texts from a variety of distinguished writers and analysts who have handled some version or other of the absolutizing part of the human spirit. Perhaps the great lesson to draw from these texts is this, that just when we think a certain class of people (who might include ourselves) are not to be included, there, with suddenness and surety, that class appears. No group, no person, is exempt by definition from the absolutizing instinct.

The documentation of the human imagination and its contribution to hope is difficult. I have for many years been preoccupied with the imagination, especially in its literary forms, and have felt regret at the paucity of writing on the subject. The imagination, like hope, cries out for future exploration. This would buttress a point I consider central: as the new mental sciences, the imagination, properly understood and carefully distinguished from fantasy, directs the movement of human beings toward reality. And that, after all, is the greatest of human goals.

Harry Stack Sullivan, *The Interpersonal Theory of Psychiatry* (New York: Norton, 1953), pp. 32-33.

I now want to present what I used to call the one-genus hypothesis, or postulate. This hypothesis I word as follows: We shall assume that *everyone is much more simply human than otherwise,* and that anomalous interpersonal situations, insofar as they do not arise from differences in language or custom, are a function of differences in relative maturity of the persons concerned. In other words, the differences between any two instances of human personality—from the lowest-grade imbecile to the highest-grade genius—are much less striking than the differences between the least-gifted human being and a member of the nearest other biological genus. Man—however undistinguished biologically—as long as he is entitled to the term, human personality, will be much more like every other instance of human personality than he is like anything else in the world. As I have tried to hint before, it is to some extent on this basis that I have become occupied with the science, not of individual differences, but of human identities, or parallels, one might say. In other words, I try to study the degrees and patterns of things which I assume to be ubiquitously human.

Daniel J. Boorstin, *The Image, or What Happened to the American Dream* (New York: Atheneum, 1962), Introduction, pp. 3–6.

[I wish to] describe the world of our making, how we have used our wealth, our literacy, our technology, and our progress, to create the thicket of unreality which stands between us and the facts of life. I recount historical forces which have given us this unprecedented opportunity to deceive ourselves and to befog our experience.

Of course, America has provided the landscape and has given us the resources and the opportunity for this feat of national self-hypnosis. But each of us individually provides the market and the demand for the illusions which flood our experience.

We want and we believe these illusions because we suffer from extravagant expectations. We expect too much of the world. Our expectations are extravagant in the precise dictionary sense of the word—"going beyond the limits of reason or moderation." They are excessive.

When we pick up our newspaper at breakfast, we expect—we even demand—that it bring us momentous events since the night before. We turn on the car radio as we drive to work and expect "news" to have occurred since the morning newspaper went to press. Returning in the evening, we expect our house not only to shelter us, to keep us warm in winter and cool in summer, but to relax us, to dignify us, to encompass us with soft music and interesting hobbies, to be a playground, a theater, and a bar. We expect our two-week vacation to be romantic, exotic, cheap, and effortless. We expect a faraway atmosphere if we go to a nearby place; and we expect everything to be relaxing, sanitary, and Americanized if we go to a faraway place. We expect new heroes every season, a literary masterpiece every month, a dramatic spectacular every week, a rare sensation every night. We expect everybody to feel free to disagree, yet we expect everybody to be loyal, not to rock the boat or take the Fifth Amendment. We expect everybody to believe deeply in his religion, yet not to think less of others for not believing. We expect our nation to be strong and great and vast and varied and prepared for every challenge; yet we expect our "national purpose" to be clear and simple, something that gives direction to the lives of nearly two hundred million people and yet can be bought in a paperback at the corner drugstore for a dollar.

We expect anything and everything. We expect the contradictory and the impossible. We expect compact cars which are spacious; luxurious cars which are economical. We expect to be rich and charitable, powerful and merciful, active and reflective, kind and competitive. We expect to be inspired by mediocre appeals for "excellence," to be made literate by illiterate appeals for literacy. We expect to eat and stay thin, to be constantly on the move and ever more neighborly, to go to a "church of our choice" and yet feel its guiding power over us, to revere God and to be God.

Never have people been more the masters of their environment. Yet never has a people felt more deceived and disappointed. For never has a people expected so much more than the world could offer.

We are ruled by extravagant expectations:

(1) Of what the world holds. Of how much news there is, how many heroes there are, how often masterpieces are made, how exotic the nearby can be, how familiar the exotic can become. Of the closeness of places and the farness of places.

(2) Of our power to shape the world. Of our ability to create events when there are none, to make heroes when they don't exist, to be somewhere else when we haven't left home. Of our ability to make art forms suit our convenience, to transform a novel into a movie and vice versa, to turn a symphony into mood-conditioning. To fabricate national purposes when we lack them, to pursue these purposes after we have fabricated them. To invent our standards and

then to respect them as if they had been revealed or discovered.

By harboring, nourishing, and ever enlarging our extravagant expectations we create the demand for the illusions with which we deceive ourselves. And which we pay others to make to deceive us.

The making of the illusions which flood our experience has become the business of America, some of its most honest and most necessary and most respectable business. I am thinking not only of advertising and public relations and political rhetoric, but of all the activities which purport to inform and comfort and improve and educate and elevate us: the work of our best journalists, our most enterprising book publishers, our most energetic manufacturers and merchandisers, our most successful entertainers, our best guides to world travel, and our most influential leaders in foreign relations. Our every effort to satisfy our extravagant expectations simply makes them more extravagant and makes our illusions more attractive. The story of the making of our illusions—"the news behind the news"—has become the most appealing news of the world.

We tyrannize and frustrate ourselves by expecting more than the world can give us or than we can make of the world. We demand that everyone who talks to us, or writes for us, or takes pictures for us, or makes merchandise for us, should live in our world of extravagant expectations. We expect this even of the peoples of foreign countries. We have become so accustomed to our illusions that we mistake them for reality. We demand them. And we demand that there be always more of them, bigger and better and more vivid. They are the world of our making: the world of the image.

Nowadays everybody tells us that what we need is more belief, a stronger and deeper and more encompassing faith. A faith in America and in what we are doing. That may be true in the long run. What we need first and now is to disillusion ourselves. What ails us most is not what we have done with America, but what we have substituted for America. We suffer primarily not from our vices or our weaknesses, but from our illusions. We are haunted, not by reality, but by those images we have put in place of reality.

To discover our illusions will not solve the problems of our world. But if we do not discover them, we will never discover our real problems. To dispel the ghosts which populate the world of our making will not give us the power to conquer the real enemies of the real world or to remake the real world. But it may help us discover that we cannot make the world in our image. It will liberate us and sharpen our vision. It will clear away the fog so we can face the world we share with all mankind.

Leslie H. Farber, "Schizophrenia and the Mad Psychotherapist," *Review of Existential Psychology and Psychiatry* (Vol. 2, 1962), pp. 224-226.

Relation and Will. Now I would like to pick up again that most important thread in this whole design, which I left dangling—with promises attached—somewhile ago: the issue of the connection between relation and will. I believe that this unholy conspiracy characterizes, in an important sense, the behavior of both therapist and schizophrenic, not only in their relationship with each other—where it achieves its most dramatic form—but also, and equally importantly, in the relationship of each to his world, to all others, and to himself. In spite of the fact that the intellectual life of the schizophrenic is as fearfully impoverished as his capacities for relation with others, we must assume that he is still human enough to hunger for relation, and, should it be even fleetingly achieved, to dread and be enraged by its loss. In a state so extreme much of his delusional and hallucinatory life will either reach for consummation, even glory, or else proclaim his repudiation of such a possibility with a web of corroborating though fantastic details. By his impoverishment he is reduced in his attempts at relation or in his repudiation of relation (and often both are intermingled) to what I choose to call his isolated will—or willfulness, if we define it as Webster does: namely, that state in which one is governed by will without yielding to reason; obstinate; perverse; stubborn. It is a most important part of schizophrenia, and one that has been relatively neglected in the literature, though aspects of it have been considered under other categories. I would say that willfulness not only accounts for much of the schizophrenic's behavior, but authors a great deal of his delusional material. Without the assistance of the imagination the will invents in its own image; this means that the will contrives plots in which will is pitted against will, its subject matter being, roughly, power. In delusion the willful one may be an outside agent with the schizophrenic as victim, but regardless of who is seen to be the willful agent and who the victim the plot represents a crude example of what Yeats called the will doing the work of the imagination. To some extent power *is* a real and ubiquitous motive in the world. Thus, if the therapist is adept at supplying texture and meaning to the plot, it is easy to see how he may come to endow his schizophrenic patient with an oracular vision of how power controls and corrupts the affairs of all men.

Willfully then, the schizophrenic grasps at and withdraws from relation—sometimes simultaneously. Sullivan once remarked that he thought that with the exception of periods of panic the schizophrenic's life with others was largely hysterical in character. Although my understanding of hysteria is quite different from Sullivan's, I think I know what led him to this observation. It was, I suspect, the violent, flamboyant, impulsive, often explosive and destructive quality of the schizophrenic's social movements which reminded him of hysteria. In this regard we should remind ourselves that one or two of the first hysterics Freud and Breuer studied would today be diagnosed as schizophrenic. To take but one example: a particular case of schizophrenic mutism may have begun in panic when talk led to such terrifying confusion about reality that distress, instead of being relieved, was not only perpetuated but intensified. But as his panic subsides, this person's muteness perhaps becomes—and may remain—a willful refusal to talk, in response to what he regards as the demand to talk being made on him by those about him. Reduced to his own will, the schizophrenic believes and perceives himself to be continually assailed by the willful demands of the world around him. Examples of schizophrenic willfulness, whether or not they had their antecedents in panic, and despite the often confusing nature of their delusional elaboration or justification, are numerous; the refusal to eat, waxy inflexibility or the refusal to move, untidiness and nakedness, even smearing—all these expressions may become willful responses to what seems to the schizophrenic to be willfulness on the part of those responsible for his care. Most of the gestures I have mentioned are those of rejection of relation, but it should be said that his sexual attempts to force intimacy can be equally willful—as with Frieda's masturbating patient—seeming almost assaultive in their grotesque lack of the nuances which usually assist the life of affection.

Not until the particular willfulness of the schizophrenic is recognized can it be understood why the therapeutic life with schizophrenics is such a bloodcurdling affair, its melodrama underscored by screaming invective, physical grappling of a brutal order, and all manner of obscenity. Even the mildest, most unassuming therapist will, if he continues in this work, soon find himself hurled into an arena where will is pitted bodily against will. And he may even come to count himself fortunate to have this semblance of relation, no matter how degraded, instead of none at all—which is his more frequent lot.

It is hardly surprising that the more violent forms of the therapy of schizophrenia should seem to be life in the raw, making all ordinary civilized existence pallid and tedious by comparison. But the problem for the therapist is more serious than this. Whether he is locked in frantic physical encounter with his patient or else trying, through monologue, to breach his patient's muteness, he is thrown back on his own isolated will in his efforts to provoke relationship. Even in defeat he may resort to a silence which is as willful as the silence of his patient. It can be said that both therapist and patient have a will to relation and a relationship of wills. But this is a rather reckless use of the word relation. Relation, understood in any decent sense, cannot be willed: it happens or doesn't happen, depending on what human qualities are brought to the event: honesty, imagination, tact, humor, and so on. By contrast, the willful encounter—a far cry from the chancy and fleeting mutuality that occurs from time to time between people, and that we designate by the honorable term relation—will have a special binge-like excitement, even though its center is hollow. Its intensity is of the moment: unlike friendship, when the moment vanishes little remains. This is the reason the addictive possibilities of this therapeutic life are considerable. (In this regard it is no accident that two of the best known therapists in the field have attempted to give the experience of loneliness ontological status in the human condition.) As the therapist returns again and again to the excitements of this drama of wills that passes for relation, he becomes increasingly impatient of relation, although it is unlikely he will cease believing—and asserting—that the capacity for relation is his special power. Gradually, but not casually, he develops into an apostle of relation who can no longer abide relation. It is an unhappy fact that when, through drugs or life situation, one finds more and more scope for willfulness, those other human qualities I have mentioned are not merely held in abeyance but fall into the atrophy of disuse. And with such atrophy the ordinary amenities of the world become not only no longer sustaining but actually disturbing, making recourse to the drug ever more compelling. As the therapist continues to will what cannot be willed, those attributes of character to expand and harden will be precisely those public, self-assertive gestures which are inauthentic to the person he might have become.

Leslie H. Farber, "Despair and the Life of Suicide," *Review of Existential Psychology and Psychiatry* (Vol. 2, 1962), pp. 129-131.

A Vaudeville of Devils. Even in such a brief account of the landscape of despair, it must be clear that despair—potentially at least—is both destroying and renewing. With this double potentiality in mind, T. S. Eliot has addressed himself to the despairer in this manner:

> I said to my soul, be still, and wait without hope
> For hope would be hope for the wrong thing; wait without love
> For love would be love of the wrong thing; there is yet faith
> But the faith and the love and the hope are all in the waiting.
> Wait without thought, for you are not ready for thought:
> So the darkness shall be light, and the stillness the dancing.[4]

While we may not share the author's rather Eastern reliance on the waiting itself as the way out of despair, still we must acknowledge how difficult it is for the despairer to still his soul—or his mind. While despair means literally the loss of hope, the movements of despair are frantically directed toward hope; but the hope born of despair may turn to the prescriptions of the isolated will. Spurning the self-illumination arising from true humility, despairing hope concerns itself pridefully with certainties—even the certainty of hopelessness may paradoxically appear as a form of hope, promising to make reasonable what is unreasonable, namely

[4] T. S. Eliot, East Coker. *Four Quartets*. New York: Harcourt, Brace, 1943, p. 15.

hopelessness itself. The despairer may, at this opaque moment, be utterly convinced of the clarity of his vision, condemning the world which preceded his despair as no more than a sentimental insanity, a silly fabrication created by his own unwillingness to discern the harsh truth about this existence. It is as if his imagination, in its fullest sense, had abdicated, and now his will could apply itself to the task of reducing what is most human, to pursuing ever further the inevitability—and therefore the essential absurdity—of all that has been and all that will be. He now seems to himself, despite his melancholy, the most reasonable and forthright of men. Like Kirillov in Dostoyevsky's *The Possessed,* he proclaims, "I am just such a scoundrel as you, as all, not a decent man. There's never been a decent man anywhere . . . all the planet is a lie and rests on a lie and on mockery. So then, the very laws of the planet are a lie and the vaudeville of devils." [5] This is the realism of a truly macabre predictability. And a "vaudeville of devils" accurately describes the stale, repetitious, lifeless routines from which the despairer yearns to escape. Surprise and mystery have vanished from his view, if not from his experience. If he contemplates a visit with friends he can no longer imagine the casual, the unexpected moment which might offer even momentary relief. No, instead he writes both scripts and concludes from his authorship that since he knows what would happen there is no reason for making such a visit. But if life itself should provide a casual moment, even with a stranger, which quite cuts through his self-absorption, wholly transforming his mood, he has no capacity to celebrate this moment. In fact, he will disown or conceal the moment rather than allow it to question his dismal certainty, and he thus learns cagily to protect his state from life's interventions. Even the rational or logical steps to his conclusions, which strike him as utterly convincing, may turn shabby if exposed to the light of discourse. So, pride urges him to keep to his own counsel, even though it means his death. Thus does the despairer appear before us to ask that most extraordinary and truly diabolical question—especially when addressed to a psychotherapist—"Is there any good in talking?" After this, we may recover our composure and succeed in engaging him imaginatively, so that real talk, does, after all, begin

[5] Fyodor Dostoyevsky, *The Possessed*. New York: The Modern Library, 1936, pp. 625–629.

to come about. Despite his absolute certainty of a few moments before that even momentary relief from the torment of despair was no longer possible, his despairing self-absorption may yield to forthright interest in the subject at hand, a yielding which goes beyond mere distraction. Relief has, in spite of everything, actually been granted him; his despairing certainty has been exposed to the real world of discourse and proved false. We might even say that a minor miracle has occurred. What are we to answer then, when, as the hour nears its end, our patient or friend, preparing to take his leave, turns to us and asks, "But haven't you something *useful* to say to me—something I can use after I leave here?" If there is an answer to this question, it has not occurred to me. I wish to comment only on one of its most curious aspects: the man who spoke these words was one who had recently been in despair and would, very likely, soon be in despair again. Yet by this question, which could occur only to a despairing mind, despair reasserted its claim on him, still without forcing upon him the anguish which is its customary companion. Contained within his question is the reminder that such fleeting moments of relief are all very well, but after all truth is truth and logic is logic, and by truth of course he means despairing truth and by logic he means despairing logic. This is to say that what he wishes to take with him to counter his despairing certainties are other certainties, maxim-like morsels, prescriptive in nature, which, like pills, will offer him some comfort when the pain returns. Almost while still celebrating the wonder of his renewal, he has with his question submitted himself again to despair.

Leslie H. Farber, "Perfectibility and the Psychoanalytic Candidate," *The Journal of Existential Psychiatry* (Vol. III, No. 11, Winter, 1963).

When I was first admitted to psychoanalytic training twenty years ago, I assembled with four other colleagues to hear a sermon by one of the senior training analysts. All that remains with me of that somber occasion is a picture of this learned man standing above us grasping the top of a rickety folding chair. He looked quite devout to me as, with eyes lowered, he rocked himself back and forth, and thus admonished us: "Though you have been accepted for psychoanalytic training, you are not psychoanalysts. Should you be asked, identify yourselves merely as psychiatrists. And by no means, are you to designate the work you do as psychoanalysis." Between him and me there seemed to be an impossible gulf—not only of esoteric skills and knowledge, but, more important, of a quality of being which I assumed was the most important reward of this long period of training I was to undergo. His admonition remains with me to this day. When pressed I find it hard to designate my insufficient person as that of a psychoanalyst; and I feel I am taking some advantage of the truth when I identify my work as psychoanalysis. My experience cannot be too different, say, from that of proselytes of the Catharist heresy in the 12th century, who were divided into the Pure and the Impure. So difficult was the attainment of Purity that this spiritual distinction often did not arrive until the moment of last rites.

This particular heresy, with its promise of earthly perfection, provoked the Church into the first mass slaughter in Western history. If psychoanalysis is a variety of heresy, it will not, I think, result in genocide at the hands of the mother Church. What I shall be more concerned with in these remarks is the effect of our heresy—if that is what it is—on its celebrants.

Let me say quickly that our heresy, while resembling in its gnostic nature, its predecessors, is a peculiarly modern and secular variety, and, unlike earlier heresies within the church, the heretical portion of its doctrine is largely unacknowledged. Stripped of the unusual scientific qualifications, it might be expressed in this manner: *however rarely the goal of perfection may be achieved, man is a creature who is, nonetheless, psychologically perfectible, by virtue of either the early and happy accident of childhood or the later and unhappy necessity of psychoanalysis.* (In keeping with such a theory, of course, the word "accident" must be understood as a rather gay metaphor for something which is in no way accidental. The idea of perfectibility is as dependent on some form of determinism as it is disdainful of the chaotic freedom which would permit someone to have an "accidental" sort of childhood. Once perfectibility is postulated, its logical mechanisms fit together to forge a deterministic, chance-proof continuity, extending its exclusive claim over past and future alike. Tucked away in this chain of causation is one of determinism's most logically baffling yet favorite propositions: if the determining factors are identified and understood, they may be manipulated; this results in the interesting phenomenon of a logically lawful and impersonal determinism, subject to will.) No sensible psychoanalyst would confess agreement with the doctrine of perfectibility when it is so nakedly stated as it is above; yet I would suggest that covertly it accounts for many of our professional miseries, particularly during our training period.

Unlike any other profession I know, with the possible exception of the priesthood, psychoanalysis places a double burden on its candidates: not only must they acquire psychoanalytic skills and knowledge, a difficult enough task in itself, but they must in addition undergo a lengthy period of psychoanalytic therapy, which at once calls into question what they had previously taken for granted—namely their characters—while promising, or stipulating, something variously called growth or maturity as the outcome of this experience. Thus, at the same time that they are asked to address themselves wholeheartedly to complex theoretical and clinical problems, they are beset through their own psychoanalysis by a degree of self-absorption which in some ways quite opposes their pursuit of their subject matter. And, the reverse dilemma is equally burdensome. At the same time that they are asked to address themselves wholeheartedly to disorganizing and reforming their own characters, they are prompted, by their didactic studies, to a scientific inspection of that very process. The difficulty of being both subject and student at once produces a disturbing self-consciousness which affects both aspects of their training. While it is quite true that the theories of psychoanalysis cannot be usefully learned and understood as though they were propositions of chemistry, they must to some extent be personally grasped and subjectively imagined, the often painful self-involvement and crippling self-doubt that attend one's own analysis are not always helpful partners to imagination. Conversely, while run-away subjectivity interferes with analytic progress, and some "objective" perfection of one's self and one's feelings is essential, this requirement is seldom served by the rather unnaturally and irrelevantly detached self-scrutiny that absorption with theoretical formulae invites. Achieving some objectivity toward oneself and assigning scholarly and hyphenated labels to one's symptoms are far from identical operations; scientific objectivity is not, if you will excuse me, subjective objectivity; it is, in fact, its opposite and enemy when the two are confused.   —pp. 285-287

It is fashionable to complain that candidates these days

are far more conforming to middle class values than were the candidates twenty years ago. In this complaint it is suggested that Freud was too unbalanced to be accepted for candidacy today, that institutes now, in offering fellowship, prefer the well-behaved and amiable to the unruly gifted and disagreeable. I think there is truth to this observation, but I am not satisfied that this change comes merely from the increasing institutionalization of a movement which, in its beginnings at least, was more inspired and Bohemian in nature. It seems more likely to me that, as the image of earthly psychological perfection, even though unacknowledged, settled in the minds of the majority of psychoanalysts, sheer discontent with the actuality of the analyzed self chafed and mounted. Perfection was demanded, and yet it could not be grasped inwardly. Unable to *be* what was required of him, the candidate turned in desperation to dramatizing his possession of the well-being he could not possess, by assuming what he hoped were its outward manifestations and appearances. In this imitation of being which is behaving, he strove to create an illusion of so-called maturity, a style of life and statement which would persuade others that he actually had realized those psychological values which continued privately to elude him. A style of life so self-imposed and so at odds with being itself, will by definition be more banal and predictable than surprising.

Predictable, however, not only in its outward conformity, but in the burden of its inward pain. When man believes in his perfectibility he experiences his own real being almost as a disease, a fatal sickness whose cure—perfection—seems unattainable for himself, and whose tormenting symptoms can only partially be eased by the exchange of seeming for being. When he measures himself not by his acts—which may reveal what he *is*—but by his actions, his image of himself becomes external, objective, and turns for its definition to a psychology of behavior. And we hardly notice that we have almost ceased to wonder what maturity, say, might individually, subjectively feel like or be, since we now know so very much about what it looks like or does. Being, however, is not easily denied. Such grand scale deception as I have described, especially in those who are trained in self-scrutiny, is usually too large an order even for those with considerable talent for acting, so that no matter how convincing the candidate's efforts may be to others, to him they are the movements of misery; every gesture he makes in imitation of the ideal (a role as recognizable as Hamlet, though requiring greater gifts) reminds him shamefully of his pretenses and painfully of his real limitations, which appear, in the shadow of the ideal, ever more huge and menacing. Thus does the noble dream of perfection make cynics of us all, destroying our infinite variety, reducing us to our facility for imitation, and rendering us despicable to ourselves.

The desire for self-improvement, striving after goals, aspiring toward an ideal—these ambitions were not suddenly thrust into human experience in the second half of the 19th century; they ante-date modern psychology by several thousand years at least. Man has always measured himself against what he is not, but might become: his goals; and against what he can never become, but can move toward: his ideals. Throughout history man has often been tyrannized by his own ambition, but his ideals could not enslave him by their very nature, so long as he could recognize and acknowledge the impossible. Ideals in the pre-Freudian past usually concerned themselves with those distinctly human virtues which were central to man's definition of himself: discrimination, judgment, intelligence, taste, restraint, humility, imagination, to name but a few. The ideal—the perfection of any such virtue—was clearly beyond human reach; but its image penetrated the human sphere just deeply enough to illuminate a direction, a path toward ever greater exercise and refinement of virtue, a path with no point of arrival for man, which lay across the very center of his life. Excepting the doctrine of a few religious heresies, little claim was made for the perfectibility of the total man. Man knew himself an imperfect creature, and his own imperfectibility was as essential to his definition of himself as were the sins he committed, the temptations that raged in his heart, the virtues he honored, the faith or hope he cherished.

With the development of psychoanalysis at the turn of the century, the perennial issue of *what is human* was invigorated by a whole new body of psychological evidence and hypothesis, all proceeding exclusively from attention to psychological disorder or pathology. In the sheer excitement of these discoveries and inventions, analysts tended to forget older sources of wisdom pertaining to the question of *what is human*. Instead, as though they were the first citizens to arrive on this planet, they attempted to derive an entire way of life from their theories of pathology. The examples are legion. If authoritarian fathers produce neurotic children, children should be raised in cooperative nurseries away from parental pressures. If oral fixation leads to schizophrenia, then decent nursing attention not only prevents schizophrenia but furnishes the conditions for a normal human being. If repressed hostility accounts for certain types of misery, then free expression of anger is evidence of maturity. In other words, when human virtue is the opposite of defect, absence of defect means presence of virtue. Complete absence of all defects means complete virtue—or perfection. Now, virtues which are the absence of defects have very little relevance to any knowledge of virtue we may have that has come to us *not* from psychology, but from any other source of information about the human: history, literature, philosophy, religion, our own experience—all of which have not only always recognized human imperfectibility, but have constantly warned man against the grave dangers of believing himself perfectible. The theories of psychoanalysis seem to tempt us to forget or even to ignore these warnings, offering us a promise and a plan for our own perfection. Such heresy, however, does not rise inevitably from our doctrines, but captures us only when we use these doctrines to estrange us from all other knowledge of ourselves.   —pp. 290–292

Erik Erikson, *Identity and the Life Cycle,* Psychological Issues (Vol. I, No. 1, 1959, New York: International Universities Press, 1959), pp. 129–132.

The Choice of the Negative Identity. The loss of a sense of identity often is expressed in a scornful and snobbish hostility toward the roles offered as proper and desirable in one's family or immediate community. Any part aspect of the required role, or all parts, be it masculinity or femininity, nationality or class membership, can become the main focus of the young person's acid disdain. Such excessive contempt for their backgrounds occurs among the oldest Anglo-Saxon and the newest Latin or Jewish families; it easily becomes a general dislike for everything American, and an irrational overestimation of everything foreign. Life and strength seem to exist only where one is not, while decay and danger threaten wherever one happens to be. This typical case fragment illustrates the superego's triumph of depreciation over a young man's faltering identity: "A voice within him which was disparaging him began to increase at about this time. It went to the point of intruding into everything he did. He said, 'if I smoke a cigarette, if I tell a girl I like her, if I make a gesture, if I listen to music, if I try to read a book—this third voice is at me all the time—"You're doing this for effect; you're a phony."' This disparaging voice in the last year has been rather relentless. The other day on the way from home to college, getting into New York on the train, he went through some of the New Jersey swamplands and the poorer sections of the cities, and he felt that he was more congenial with people who lived there than he was with people on the campus or at home. He felt that life really existed in those places and that the campus was a sheltered, effeminate place."

In this example it is important to recognize not only an over-weening superego, over-clearly perceived as an inner voice, but also the acute identity diffusion, as projected on segments of society. An analogous case is that of a French-American girl from a rather prosperous mining town, who felt panicky to the point of paralysis when alone with a boy. It appeared that numerous superego injunctions and identity conflicts had, as it were, short-circuited in the obsessive idea that every boy had a right to expect from her a yielding to sexual practices popularly designated as "French."

Such estrangement from national and ethnic origins rarely leads to a complete denial of *personal identity*, although the angry insistence on being called by a particular given name or nickname is not uncommon among young people who try to find a refuge from diffusion in a new name label. Yet confabulatory reconstructions of one's origin do occur: a high-school girl of Middle-European descent secretly kept company with Scottish immigrants, carefully studying and easily assimilating their native dialect and their social habits. With the help of history books and travel guides she reconstructed for herself a childhood in a given milieu in an actual township in Scotland, apparently convincing enough to some descendants of that country. Prevailed upon to discuss her future with me, she spoke of her (American-born) parents as "the people who brought me over here," and told me of her childhood "over there" in impressive detail. I went along with the story, implying that it had more inner truth than reality to it. The bit of reality was, as surmised, the girl's attachment, in early childhood, to a woman neighbor who had come from the British Isles; the force behind the near-delusional "truth" was the paranoid form of a powerful death wish (latent in all severe identity crises) against her parents. The semideliberateness of the delusion was indicated when I finally asked the girl how she had managed to marshal all the details of life in Scotland. "Bless you, sir," she said in pleading Scottish brogue, "I needed a past."

On the whole, however, our patients' conflicts find expression in a more subtle way than the abrogation of personal identity: they rather choose a *negative identity,* i.e., an identity perversely based on all those identifications and roles which, at critical stages of development, had been presented to the individual as most undesirable or dangerous, and yet also as most real. For example, a mother whose first-born son died and who (because of complicated guilt feelings) had never been able to attach to her later surviving children the same amount of religious devotion that she bestows on the memory of her dead child may well arouse in one of her sons the conviction that to be sick or dead is a better assurance of being "recognized" than to be healthy and about. A mother who is filled with unconscious ambivalence toward a brother who disintegrated into alcoholism may again and again respond selectively only to those traits in her son which seem to point to a repetition of her brother's fate, in which case this "negative" identity may take on more reality for the son than all his natural attempts at being good: he may work hard on becoming a drunkard and, lacking the necessary ingredients, may end up in a state of stubborn paralysis of choice. In other cases, the negative identity is dictated by the necessity of finding and defending a niche of one's own against the excessive ideals either demanded by morbidly ambitious parents or seemingly already realized by actually superior ones: in both cases the parents' weaknesses and unexpressed wishes are recognized by the child with catastrophic clarity. The daughter of a man of brilliant showmanship ran away from college and was arrested as a prostitute in a Negro quarter of a Southern city; while the daughter of an influential Southern Negro preacher was found among narcotic addicts in Chicago. In such cases it is of utmost importance to recognize the mockery and the vindictive pretense in such role playing; for the white girl had not really prostituted herself, and the colored girl had not really become an addict—yet. Needless to say, however, each of them had put herself into a marginal social area, leaving it to law-enforcement officers and to psychiatric agencies to decide what stamp to put on such behavior. A corresponding case is that of a boy presented to a psychiatric clinic as "the village homosexual" of a small town. On investigation, it appeared that the boy had succeeded in assuming this fame without any actual acts of homosexuality except one, much earlier in his life, when he had been raped by some older boys.

Such vindictive choices of a negative identity represent, of course, a desperate attempt at regaining some mastery in a situation in which the available positive identity elements cancel each other out. The history of such a choice reveals a set of conditions in which it is easier to derive a sense of identity out of a *total* identification with that which one is *least* supposed to be than to struggle for a feeling of reality in acceptable roles which are unattainable with the patient's inner means. The statement of a young man, "I would rather be quite insecure than a little secure," and that of a young woman, "At least in the gutter I'm a genius," circumscribe the relief following the total choice of a negative identity. Such relief is, of course, often sought collectively in cliques and gangs of young homosexuals, addicts, and social cynics.

A relevant job ahead of us is the analysis of snobbism which, in its upper-class form, permits some people to deny their identity diffusion through a recourse to something they did not earn themselves, namely, their parent's wealth, background, or fame. But there is a "lower lower" snobbism, too, which is based on the pride of having achieved a semblance of nothingness. At any rate many a late adolescent, if faced with continuing diffusion, would rather *be nobody or somebody bad, or indeed, dead—and this totally, and by free choice—than be not-quite-somebody*. The word "total" is not accidental in this connection, for I have endeavored to describe in another connection a human proclivity to a "totalistic" reorientation when, at critical stages of development, reintegration into a relative "wholeness" seems impossible.

Sebastian Moore, O.S.B., "A Catholic Neurosis?", *The Clergy Review* (new series, Vol. XLVI, No. 11, November, 1961), pp. 641–647.

The subject of this essay is a delicate one. I want only to

express a conviction that has grown on me in recent years: that one encounters among Catholics certain ways of behaving in the exchanges of social life: that these ways of behaving can be understood in the light of a certain hypothesis: that this hypothesis is that of a neurosis found in Catholics at the present time. My plan is to give a random list of the phenomena, then to suggest what is the root of the trouble.

To begin with, let it be clear that the case for a Catholic neurosis cannot be scientifically established. It will always be possible to reduce the phenomena listed to other causes, or even to deny their existence. The following suggestion is therefore only in the realm of hypothesis. It is offered only on the understanding that self-criticism is a good thing, that the difficulty often is to know *how* to criticize oneself relevantly, and thus therefore any suggestion may be welcome.

Every man needs some ideas, some principles for interpreting life to him and for guiding him in its conduct. But there needs to be some *balance* between this ideal structure and the unique life which it is guiding. A man needs to "realize" his ideas, to feed into them a personal discovery of their meaning and usefulness. Now, with the Catholic, this ideal structure is most imposing. It is the creation of Christian faith working in great and holy minds, bringing forth their best insights. From the meditations of Augustine, from the speculations of Aquinas, and from numberless other sources, there has built up this great body of objective truth. The effect is peculiarly accumulative in the Church, whose law it is that every significant Christian insight feeds and increases a common mind. And whether or not your individual Catholic is overtly aware of all that he carries, he does carry it. At moments he will surprise his non-Catholic friend by showing an astounding *certainty* about life and death and God and after-death, problems about which the greatest minds have anguished without conclusion. Now, this effortless certainty is a wonderful thing, and I have sometimes pointed to it, while instructing a convert, as showing the real meaning of infallibility. Still, if I am right in saying there must be some balance between a man's ideal structure and his life as experienced, there is going to be a serious imbalance in the case of the Catholic. Between him and what *he* feels and, fumblingly, thinks about life—"life" meaning girls, money, marriage, fun and drudgery—there comes what great and noble souls have thought about it, twice-born souls who have seen the true perspectives and made the consequent sacrifice. So he oscillates between two standards. This oscillation is not the same thing as the tension between good and evil, between the dictates of conscience and the importunities of the flesh. It is a division of the mind rather than of the will. It is better described as a neurosis than as a straight spiritual conflict. And it is the Catholic ideal structure, getting between the individual and his rudimentary common sense, that tends to inhibit a commonsense approach to the problems of daily living.

The neurosis will be more active in those whose manner of life commits them more closely to the Church, and that is why the symptoms I have listed are those shown by us religious. This is a hard saying and takes no account of the numberless souls who have grown, in religious and priestly life, into fine men and women. But I'm not writing about them. I'm not even writing about the redeeming feature (in the strong theological sense) in our own lives. I'm writing about the other side of the picture. I want to understand why it is that a religious community may fail, sometimes to an alarming degree, to develop the natural virtues of community life. After all, it is this sort of thing that our layman in religious employ finds himself up against. He misses in his employers a type of straight dealing and sanity that is more easily found among men not embarrassed by supernatural awareness. And I want us priests to ask ourselves: Am I such a small man that I cannot worthily represent to others an infallible and inflexible authority? And let us avoid the stop-thought that immediately offers itself: Of course no one is *worthy!*

This division to which the Catholic soul is liable can have many effects. The principal of these is apathy, or what a seminary professor of my acquaintance once referred to as "Catholic pessimism." He was speaking of the seminary itself, where the ideal structure is built up in all its imposing coherence. The effect of being continually exposed to the truth which is doing one no good is distressing to the soul. There can even result a kind of unbelief, an exhaustion of the spirit, which is all the worse for being partly unconscious. In this connection we ought to look up what the old masters have to tell us about accidie, which may be loosely rendered as "spiritual bloody-mindedness."

And outside the seminary! The young teenagers who go straight from a Catholic school into the factory, what of them, what is in their minds, what *can* be there? What relation will there be between the formulas they have learned and the life they are beginning to discover?

Karin Stephen, *The Wish to Fall Ill* (London: Cambridge, 1960), pp. 75–77.

The point of fundamental importance which I am anxious here to emphasize is that what upsets the smooth functioning of the pleasure instinct, and leads to all the psychogenic abnormalities which we are trying to investigate, is *disappointment*. According to what a child does about this, he grows up mentally healthy or ill. This fundamental problem of how to deal with disappointment runs right through the history of the child's gradually developing relations to external reality and especially its emotional relations connected with these early sensual pleasures of which I have just spoken and which I am proposing to regard as constituting the immature stages in the developmental history of sexuality. These pleasure-cravings of childhood are intense: but since it is hardly possible, even under the most favorable conditions, to enjoy nothing but unbroken satisfaction, bitter disappointment is a situation which every baby meets almost from the very beginning of its existence.

At this time its power of tolerating any state of tension, with the accompanying anxiety and fear, is very weak; real self-control is not within its power, and it has at its disposal only three alternatives, despair or rage or repression. Despair means the extinction of pleasure—emotional death. But undisguised rage lays the child open to all the terrors that must beset any small creature which attempts to rear itself up against a huge and powerful enemy. And for the human child there are further complications, one being the conflict which is set up by its rage at being disappointed and its already existing love for the ones who disappoint it, and the other being its utter dependence on these very ones against whom its rage is directed. If it bites the hand or breast that feeds it, the food is withdrawn. The child seems commonly to regard disappointment as punishment for its own attacks and in this way it loses courage.

Repression evades this difficult situation by disassociating pleasure-hunger without destroying it. Thus it avoids conscious *dis*pleasure and the open rage which at first accompanies this: it simply evades the immediate danger by shutting off the entire conflict just as it stands, so that the whole emotional complex—craving, love, rage, and fear—are all excluded from consciousness, thus behaving towards mental pain in a way comparable to the escape from excessive physical pain by fainting. This is in the long run a bad solution, however, because it provides no discharge for the craving, and while the conflict remains unresolved the craving will go on, though now entirely outside consciousness, so long at least as repression is successfully maintained.

This was the situation in which Freud found that many of his patients were, even though years had passed since the original disappointments occurred. They had not got over them. They were still unconsciously living in the old infantile situation in which their early disappointments befell them, still craving the infantile satisfactions and still torn by the old conflicts between love on this early infantile model and rage and fear. Freud considered that these early situations had become as it were embalmed and preserved in this way right on into adult life, because in early childhood the problem of how to deal with disappointment had not been well solved. At that time it was met by not admitting reality, by pretending all was well when it was not, and dissociating into the unconscious the wishes and fancies which, openly recognized, would have aroused an active conflict between love, rage and fear.

Neurosis, it thus appears, is really a flight from the pain of facing reality at some point. When the child finds it cannot or dare not satisfy some desire, it may refuse to admit this reality and repress the desire, all the while clinging to it obstinately in the unconscious, though perhaps being quite unaware in consciousness of disappointment.

The ꞓre fact of having dealt with disappointment by repression is, however, not enough to distinguish the neurotic from the normal person, since this reaction is, to some extent, universal in all human beings. Normally, however, the unavoidable repression of early childhood seems to be more or less outgrown. Desires which were, perhaps, repressed at their first appearance get modified in the ordinary course of development and reappear in more acceptable forms, putting up substitute outlets which are more attainable. Fears which were realities in childhood are ultimately seen through and discarded, wishes appropriate only to infancy are really outgrown.

With the neurotic things turn out otherwise. The original disappointment is never accepted, and the primitive demands of instinct are retained in their original form, unmodified. One patient said to me, half in joke, half in anger, "The Constant Nymph simply isn't in it with me!" On another ocasion she compared herself with the famous Pears' Soap cartoon of the baby in the bath howling for the lost soap, underneath which is written, "He won't be happy till he gets it." This is indeed the neurotic situation—they simply *will not* take any substitute for the original pleasures which were denied them. Their primitive instinctive cravings continue unchanged. Time does not alter them, they do not mature, and experience seems unable to touch them. They remain embedded in the unconscious-like fossils, shut off from the air, retaining their old form. The early infantile wishes and fears which were originally repressed remain infantile ever after, little foreign bodies like splinters in the otherwise developing and maturing character.

R. J. Lifton, *Thought Reform and the Psychology of Totalism* (New York: W. W. Norton, 1961).

The language of the totalist environment is characterized by the thought-terminating cliché. The most far-reaching and complex of human problems are compressed into brief, highly reductive, definitive-sounding phrases, easily memorized and easily expressed. These become the start and finish of any ideological analysis. In thought reform, for instance, the phrase "bourgeois mentality" is used to encompass and critically dismiss ordinarily troublesome concerns like the quest for individual expression, the exploration of alternative ideas, and the search for perspective and balance in political judgments. And in addition to their function as interpretive shortcuts, these clichés become what Richard Weaver has called "ultimate terms"; either "god terms," representative of ultimate good; or "devil terms" representative of ultimate evil. In thought reform, "progress," "progressive," "liberation," "proletarian standpoints," and "the dialectic of history" fall into the former category; "capitalist," "imperialist," "exploiting classes," and "bourgeois" (mentality, liberalism, morality, superstition, greed) of course fall into the latter. Totalist language, then, is repetitiously centered on all-encompassing jargon, prematurely abstract, highly categorical, relentlessly judging, and to anyone but its most devoted advocate, deadly dull: in Lionel Trilling's phrase, "the language of nonthought."

To be sure, this kind of language exists to some degree within any cultural or organizational group, and all systems of belief depend upon it. It is in part an expression of unity and exclusiveness: as Edward Sapir put it, " 'He talks like us' is equivalent to saying 'He is one of us'!" The loading is much more extreme in ideological totalism, however, since the jargon expresses the claimed certitudes of the sacred science. Also involved is an underlying assumption that language—like all other human products—can be owned and operated by the Movement. No compunctions are felt about manipulating or loading it in any fashion; the only consideration is its usefulness to the cause.

For an individual person, the effect of the language of ideological totalism can be summed up in one word: constriction. He is, so to speak, linguistically deprived, and since language is so central to all human experience, his capacities for thinking and feeling are immensely narrowed. This is what Hu meant when he said, "using the same pattern of words for so long . . . you feel chained." Actually, not everyone exposed *feels* chained, but in effect everyone *is* profoundly confined by these verbal fetters. As in other aspects of totalism, this loading may provide an initial sense of insight and security, eventually followed by uneasiness. This uneasiness may result in a retreat into a rigid orthodoxy in which an individual shouts the ideological jargon all the louder in order to demonstrate his conformity, hide his own dilemma and his despair, and protect himself from the fear and guilt he would feel should he attempt to use words and phrases other than the correct ones. Or else he may adopt a complex pattern of inner division, and dutifully produce the expected clichés in public performances while in his private moments he searches for more meaningful avenues of expression. Either way, his imagination becomes increasingly dissociated from his actual life experiences and may even tend to atrophy from disuse.   —pp. 429-430

. . . Ideological totalism itself may offer a man an intense peak experience: a sense of transcending all that is ordinary and prosaic, of freeing himself from the encumbrances of human ambivalence, of entering a sphere of truth, reality, trust, and sincerity beyond any he had ever known or even imagined. But these peak experiences, the result as they are of external pressures, distortion and threat, carry a great potential for rebound, and for equally intense opposition to the very things which initially seemed so liberating. Such imposed peak experiences—as contrasted with those more freely and privately arrived at by great religious leaders and mystics—are essentially experiences of personal closure. Rather than stimulating greater receptivity and "openness" to the world, they encourage a backward step into some form of "embeddedness"—a retreat into doctrinal and organizational exclusiveness, and into all-or-nothing emotional patterns more characteristic (at least at this stage of human history) of the child than of the individual adult.

And if no peak experience occurs, ideological totalism does even greater violence to the human potential: it evokes destructive emotions, produces intellectual and psychological constrictions, and deprives men of all that is most subtle and imaginative—under the false promise of eliminating these very imperfections and ambivalences which help to define the human condition. This combination of personal closure, self destructiveness and hostility towards outsiders leads to the dangerous group excesses so characteristic of ideological totalism, in any form. It also mobilizes extremist tendencies in those outsiders under attack, thus creating a vicious circle of totalism.   —p. 439

J. Piaget, *Judgment and Reasoning in the Child* (New Jersey: Littlefield Adams and Company, 1959).

The problem remains as to why the child's field of consciousness should be so narrow and why individuals should be perceived singly without any relations to each other nor to the child himself. Now, if the child makes no attempt to find the connections which unite individuals severally, if he regards them as something absolute, without taking account of the relativity of their characters and of their points of view, might it not be because he has never compared himself to these individuals? In other words, if he fails to understand why a friend of his can be both fairer than another friend and darker than a third, might this not be because the child has never suspected that such and such a person whom he has always considered fair may be looked upon as having chestnut-coloured hair by children who are themselves very fair, and so on? In short, is it not because he has always taken his own point of view as something absolute that the child remains ignorant of the habits of relativity and comparison, and that his field of consciousness is still restricted? Thus the difficulty in handling the logic of relations would seem to be a new consequence of childish ego-centrism; ego-centrism leads to naïve realism, and this realism, which is by definition the ignorance of all relations, leads to logical difficulties every time there is a question of substituting the logic of relations for that of membership or inclusion.

These psychological factors show up very clearly in the case of the brother and sister relationship. One must be very careful, in examining children in the manner we have described, not to interpret their mistakes as actual fallacies, i.e., as mistakes in reason. The child's attitude betrays only a deficiency of attention, or, strictly speaking, a faulty point of view, due to the fact that he has not yet asked himself the question as we ask it. He has always considered his brothers and sisters from his own point of view, calling them brothers and sisters, counting them up without including himself, or counting the family only as a whole. But the thought of their individual viewpoints has never crossed his mind; he has never asked himself what he was to them. . . . —p. 89

In virtue of the 'innocence' of his judgment, the child reasons as though he were the only thinker in question: his point of view about his family seems to him the only one possible and excludes all others. For him therefore it is not a subjective point of view, but that of absolute reality. Consequently, as he is not conscious of his own subjectivity, or more simply of himself, he places himself on a completely different plane from his brothers, and this is what prevents him from seeing that he is a brother to his brothers on precisely the same grounds as they are brothers to him.

Thus when all is said and done, it is once more to the ego-centrism of thought that we must appeal in order to explain the incapacity for even the most elementary relativism of thought. To understand a relation—that for instance of brother to brother—means thinking of at least two points of view at the same time, those of each of the brothers. Absolute notions like those of 'boy,' etc., presuppose only one point of view. The judgment 'Paul is a boy' remains the same whatever may be the perspective adopted.

The full importance of the ego-centric illusion will now be manifest. The explanation just given with regard to the notion of brother holds for all relative notions. If for the child things are absolutely to the right or to the left, or as we have just seen, absolutely dark or fair, and so on, it is because up to a certain age the child fails to realize the very simple fact that one of his companions whom he holds to be big, or dark, or horrid may perfectly well be regarded by a third party as small, or fair, or nice, without the third party being necessarily either a fool or a knave. —p. 91

... The idea of right and left in so far as it is a relative notion passes three successive stages which correspond to three successive points in the desubjectification or socialization of thought: the first stage (5-8) in which left and right are considered only from the child's own point of view; the second (8-11) in which they are also considered from that of the other person, of the person who is speaking to him; finally, the third stage (11-12), which marks the moment when right and left are also considered from the point of view of the things themselves. Now these three stages correspond exactly to the three social stages we established before: the age 7-8 marks the decline of primitive ego-centrism and that of 11-12 the discovery of formal thought which reasons from every point of view at once. But let us turn to the facts before us.

The Binet-Simon tests tell us that the age of 6 is that at which a child can show his left hand and his right ear. But this does not necessarily mean that at that age right and left are known and handled as *relations*. These notions may very well still be 'absolute,' i.e., there may be a left and right 'in themselves,' just as for the Greeks there was a 'high' and a 'low' independently of weight. The child's own body would naturally determine this absolute right and left to begin with, and an enormous amount of adaptation would still be necessary before the child could realize, first that there was a right and left for everyone else, and later that objects themselves can be to the right or the left of each other even though their disposition in space is relative. —p. 107

... the child's difficulty arises from the fact that he juxtaposes territories but does not connect them. He realizes that Geneva is in Switzerland but not that it 'forms a part' of Switzerland. The difficulty lies in the relation of part to whole, and this is our reason for including the question of the definition of the word 'country' in a chapter devoted to the child's use of relations.

Three stages mark the evolution of the idea of country. During the first, country is simply a unit along with towns and districts, and of the same magnitude as these. Switzerland is therefore alongside of Geneva and Vaud. During the second, town and districts are in the country but do not form part of it. Thus Switzerland surrounds Geneva and Vaud. These are in Switzerland but do not really 'form part of' Switzerland. Finally in the third stage the correct relation is discovered.   —p. 121

The child does not realize that certain ideas, even such as are obviously relative for an adult are relations between at least two terms. Thus he does not realize that a brother must necessarily be the brother of somebody, or that a part must necessarily be part of a whole, but thinks of all these notions as existing in themselves, absolutely. Or again he defines a family, not by the relation of kinship which unites its members, but by the space they occupy, by the immediate point of view from which he sees them grouped around him in a house. It should be noted that such behaviour is universal, and that the list of examples might have been added to indefinitely. We are indebted, for example, to the kindness of Mme. Passello, a Geneva school-mistress, for the knowledge of the fact that at the age of 7 the notions of 'friend' and 'enemy' are still devoid of relativity. An enemy is *"a soldier,"* *"someone who fights,"* *"a horrid person,"* *"someone who is horrid,"* *"someone who wants to hurt you,"* etc. It is therefore not a person who is an enemy in relation to someone else, but an enemy in himself. Similarly for a friend.

We discovered innumerable examples of the same kind with Mlle. Hahnloser in connection with the word 'foreigner.' At the age when children can say that foreigners are people from another country (about 9-10), they are still ignorant of the fact that they are themselves foreigners for these people. All the more reason therefore for their ignorance of the reciprocity of this relation when the term is reserved for people coming from another country but living in Geneva. Such examples could be multiplied indefinitely. —p. 121

John H. Weakland, "The Double-Bind Hypothesis of
Schizophrenia and Three-Party Interaction," *The Etiology of
Schizophrenia*, ed. by Don D. Jackson, M.D. (New York:
Basic Books, 1960), pp. 376-379.

(1) *In a double-bind situation, a person is faced with a
significant communication involving a pair of messages, of
different level or logical type, which are related but incongruent with each other.*

(2) *Leaving the field is blocked.* Such escape, presumably
followed by establishment of more satisfactory communication
elsewhere, would be one potential avenue of natural and
adequate response. Its unavailability usually is an outcome
of dependence on the person (or persons) giving the contradictory messages. When dependency is inherent in a situation
(as with childhood or illness) this point is obvious. More
complex, however, are the important situations where dependency (or effective belief in it) is fostered by other messages of total double-bind communication, to a degree far
beyond the physical or emotional "realities" of the person's
current life situation.

(3) *It is therefore important to respond adequately to the
communication situation, which includes responding to its
duality and contradiction.* Two contradictory significant messages mean two incongruent behavioural injunctions, because
every message instigates behavioural response. Lack of recognition and response to the duality and incongruence of
the messages received leads to further difficulties on the re-
cipient's part at several levels of behaviour: failure to discriminate the order of messages being received; consequent
subjective confusion and distortion of ideas and affects; and
speech or action that manifests confusion and division either
directly or by an all-or-nothing reaction to one aspect of the
sender's message. Further, such inadequate and incomplete
responses are very apt to provoke a further message condemning the response: e.g., "Why are you so silent when I
speak to you?" or "You always get excited so easily." The
total sequence, then, has the form of a larger more encompassing double bind, and the situation is still further
aggravated.

It appears that such incongruent communication can be
handled adequately only by a response that recognizes and
points up the incongruity. This might be done by (a) overtly
labeling the incongruity as such—i.e., by moving to a dif-

ferent level of communication and explicitly discussing the original communication situation. It might also be done by (b) giving a manifestly dual message in reply, or by (c) a humourous response exposing the nature of the double-bind incongruence, for humour always involves multiple message levels and incongruities. As an illustration we can consider possible responses to a mild sort of incongruent message situation: "Wouldn't you like to open that window," said in a way or context that suggests that the speaker is really the one who wants it open, yet does not acknowledge this. Then: (a) "You speak as though you're asking what I like, but you really seem to be telling me what to do." (b) "I wouldn't like to but if it's important to you I'll do it." (c) "Thank you for being thoughtful of me, but can it be opened from below?" But this is not to say that any of these responses is easy to carry off, even though we are throughout this paper considering the double-bind pattern in terms of a type of maneuver and various possible outcomes, not just the "successfully completed" bind.

(4) *An adequate response is difficult to achieve because of the concealment, denial, and inhibition inherent in or added to the basic contradictory pair of messages.* The communicational factors that may serve to restrain awareness and/or comment on duality and contradiction are many; some are gross and others very subtle, some explicit and others implicit, some verbal and others tonal, gestural, or contextual, some positive and others negative. It is probable that this variety and subtlety have played a major part in obscuring, for both patients and psychiatrists, the existence of the double-bind communication pattern and its etiological significance for schizophrenia. Related to this has been psychiatric overemphasis on specific trauma and neglect of repetitive patterns in basic learning situations. A few such factors of particular importance may be mentioned here, as they operate in two-party double-bind situations; some counterparts in three-party situations will be considered later.

(a) *Concealment:* Two major barriers to the overt recognition of the basic inconsistency in the double-bind communication are inherent in its nature. First, the messages, being of different level or logical type, do not confront one another directly, whether one verbal message qualifies another incongruously or a verbal message conflicts with tone or gesture. There is no clear confrontation—"A is true. No, A is false"—even if the two messages convey different and incompatible behavioural injunctions. In this connection, it is important to remember that objectively very slight signals—thus ones easily ignored or denied—can drastically modify or even reverse the significance of much more obvious or lengthy messages. Second, the fact that only one person is addressing the receiver carries an implication of "only one message," or at least of consistent messages, in a given situation. This is further reinforced by the fact that this person is important to the receiver; not only can he not be escaped or ignored, but also his messages are hard to doubt or question. These various factors may all be seen in such a simple example as a mother who says, "Come here to me, dear," with a slight edge of concealed hostility in her tone, or a little bodily withdrawal. The incongruence is real, but it is well concealed, and it is not easy to call one's mother to account on the basis of such apparently minor evidence.

(b) *Denial:* Obviously, the operation of the factors just mentioned can be reinforced by adding to the basic pair of incongruent messages other messages overtly denying that contradiction exists—and perhaps putting the onus on the receiver by claiming that he misunderstood, by emphasizing the unity of the sender or his important position vis-a-vis the receiver, and so on. Continuing the example above, if the child should go so far as to remark on the mother's tone, there might be a reply like, "You just imagined that, dear; you know how much mother loves you."

(c) *Inhibition:* Reinforcement much like that obtained by denial may also occur via "no message"—i.e., by strongly *ignoring* the actual complexities of communication and the possibilities of inconsistency and by acting as though they were out of the question. Investigation of the communication situation may also be inhibited by direct prohibition of comment or by various threats, such as signs of parental withdrawal or disturbance if any questioning is attempted. All of these factors are further reinforced when, as seems common in double-bind situations, the binder stresses his own benevolent position and concern for the other's welfare. In accordance with these possibilities, our hypothetical mother might behave as though her incongruent statement is perfectly simple and straightforward; if this were questioned she might reply, "Don't worry yourself making something out of nothing, dear; just leave things to mother,"; or she might appear confused or hurt by an unjustified attack on her maternal love and nobility; or she might simply appear completely unable to see the point of the question raised, a reaction that can be one of the more devastating forms of withdrawal.

Whenever any such message of concealment, denial, or inhibition is added to reinforce an original double-bind communication. the combination produces another double-bind structure, on a wider scale. For example, when the occurrence of a pair of incongruent messages is followed by a further message denying that there was any contradiction, this combination comprises another pair of incongruent messages, of different levels, whose incongruence is difficult to detect and handle. And this process may repeat itself, enlarging each time. If the child is still questioning about the mother's denial, then mother might say, "Something must have upset you to make you behave that way to your own mother, who loves you so." The pathogenic power of double-bind communication patterns and the difficulty of altering them seems importantly related to this progressive and cumulative tendency.

Marion Milner, *On Not Being Able To Paint* (New York: International Universities Press, 1957), pp. 89-91.

There was one drawing which seemed to be depicting the fact of (this) loss and gain, particularly in connection with those aspects of our dreams which are usually called ideals. It was called "The Eagle and the Cave-man."

Those little figures are suspended above the earth by curious square balloons like Chinese lanterns which look as though they are beginning to crumble. Also there are brickbats flying about and then also the eagle is just going to fly across the supporting strings. Altogether I think the mannikins hanging on to the lanterns are going to have to come down to earth pretty quickly. And what are they going to find there? Footsteps of a cave-man who has emerged out of a crack in the mountain and gone along to the fire. But there are no footsteps away from the fire, I wonder where he has got to? I do believe he has plunged into the fire and emerged again as the eagle. What's an eagle? A bird that sees. It seems to be the power of seeing that is destroying the mannikin's aethereal supports and bringing them down to earth. I always did feel that hitching one's wagon to a star might end in hanging most uncomfortably in mid-air.
 . . . Thus I thought the eagle picture was saying that

to stop looking to the sky for one's supports was not necessarily to lose all that distinguishes one from the animal and the cave-man; and in saying this it did seem to show a step towards willingness to bring dreams down to earth and letting them interact with the facts. I thought also it showed a growing realization that to be so 'indirect and lumbering' that one confused the spiritual reality of the internal dream with what in fact can be found externally was a fatal idolatry. Such confusion must surely lead to an inner tension that was intolerable; to escape it one would tend either to distort the facts and pretend they were better than they actually were, giving everything a rosy light; or else one would degrade the dream, turn against it and deny that one had ever loved it or that it had any value. In fact I saw now that disillusion, opening one's eyes to what are called the stern facts of life, meant recognizing that the inner dream and the objective fact can never permanently coincide, they can only interact. But I also saw that in order to do this one has to reckon not only with one's hate of the external world, when it fails to live up to one's expectations, but also hate of oneself when one similarly fails. Thus the same problem of the gap between the ideal and the actual applied within oneself, the gap between what one is and what one would like to be. Certainly I had long been aware that failure to recognize the inevitability of the gap led to much self-deception and fruitless straining. But what I found now was that, at times, if one could bring oneself to look at the gap, allow oneself to see both the ideal and the failure to live up to it in one moment of vision, and without the urge to interfere and alter oneself to fit the ideal, then the ideal and the fact seemed somehow to enter into relation and produce something quite new, something that had nothing to do with being pleased with oneself for having lived up to an ideal or miserable because of having failed to. In fact it almost seemed that the wide-seeing eagle of the drawing was a way of saying something about a growing belief in a certain watching capacity of the mind; a watching capacity which, when separated from the interfering part, became the light that could meet darkness and redeem the denied greeds and hates and despairs of the bodily life. For it was a watching part, which, by being able to see the two opposing differences of standard, or ideal, and actuality, in relation to each other, was by this very act able to bring about an integration, a new way of being which somehow combined the essence of both.

Harry Stack Sullivan, M.D., *Schizophrenia as a Human Process* (New York: Norton, 1962), pp. 220-224.

. . . He [the schizophrenic] has come upon certain situations which were most serious in their negative effect upon his self-esteem; and after encountering these situations (which include as significant factors only other people), after, perhaps, a rebuff to his self-assertion, he has shown a significant and characterizable failure to react by any of the methods of reacting to rebuff which are more or less well known to all of us from our personal experience (which, in turn, might well be made the subject of study if anyone can be encouraged to leave the realm of more pure science and take up so personal a matter).

We find that the stricken individual, following the peculiar and characterizable failure to react to rebuff, has lost a great part of that confidence in the integrity of the universe, the goodness of God, and so on, which is our common human heritage from infancy; and that from thence onward he goes on feeling decidedly uncertain about life. Apparently, if one is sufficiently uncertain about life, one loses the cognitive assets which serve us in distinguishing products of autistic or purely subjective reverie from products which include important factors residing in so-called external reality; and when one has lost this ability to distinguish between such reveries and such objects having more external points of reference, one begins to sink into mental processes significantly like those that we experience when we are asleep.

With the appearance of a partition in which considerable waking time is spent in a condition in which one is without the ability to tell what has true, genuine, and consensually acceptable, external references, and what instead is purely personal fantasy, there appears a peculiar disorder of social activity (and I might say even of nonsocial activity), and it is these peculiarities that seem to constitute the essence of schizophrenic behavior.

Now it appears that one does not thus lose one's ability to distinguish externally conditioned realities excepting after certain very significant losses of self-respect, and it appears also true that such significant losses of self-respect arise from but a small group of weaknesses or alleged weaknesses in the individual. Only from this two-factor situation does there derive a state in which dominating autistic reveries or fantasies take the place of the more realistic thinking; these reveries arise from and work out the comparatively few important tendencies in the individual to one or more of which the rebuffs had application—rebuffs which led to the failure of self-esteem and belief in the dependability of the universe. The reveries, therefore, take a markedly asocial or actually antisocial type, and the patient becomes a difficult person to have in the house, the school, or elsewhere.

It occurred to me some time since that if in receiving these patients we regarded them as persons, we attempted to discover what continued to be of interest to them, and we attempted to adjust the environment to which they are exposed in a fashion in harmony with these particular findings, we might then discover a rather remarkable recovery rate, if you will. In other words, we might find a way of restoring a lot of these people. I am now rather convinced that that notion is true, and the contribution, if any, that I can lay before you— in the hope solely that it will bring out a great deal of response from you—is the following:

We find that the schizophrenic is an extremely shy individual, extremely sensitive, possessed of a singular ability to get his feelings hurt, who has rather naturally erected an enormous defensive machinery between himself and intimate contact with other people.

Now, given such a person, one might expect that a detachment from reality, from externally conditioned reality, and a getting lost in autistic reverie would be moderately easy to achieve. At the same time, the fact remains that these patients continue to be very sensitive. You must take my word for that, because it is not recorded in the well-known textbooks.

I found some people running around loose who seemed to have a good deal of this same sensitiveness but who still seemed like myself to maintain a measure of contact with external conditioned reality; and when we put these people in positions to care for some particularly young schizophrenics, the results achieved approximate miracles, so far as the well-known traditions about schizophrenics are concerned.

We found that situations of affection, striving for esteem among others, cultivation of favorable reactions on the part of these particularly selected attendants, and so on, went on very much as they are supposed to go on in ordinary human society.

That was promising. But many of these chosen employees didn't seem to function satisfactorily; and so we looked further, and we discovered that if we changed the attitudes of these sensitive, shy, and ordinarily considered handicapped employees so that they had some notion of the schizophrenic as a person—in other words, if they ceased to regard him in more or less traditional ideology as "insane," but instead had stressed to them the many points of significant resemblance between the patient and the employee—we created a much more useful social situation; we found that intimacy between patient and employee blossomed unexpectedly, that things which I cannot distinguish from genuine human friendships sprang up between patient and employee, that any signs of the alleged apathy of the schizophrenic faded, to put it mildly, and that the institutional recovery rate became high. In other words, in an environment intelligently adjusted to the schizophrenic, the schizophrenic seemed to prosper and to be able to do almost everything but get quite ready to go back into the world. . . .

Notes

Introduction

1. Robert Jay Lifton, *Thought Reform and the Psychology of Totalism* (New York: Norton, 1961), p. 435. Other studies of Chinese brainwashing include: Edgar Schein, Inge Schneier and Curtis H. Barker, *Coercive Persuasion* (New York: Norton, 1961); my own study of the totalistic mind may be found in *The Integrating Mind* (New York: Sheed & Ward, 1962). *Coercive Persuasion* notes the brainwashed prisoners' repeated theme: "If only *I had been what I thought I was*, I would have been able to resist" (p. 149). One might turn the idea around: "If only I had been able to accept what I was, I would have been able to resist."

Part One, Chapter 1—On Hope

1. I shall not in this book speak directly about one important and familiar kind of hope: hope that present good circumstances shall continue. I have two reasons: I wish to discuss hope in terms that apply usefully to the troubled and the mentally ill, who lack this form of hope; second, the hope that a present good will not be lost is, in many ways, included within the hope that there is a way out of a difficulty.

2. George Kelly analyzes the purposiveness of suicide in "Suicide, the Personal Construct Point of View," in *The Cry for Help*, edited by Norman L. Farberow and Edwin S. Shoreidman (New York: McGraw-Hill, 1961), pp. 255-280.

3. Kurt Lewin, *Field Theory in Social Science, Selected Papers,* edited by Dorwin Cartwright (New York: Harper Torchbooks, 1951), p. 53.

4. For contrast, see Therese F. Benedek, "Toward the Biology of Depressive Constellation," *Journal of the American Psychoanalytic Association* (Vol. 4, 1956), p. 403: "The effect of frustration is the opposite to that of hope. Frustration gives rise to the sensation of inability to span an unpleasant situation in the present and project one's expectation to a gratification in the future."

5. M. A. Sechehaye, *Symbolic Realization* (New York: International Universities Press, 1961), p. 140.

6. For a psychoanalytic view of one relation between hope and help, see the work of Leo Nageberg, "The Meaning of Help in Psychotherapy," *Psychoanalysis and the Psychoanalytic Review* (Vol. 46, No. 4, 1959), pp. 50-63.

Part One, Chapter 2—On Hopelessness

1. Allen Wheelis, *The Quest for Identity* (New York: Norton, 1958), p. 128.

2. In "The Meaning of Passivity," *Psychiatric Quarterly* (Vol. 29, 1955, pp. 595-611), Henry Hart describes the flexibility of the healthy ego, pointing out that passivity (and hopelessness) are not necessarily pathological, but are correlatives of activity (and hopefulness) in the normal individual.

3. Leslie Farber, "Perfectibility and the Psychoanalytic Candidate," *The Journal of Existential Psychiatry* (Vol. III, No. 2, Winter 1963), p. 29.

4. Sebastian Moore, O.S.B., "A Catholic Neurosis," *The Clergy Review* (Vol. XLVI, 1961), p. 643.

5. Norman Cohn, *The Pursuit of the Millennium* (New York: Harper, 1961).

6. Paul Tillich, "What Is Basic in Human Nature?" *The American Journal of Psychoanalysis* (Vol. XXII, 1922), p. 121.

7. R. A. Spitz's studies of the effects of maternal deprivation are crucial to understanding hopelessness. See "Hospitalism: an Inquiry into the Genesis of Psychiatric Conditions in Early Childhood," in *Psychoanalytic Study of the Child* (New York: International Universities Press, 1945), Vol. I, pp. 53-74; and "Hospitalism: a Follow-Up Report," (*ibid.*, 1946), Vol. II, pp. 113-117.

8. The classic example is Plato's *Meno*. Much of the substance of the Platonic dialectic involves the progressive cancellation of hypotheses until a true idea is reached.

9. ". . . the essence of normality is flexibility, in contrast to the freezing of behavior into patterns of unalterability that characterizes every manifestation of the neurotic process, whether in impulses, purposes, acts, thoughts, or feelings," in Lawrence S. Kubie, "The Fundamental Nature of the Distinction between Normality and Neurosis," *The Psychoanalytic Quarterly* (Vol. XXIII, 1954), p. 182. See also, Franz Alexander and Thomas M. French, *Psychoanalytic Therapy: Principles and Application* (New York: Ronald Press, 1946). Alexander and French maintain that neurosis is the result of the interruption and distortion of the learning process and, conversely, that therapy is the continuation of the learning process.

Part One, Chapter 3—The Hopeless as Entrapment

1. George Orwell, *1984* (New York: Harcourt Brace, 1949), "Appendix on Newspeak."

2. A. H. Maslow, *Motivation and Personality* (New York: Harper, 1954), p. 38.

3. In "The Meaning of Masochism," *American Journal of Psychotherapy* (Vol. 7, 1953), pp. 473-478, Irving Beiber notes that masochism is not a primary negative impulse but an attempt at adaptation.

4. Harry Stack Sullivan, *Clinical Studies in Psychiatry* (New York: Norton, 1956), p. 185.

5. Igor Stravinsky, *Poetics of Music in the Form of Six Lessons* (New York: Vintage, 1956), pp. 66-69.

6. See especially William Goldfarb and Irving Mintz, "Schizophrenic Child's Reaction to Time and Space," *Archives of General Psychiatry* (Vol. 5, 1961), pp. 535-543.

7. See Arthur Burton and Louis G. Heller, "The Touching of the Body," *Psychoanalytic Review* (Vol. 51, 1954), pp. 122-134.

8. Muriel Hall Hyroop points out that overcoming hopelessness is communicated from the outside not only in acute neurosis but from the earliest stages of childhood. See "The Significance of Helplessness," *American Journal of Psychotherapy* (Vol. 7, 1953), pp. 672-683.

9. L. Takeo Doi, "Some Thoughts on Helplessness and the Desire to be Loved," *Psychiatry, Journal for the Study of Interpersonal Processes* (Vol. 26, No. 3, 1963), pp. 270-71.

Part One, Chapter 4—Hopelessness and Confusion

1. Sigmund Freud, *A General Introduction to Psychoanalysis* (New York: Liverwright, 1935), p. 376.

2. Paul Schilder, *Medical Psychology* (New York: International Universities Press, 1953), p. 345 *et passim*.

3. Betty Frieden in the New York *Herald Tribune*, July 15, 1964.

4. Elsa Morante, *Arturo's Island* (New York: Knopf, 1959), pp. 135-136.

5. Lawrence S. Kubie, "Social Forces and the Neurotic Process," in *Explorations in Psychiatry* (New York: Basic Books, 1957), p. 87.

6. See R. D. Laing, *The Divided Self* (Chicago: Quadrangle Books, 1960) for a thoughtful discussion of this phenomenon.

7. John H. Weakland, "The 'Double-Bind' Hypothesis of Schizophrenia and Three-Party Interaction," in *The Etiology*

of Schizophrenia, edited by Don D. Jackson (New York: Basic Books, 1960), p. 375.

8. Ashley Montagu, "Culture and Mental Illness," *The American Journal of Psychiatry* (Vol. 118, 1961), p. 20.

Part One, Chapter 5—The Absolutizing Instinct

1. The best analysis I know of the relationship of the idea of the absolute to psychiatric theory is Wilfrid Daim's *Transvaluation de Psychanalyse* (Paris: Aubier, 1956).

2. Otto Fenichel, *The Psychoanalytic Theory of Neurosis* (New York: Norton, 1945), p. 237.

3. Job 25:4-6.

4. Job 26:2-3.

5. Job 31:37.

6. Job 36:10.

7. See Wilfrid Daim, "On Depth-Psychology and Salvation," *Journal of Psychotherapy as a Religious Process* (No. 2, 1955), pp. 24-37.

8. Hannah Arendt brilliantly describes how the instinct develops in the political order in *The Origins of Totalitarianism* (New York: Meridian, 1958). Useful essays in the area appear in *Totalitarianism,* edited by Carl J. Friedrich (Cambridge: Harvard University Press, 1954).

9. For an important treatment of the pathology of mourning, see Karl Abraham, "Notes on the Psychogenesis of Melancholia," in his *Selected Papers, 1927* (London: Hogarth, 1927), pp. 453-464.

10. For a treatment of the relationship of ambivalence to the experience of guilt, see Donald W. Winnicott, "Psychoanalysis and the Sense of Guilt," in *Psychoanalysis and Contemporary Thought,* edited by John D. Sutherland (New York: Grove Press, 1959), pp. 35ff.

11. Norman Cohn, *op. cit.,* p. 185.

12. Charles H. Cook, Jr., "Ahab's 'Intolerable Allegory,' " *Boston University Studies in English* (Vol. I, 1955-6), pp. 45-52.

13. William Golding, *The Spire* (New York: Harcourt Brace and World, 1964), p. 76.

14. Indispensable in this area is the critical bibliography assembled by William Meissner, S.J.: *Annotated Bibliography in Religion and Psychology* (New York: Academy of Religion and Mental Health, 1961).

15. Edith Weigert develops the importance of trust in "Loneliness and Trust—Basic Factors of Human Experience," *Psychiatry, Journal for the Study of Interpersonal Processes* (Vol. 25, 1960), pp. 121-131; Erik H. Erikson, *Iden-*

tity and the Life Cycle (New York: International Universities Press, 1959); Christine Olden, "On Adult Empathy with Children," *Psychoanalytic Study of the Child* (Vol. 8, 1953), pp. 112-126; Fred Berthold, *The Fear of God* (New York: Harper, 1959).

16. Sigmund Freud, *A General Introduction to Psychoanalysis* (New York: Liveright, 1935), p. 387.

17. Romans 8:24.

18. Wilfrid Daim, "On Depth Psychology and Salvation," *loc. cit.*

Part Two, Chapter 1—On Wishing and Hoping

1. Ernest Becker observes in "Anthropological Notes on the Concept of Aggression," *Psychiatry* (Vol. 25, 1962), p. 338: "There seems to be every reason for a final, complete departure from the traditional Freudian idea of aggression as a primary destructive drive. . . . One might understand aggression to exist where alternative creative means of deriving a feeling of self-value have not been made available . . ."

2. Melitta Schmidberg warns that obsessive decisiveness is often a ploy used to deny the presence of obsessional indecision. See "A Note on Obsessional Indecision," *Psychoanalytic Review* (Vol. 35, 1948), pp. 312-313.

3. Otto Fenichel, *Collected Papers,* Vol. I (New York: Norton, 1954), p. 297.

4. *Ibid.,* p. 293.

5. *Ibid.,* p. 292.

6. *The Confessions,* VII:9 (translation of Rex Warner, New York: New American Library, 1963), pp. 176-177.

7. Ronald Knox, *Enthusiasm* (Oxford: Oxford University Press, 1950), p. 23.

8. *Ibid.,* p. 591.

9. See Edith Weigert, "The Nature of Sympathy in the Art of Psychotherapy," *Psychiatry* (Vol. 24, No. 2, 1961), pp. 187-196. Dr. Weigert makes it clear that the psychiatrist's role is to visualize the patient's wholeness "despite the various states of confusion" and to "mobilize his genuine emotions towards freedom."

10. For a review of the theories of sublimation, see J. C. Flugel, *Studies in Feeling and Desire* (London: Duckworth, 1955). Flugel's own theory resembles the one that I have described.

Part Two, Chapter 2—The Absolute Wish Versus the Willful Act

1. Sigmund Freud, *The Interpretation of Dreams,* in *The Standard Edition of the Complete Psychological Works*

of Sigmund Freud, edited by James Strachey, Anna Freud, Alix Strachey, and Alan Tyson (London: Hogarth Press, 1954), Vol. V, p. 567.

2. *Ibid.*, p. 589.

3. *Ibid.*, p. 569.

4. *Ibid.*, p. 372.

5. For a psychoanalytic treatment of this corrective process in human thinking, see C. de Morchaux, "The Psychoanalytic Study of Thinking: Thinking and Negative Hallucination," *International Journal of Psychoanalysis* (Vol. 43, 1962), pp. 311-314.

6. For a useful distinction between neurotic fantasy and the work of the imagination, see Northrop Frye, "The Imaginative and the Imaginary," *American Journal of Psychiatry* (Vol. 119, 1962), pp. 289-298.

7. T. S. Eliot, "The Wasteland," lines 60-64, in *The Complete Poems and Plays, 1909-1950* (New York: Harcourt Brace, 1952), p. 39.

8. *Ibid.*, lines 115-116, p. 40.

9. *Ibid.*, lines 249-256, p. 44.

10. *The Imitation of Christ*, Book III, Chapter 5, Verse 2.

11. Leslie Farber describes it this way: "Once isolated as willfulness, the will can no longer step outside itself, so that its inventiveness must be within its own terms. While willfulness may seize other categories, under its dominion the categories lose their original substance, serving only as illusions of themselves." "Will and Willfulness in Hysteria," *Review of Existential Psychology and Psychiatry* (Vol. 1, 1961), p. 241.

12. Albert Camus, *The Rebel* (New York: Vintage, 1956), pp. 51-52.

Part Two, Chapter 3—Mutuality Versus Alienation

1. Albert Camus, *The Stranger* (New York: Vintage, 1956), pp. 151-153.

2. Gilbert Murray, *Aeschylus, the Creator of Tragedy* (New York: Oxford, 1940), pp. 203-204.

3. Hans Jonas, *The Gnostic Religion* (Boston: Beacon Press, 1963), p. 49.

4. Hans Jonas, *ibid.*, p. 108.

5. For a study of the human relationship called mutuality —especially that of mother and child—see Erik Erikson, *Identity and the Life Cycle*. For a description of the deceptive imitations of mutuality, see L. C. Wynne, I. Rychoff, J. Day and S. H. Hersh, "Pseudo-Mutuality in the Family Relations of Schizophrenics," *Psychiatry* (Vol. I, 1958), pp. 205-220. In

pseudo-mutuality there is a "predominant absorption in fitting together, at the expense of differentiation of the identities of the persons in the relations." Divergence is seen "as leading to disruption of the relations and therefore must be avoided; but if divergence is avoided, growth of the relation is impossible" (p. 207).

6. R. W. B. Lewis, *The American Adam* (Chicago: University of Chicago Press, 1955), p. 45.

7. Cited by Lewis, *loc. cit.*

8. The temptation to reach for this magical point is laid bare by Leslie Farber in "Perfectibility and the Psychoanalytic Candidate," *The Journal of Existential Psychiatry* (Vol. III, 1963), p. 291.

9. See Stanislaus Lyonnet, S.J., "St. Paul: Liberty and Law," in *The Bridge*, Vol. IV (New York: Pantheon, 1962), pp. 229-251.

10. For a description of autonomous wishing and authority in the creation of the dynamic self, see Rollo May, "Religion, Psychotherapy and the Achievement of Self-hood," *Pastoral Psychology* (January 1952), pp. 26-37.

11. "Will and Willfulness in Hysteria," *op. cit.*, p. 241.

12. *Cf.* Daniel 9:21 (Douay).

Part Two, Chapter 4—Hope and Waiting

1. See Harry Stack Sullivan, *The Psychiatric Interview* (New York: Norton, 1954), p. 184: "Apathy is a curious state; as nearly as I can discover, it is a way used to survive defeats without material damage, although if it endures too long one is damaged by the passage of time. Apathy seems to me to be a miracle of protection by which a personality in utter fiasco rests until it can do something else."

2. Ernest Federn, in "The Therapeutic Personality," *Psychoanalytic Quarterly* (Vol. 36, 1962, pp. 29-34), emphasizes the need for the analyst to respect his momentary quiescence of the patient, to synchronize *with* the patient and his suffering.

3. Sigmund Freud, *The Interpretation of Dreams, op. cit.*, Vol. 5, p. 588.

4. *Ibid.*, p. 600.

5. Ernest Jones, *The Life and Work of Sigmund Freud,* Vol. II (New York: Basic Books, 1957), p. 323.

6. There is a remarkable relationship between what psychiatry calls the secondary processes of the human drives and the religious orientation of human wishing. It is basic to psychoanalytic theory that the id is the place of the primary instinctual drives and that the ego adds the elements of secondarity, maturity, goals and hierarchy. This is the ele-

mentary meaning of Freud's dictum that, Where Id was, let Ego reign. But it is not clear that in Freud the ego emerges as a positive, creative, wishing world in its own right. The same doubt can be expressed about the final intentions of certain schools of religious asceticism. Ignatius, however, offers a positive asceticism in his description of "discernment of spirits" in his *Spiritual Exercises*. He suggests helps for examining the quality of our thoughts and wishes, but the wishing remains from beginning to end. There is no breaking of the will, to use an unfortunate pious phrase. Ignatius' theory is a theory of examined wishing. A parallel problem is that of creativity. In dealing with it we can use the same topography: "The unique quality of the creative man is that he is both sufficiently free and strong to allow his impulses and their ideational representations to come to consciousness and sufficiently strong to be able to delay and hold them in order to validate them by empirical or logical criteria (science) or communicability (art)." David Rapaport, *Organization and Pathology of Thought* (New York: Columbia University Press, 1951), p. 439, n. 3.

7. Samuel Beckett, *Waiting for Godot* (New York: Grove Press, 1954).

8. *Loc. cit.*

9. *Loc. cit.*

Part Three, Prologue

1. Gabriel Marcel, *Homo Viator* (New York: Harper, 1962).

2. Norman O. Brown, *Life Against Death* (New York: Vintage, 1959), p. 84.

3. The critical and far-reaching effects of the phenomenon of separation in mental illness, particularly in the early development of children, are described by J. Bowlby in "Separation Anxiety," *International Journal of Psychoanalysis* (Vol. 41, 1960), pp. 99-113. The article contains an exhaustive, 78-item bibliography (pp. 111-113). Of significance are additional articles by Bowlby: "The Influence of Early Environment in the Development of Neurosis and Neurotic Character," *International Journal of Psychoanalysis* (Vol. 21, 1940), pp. 154-178; "Forty-Four Juvenile Thieves: Their Characters and Home Life," *ibid.*, (Vol. 25, 1944); "Maternal Care and Mental Health," *W. H. C. Monograph, No. 2* (1951); "Some Pathological Processes Set in Train in Early Mother-Child Separation," *Journal of Mental Science* (Vol. 99, 1953), pp. 265-272; "An Ethnological Approach to Research in Child Development," *British Journal of Medical Psychology* (Vol. 30, 1957), pp. 230-240; "The Nature of the

Child's Tie to his Mother," *International Journal of Psychoanalysis* (Vol. 39, 1958), pp. 350-372.

4. André Malraux, *The Psychology of Art*, Vol. III (New York: Pantheon, 1949), p. 152.

5. Marion Milner, *On Not Being Able to Paint* (New York: International Universities Press, 1957), p. 14.

Part Three, Chapter 1—The Science of the Bare Fact

1. See Francis Fergusson, *Dante's Drama of the Mind* (Princeton: Princeton University Press, 1953).

2. For a philosophical treatment of rest in a psychology of human faculties, see Frederick E. Crowe, S.J., "Complacency and Concern in the Thought of St. Thomas," *Theological Studies* (Vol. 20, 1959), pp. 1-40; pp. 198-251; pp. 343-346. Crowe notes that, "Desire is a tendency and movement, but love, like delight, implies presence already of the good and hence a state of rest" (p. 3).

3. Erikson describes the role played by mutuality in each stage of the development of identity in his *Identity and the Life Cycle*. See especially pp. 139-147.

4. Marion Milner describes the distinction between neurotic fantasy and the creative relationship of dreams and ideals to reality in *On Not Being Able to Paint*.

5. William F. Lynch, S.J., *Christ and Apollo* (New York: Sheed and Ward, 1961).

6. T. S. Eliot, "The Function of Criticism," *Selected Essays* (London: Faber & Faber, 1958), p. 31.

7. See Charles Odier, *Anxiety and Moral Thinking* (New York: International Universities Press, 1963), pp. 157-159.

8. Agostino Gemelli, O.F.M., *Psychoanalysis Today* (New York: Kenedy, 1955), p. 136.

9. Erik Erikson, *Identity and the Life Cycle*, p. 131.

10. *Loc. cit.*

11. Albert Camus, *The Rebel*, p. 261.

Part Three, Chapter 2—The Human Reality

1. See Harry Stack Sullivan, *Clinical Studies in Psychiatry*, pp. 194-195.

2. See especially David Rioch, "The Psychophysiology of Death," in *The Physiology of the Emotions*, edited by Alexander Simon (Springfield: John C. Thomas, 1961), p. 182. Dr. Rioch is commenting on *Man Against Fire* by S. L. A. Marshall (New York: Morrow, 1947).

3. Adapted from William Goldfarb and Irving Mintz, "Schizophrenic Child's Reactions to Time and Space," *Archives of General Psychiatry* (Vol. 5, 1961), pp. 535-543.

4. Martti Siirala, in a mimeographed paper for private distribution.

5. Chris Argyris, *Personality and Organization* (New York; Harper, 1957), p. 68.

6. Mal. Brennan, *The Making of a Moron* (New York: Sheed and Ward, 1953), cited in Argyris.

7. Chris Argyris, *op. cit.,* p. 90.

8. *Loc. cit.*

9. *Loc. cit.*

Part Three, Chapter 3—Reality Is Not Conflictual

1. Hans Jonas, *op. cit.,* p. 57.

2. Karl Menninger, with Martin Mayman and Paul Pruyser, *The Vital Balance* (New York: Viking, 1963), p. 216.

3. Bruno Bettelheim, *Dialogues with Mothers* (New York: Macmillan, 1954).

4. Thomas M. French, *The Integration of Behaviour,* Vol. I, *Basic Postulates* (Chicago: University of Chicago Press, 1952). See also, Franz Alexander and Thomas M. French, *Psychoanalytic Therapy, Principles and Application,* pp. 125ff.

5. Frederich Nietzsche, *Beyond Good and Evil* (Chicago: Regnery, 1955), p. 58.

Part Three, Epilogue on the Imagination

1. Emile Mâle, *A History of Christian Art* (New York: Pantheon, 1951).

2. Geoffrey Gorer, "The Pornography of Death," in *The Berkley Book of Modern Writing, #3,* edited by William Phillips and Philip Rahv (New York: Berkley Publishing Corp., 1956), pp. 56-62. Gorer notes: "Nevertheless, people have come to terms with the basic facts of birth, copulation and death, and somehow accept their implications; if social prudery prevents this being done in an open and dignified fashion, then it will be done surreptitiously. If we dislike the modern pornography of death, then we must give back to death—natural death—its parade and publicity, re-admit grief and mourning. If we make death unmentionable in polite society—'not in front of the children'—we almost insure continuation of the 'horror comic.' No censorship has ever been really effective" (p. 62).

3. Mario Praz, *The Romantic Agony* (London: Oxford University Press, 1951).

4. Jean Piaget, *Judgment and Reasoning in the Child* (Paterson, N. J.: Littlefield, Adams, 1959). See especially page 134.

5. See materials in the Supplement from R. J. Lifton, *Thought Reform and the Psychology of Totalism.*

Bibliography

J. Abraham and E. Vann, *Maternal Dependency* (New York: International Universities Press, 1953).

Karl Abraham, "Notes on the Psychogenesis of Melancholia," *Selected Papers, 1927* (London: Woolf, 1927).

Action For Mental Health: Final Report of the Joint Commission On Mental Illness and Health—1961 (New York: Basic Books, 1961).

Nathan W. Ackerman, M.D., *The Psychodynamics of Family Life* (New York: Basic Books, 1958).

Franz Alexander and Thomas Morton French, *Psychoanalytic Therapy: Principles and Application* (New York: Ronald Press, 1946).

Gordon W. Allport, *Becoming* (New Haven: Yale University Press, 1955).

Hannah Arendt, *The Origins of Totalitarianism* (New York: Meridian Books, 1958).

Chris Argyris, *Personality and Organization* (New York: Harper, 1957).

Silvano Arieti, "Introductory Notes on the Psychoanalytic Therapy of Schizophrenics," in *Psychotherapy of the Psychoses*, edited by Arthur Burton (New York: Basic Books, 1961).

Dominick A. Barbara, "The Demosthenes Complex," *The Psychoanalytic Review* (Vol. 44, 1957).

Henry Bars, *Faith, Hope, and Charity* (New York: Hawthorne, 1961).

Ernest Becker, "Anthropological Notes on the Concept of Aggression," *Psychiatry* (Vol. 25, 1962).

Irving Beiber, "The Meaning of Masochism," *American Journal of Psychotherapy* (Vol. 7, 1953).

Therese F. Benedek, "Toward the Biology of the Depressive Constellation," *Journal of the American Psychoanalytic Association,* (Vol. 4, 1956).

Edmund Bergler, M.D., *The Super Ego* (New York: Grune & Stratton, 1952).

A. Bernard, *Théologie de l'espérance selon Saint Thomas*

[Coll. Bibliotheque Thomiste], (Paris: Vrin, 1959).

Fred Berthold, Jr., *The Fear of God: The Role of Anxiety in Contemporary Thought* (New York: Harper, 1959).

Bruno Bettelheim, *Dialogues With Mothers* (New York: Macmillan, 1954).

W. Earl Biddle, M.D., *Integration of Religion and Psychiatry* (New York: Macmillan, 1955).

Murray Bowen, "A Family Concept of Schizophrenia," in *The Etiology of Schizophrenia*, edited by Don D. Jackson (New York: Basic Books, 1960).

John Bowlby, "Separation Anxiety," *International Journal of Psychoanalysis* (Vol. 41, 1960).

Oliver Brachfeld, *Inferiority Feelings in the Individual and the Group* (New York: Grune and Stratton, 1951).

Charles Brenner, *An Elementary Textbook of Psychoanalysis* (New York: Doubleday, 1957).

Francis J. Braceland (ed.), *Faith, Reason and Modern Psychiatry* (New York: Kenedy, 1955).

A. A. Brill, *Basic Principles of Psychoanalysis* (New York: Doubleday, 1949).

Norman O. Brown, *Life Against Death* (New York: Vintage, 1958).

Eugene B. Brody and Frederick C. Redlich (ed.), *Psychotherapy with Schizophrenics* (New York: International Universities Press, 1952).

Donald L. Brunham, "Autonomy and Activity-Passivity in the Psychotherapy of a Schizophrenic Man," in *Clinical Studies of Personality,* edited by Arthur Burton and Robert E. Harris (New York: Harper, 1955).

Arthur Burton (ed.), *Psychotherapy of the Psychoses* (New York: Basic Books, 1961).

Arthur Burton and Louis G. Heller, "The Touching of the Body," *The Psychoanalytic Review* (Vol. 51, 1964).

A. M. Carré, *Hope or Despair* (London: Harwill, 1955).

Norman Cohn, *The Pursuit of the Millennium* (New York: Harper, 1961).

W. Conlon, "The Certitude of Hope," *The Thomist* (Vol. 10, 1947).

Charles H. Cook, Jr., "Ahab's 'Intolerable Allegory'," *Boston University Studies in English* (Vol. 1, 1955-56).

Frederick E. Crowe, S.J., "Complacency and Concern in the Thought of St. Thomas," *Theological Studies* (Vol. 20, 1959).

Wilfrid Daim, "On Depth-Psychology and Salvation," *The Journal of Psychotherapy as a Religious Process* (Vol. 2, 1955).

————. *Transvaluation de Psychanalyse* (Paris: Aubier. 1956).

J. Danielou, "Hope," *Jubilee* (March 1959).

P. de Letter, "Hope and Charity in St. Thomas," *The Thomist* (Vol. 13, 1950).

C. de Morchaux, "The Psychoanalytic Study of Thinking: Thinking and Negative Hallucination," *International Journal of Psychoanalysis* (Vol. 43, 1962).

G. Desbuquois, S.J., *Dans le mystere . . . l'espérance* (Paris: Editions Spes, 1934).

L. Takeo Doi, "Some Thoughts on Helplessness and the Desire To Be Loved," *Psychiatry, Journal for the Study of Interpersonal Processes* (Vol. 26, No. 3, 1963).

J. Dominian, *Psychiatry and the Christian* (New York: Hawthorn Books, 1962).

Emile Durkheim, *The Elementary Forms of the Religious Life* (Glencoe, Ill.: The Free Press, 1954).

Ruth Eissler (ed.), *Psychoanalytic Study of the Child,* Vol. 1 (New York: International Universities Press, 1945).

Erik H. Erikson, *Identity and the Life Cycle* (New York: International Universities Press, 1959).

Erik H. Erikson, *Young Man Luther: A Study in Psychoanalysis and History* (New York: Norton, 1958).

W. R. Fairbairn, "Synopsis of an Object-relations Theory," *International Journal of Psychoanalysis* (Vol. 44, April 1963).

Leslie H. Farber, "Despair and the Life of Suicide," *Review of Existential Psychology and Psychiatry* (Vol. 2, 1962).

————. "Faces of Envy," *Review of Existential Psychology and Psychiatry* (Vol. 1, 1961).

————. "Perfectibility and the Psychoanalytic Candidate," *The Journal of Existential Psychiatry* (Vol. 3, 1963).

————. "Schizophrenia and the Mad Psychotherapist," *Review of Existential Psychology and Psychiatry* (Vol. 2, 1962).

————. "The Therapeutic Despair," *Psychiatry, Journal for the Study of Interpersonal Processes* (Vol. 21, 1958).

————. "Will and Willfulness in Hysteria," *Review of Existential Psychology and Psychiatry* (Vol. 1, 1961).

Otto Fenichel, *The Psychoanalytical Theory of Neurosis* (New York: Norton, 1945).

Leslie A. Fiedler, *No! In Thunder* (Boston: Beacon Press, 1960).

J. C. Flugel, *Studies in Feeling and Desire* (London: Duckworth, 1955).

Nandor Fodor, "People Who Are Christ," *Psychoanalysis and the Psychoanalytic Review* (Vol. 45, 1958).

Victor E. Frankl, *The Doctor and the Soul* (New York: Knopf, 1955).

Thomas M. French, M.D., *The Integration of Behavior* (5 vols.), *Volume 1, Basic Postulates* (Chicago: University of Chicago Press, 1952).

Warren G. French, "The Phony World and the Nice World," *Wisconsin Studies in Contemporary Literature* (Vol. 4, 1963).

Sigmund Freud, *A General Introduction to Psychoanalysis* (New York: Doubleday, 1953).

————. *The Standard Edition of the Complete Psychological Works of Sigmund Freud,* edited by James Strachey, Anna Freud, Alix Strachey, and Alan Tyson (London: Hogarth Press and the Institute of Psychoanalysis).

————. "The Interpretation of Dreams," Vols. 4 and 5.

————. "Studies in Hysteria," Vol. 2.

————. "The Psychopathology of Everyday Life," Vol. 6.

————. "Five Lectures on Psychoanalysis," Vol. 11.

————. "Totem and Taboo," Vol. 13.

————. "The Unconscious," Vol. 13.

————. "Introductory Lectures on Psychoanalysis," Vols. 15 and 16.

————. "Beyond the Pleasure Principle," Vol. 18.

————. "The Ego and the Id," Vol. 19.

Carl J. Friedrich (ed.), *Totalitarianism* (Cambridge: Harvard University Press, 1954).

Northorp Frye, "The Imaginative and the Imaginary," *American Journal of Psychiatry* (Vol. 119, 1962).

L. B. Gillon, "Certitude de notre espérance," *Revue Théologique* (Vol. 45, 1939).

Agostino Gemelli, O.F.M., *Psychoanalysis Today* (New York: Kenedy, 1955).

William Goldfarb, M.D., and Irving Mintz, M.S.S.W., "Schizophrenic Child's Reaction to Time and Space," *Archives of General Psychiatry* (Vol. 5, 1961).

Paul Goodman, *Growing Up Absurd* (New York: Random House, 1960).

Geoffrey Gorer, *The American People: A Study in National Character* (New York: Norton, 1948).

————. "The Pornography of Death," in *The Berkley Book of Modern Writing #3,* W. Phillips and P. Rahv (ed.). (New York: Berkley Publishing Corp., 1956).

Andrew Greeley, "Myths, Symbols, and Rituals in the Modern World," *The Critic* (Vol. 20, 1961).

P. Greenacre, "The Predisposition to Anxiety," *Psychoanalytic Quarterly* (Vol. 10, 1941).

————. "A Study of the Nature of Inspiration," *Journal of the American Psychiatric Association* (Vol. 12, 1964).

Ralph R. Greenson, "Empathy and Its Vicissitudes," *The International Journal of Psychoanalysis* (Vol. 41, 1960).

Ihab Hassan, *Radical Innocence: Studies in the Contemporary American Novel* (Princeton: Princeton University Press, 1961).

M. L. Hayward, "Schizophrenia and the Double-Bind," *Psychoanalytic Quarterly* (Vol. 34, 1960).

Christopher M. Heinicke, "Some Effects of Separating Two-Year-Old Children From Their Parents," *Human Relations* (Vol. 9, 1956).

Paul H. Hoch, and Joseph Zubin (ed.), *The Future of Psychiatry* (New York: Grune & Stratton, 1962).

Hans Hoffman, *Religion and Mental Health* (New York: Harper, 1961).

Karen Horney, *The Neurotic Personality of Our Time* (New York: Norton, 1937).

Muriel Hall Hyroop, "The Significance of Helplessness," *American Journal of Psychotherapy* (Vol. 7, 1953).

K. S. Isaacs, *et al.*, "Faith, Trust, and Gullibility," *International Journal of Psychoanalysis* (Vol. 44, 1963).

Don D. Jackson (ed.), *The Etiology of Schizophrenia* (New York: Basic Books, 1960).

Marie Jahoda, *Current Concepts of Positive Mental Health* (New York: Basic Books, 1958).

Richard L. Jenkins, *Breaking Patterns of Defeat* (Philadelphia: Lippincott, 1954).

Robert O. Johann, "On the Meaning of Hope," *The Theologian* (Vol. 8, 1952).

Hans Jonas, *The Gnostic Religion* (Boston: Beacon Press, 1963).

Carl Gustav Jung, *Psychology and Religion* (New Haven: Yale University Press, 1938).

George A. Kelly, "Suicide: The Personal Construct Point of View," in *The Cry for Help*, edited by Norman L. Farberow and Edwin S. Shoreidman (New York: McGraw-Hill, 1961).

Melanie Klein, *Contributions to Psycho-Analysis 1921-45* (London: Hogarth, 1948).

Robert P. Knight (ed.), *Psychoanalytic Psychiatry and Psychology* (New York: International Universities Press, 1954).

A. Kobler and E. Stollind, *The End of Hope: A Socio-Clinical Study of Suicide* (New York: Macmillan, 1964).

Ernest Kris, *Psychoanalytic Explorations in Art* (New York: International Universities Press, 1952).

Lawrence S. Kubie, *Neurotic Distortions of the Creative Process* (Lawrence, Kans.: University of Kansas Press, 1958).

——————. *Practical and Theoretical Aspects of Psychoanalysis* (New York: International Universities Press, 1950).

——————. "The Fundamental Nature of the Distinction Between Normality and Neurosis," *The Psychoanalytic Quarterly* (Vol. 23, 1954).

——————. "Social Forces and the Neurotic Process," in *Explorations in Social Psychiatry* (New York: Basic Books, 1957).

Dom Marc-François Lacan, "Nous sommes sauvés par l'espérance," *A La Rencontre de Dieu, Memorial Albert Gelin* (Vol. 205, No. 5).

R. D. Laing, *The Divided Self, A Study of Sanity and Madness* (Chicago: Quadrangle Books, 1960).

Louis Levin and Leo W. Schwarz, *Psychiatry and Religious Experience* (New York: Random House, 1958).

Kurt Lewin, *Field Theory in Social Science, Selected Papers*, D. Cartwright (ed.), (New York: Harper Torchbooks, 1951).

Robert J. Lifton, *Thought Reform and the Psychology of Totalism* (New York: Norton, 1961).

Davide Limentani, "Symbiotic Identification in Schizophrenia," *Psychiatry* (Vol. 19, 1956).

Hans W. Loewald, M.D., "Psychoanalysis and Modern Views on Human Existence and Religious Experience," *Christianity and Psychoanalysis, The Journal of Pastoral Care* (Vol. 6, 1952).

W. F. Lynch, S.J., *Christ and Apollo* (New York: Sheed and Ward, 1961).

Stanislaus Lyonnet, S.J., "St. Paul: Liberty and Law," in *The Bridge* Vol. 4 (New York: Pantheon, 1962).

Marion Magid, "The Innocence of Tennessee Williams," *Commentary* (January 1963).

M. S. Mahler, M. Furer, "Certain Aspects of the Separation Individuation Phase," *Psychoanalytic Quarterly* (Vol. 32, 1963).

Norman R. F. Maier, *Frustration, The Study of Behavior Without a Goal* (New York: McGraw-Hill, 1949).

Andre Malraux, *The Psychology of Art*, Vol. 3 (New York: Pantheon, 1949).

Gabriel Marcel, *Homo Viator: Introduction to a Metaphysics of Hope* (Chicago: Henry Regnery, 1951).

A. H. Maslow, *Motivation and Personality* (New York: Harper and Brothers, 1954).

Rollo May, "Religion, Psychotherapy and the Achievement of Selfhood," *Pastoral Psychology* (Vol. 2, No. 17, 1951), and (No. 18, 1952).

Dwight McDonald, *Against the American Grain* (New York: Random House, 1962).

Paul McReynolds, "Anxiety, Perception, and Schizophrenia," in *The Etiology of Schizophrenia,* edited by Don D. Jackson (New York: Basic Books, 1960).

Margaret Mead, *From the South Seas: Studies in Adolescence and Sex in Primitive Societies* (New York: Wm. Morrow and Co., 1939).

W. W. Meissner, S.J., *Annotated Bibliography in Religion and Psychology* (New York: Academy of Religion and Mental Health, 1961).

Karl Menninger, *Man Against Himself* (New York: Harcourt Brace, 1938).

—————. *Theory of Psychoanalytic Technique* (New York: Basic Books, 1958).

—————. "Hope," *American Journal of Psychiatry* (Vol. 116, 1959), 481-491.

Karl Menninger, with Martin Mayman and Paul Pruyser, *The Vital Balance* (New York: Viking, 1963).

William C. Menninger, *Psychiatry in a Troubled World* (New York: Macmillan, 1948).

Emile Mersch, "La sainte vertu d'espérance," in *Morale et Corps Mystique.*

Milton H. Miller and Seymour L. Halleck, "The Critics of Psychiatry: A Review of Contemporary Critical Attitudes," *The American Journal of Psychiatry* (Vol. 119, 1962-63).

Marilyn Milner, "Psycho-analysis and Art," in *Psychoanalysis and Contemporary Thought,* edited by John D. Sutherland (London: Hogarth Press, 1958).

Marion Milner, *On Not Being Able to Paint* (New York: International Universities Press, 1957).

Ashley Montagu, "Human Nature and Religion," *Journal of Existential Psychiatry* (Vol. 1, 1961).

—————. "Culture and Mental Illness," *The American Journal of Psychiatry* (Vol. 118, 1961).

—————. "Man and Human Nature," *American Journal of Psychiatry* (Vol. 112, 1955).

Sebastian Moore, O.S.B., "A Catholic Neurosis," *The Clergy Review* (Vol. 46, 1961).

Leo Nageberg, "The Meaning of Help in Psychotherapy," *Psychoanalysis and the Psychoanalytic Review* (Vol. 46, No. 4, 1959).

Charles Odier, *Anxiety and Magic Thinking* (New York: International Universities Press, 1956).

Marc Oraison, *Love or Constraint?* (New York: Kenedy, 1959).

Jean Piaget, *Judgment and Reasoning in the Child* (Paterson, N. J.: Littlefield, Adams, 1959).

J. Pieper, "Sur l'espérance des Martyrs," in Semaine des Intellectuels Catholiques' *Espoir Humain et Espérance Chretienne* (Paris, 1951).

Joseph Pieper, *Uber Die Hoffnung* (Munchen: 1949).

S. Pinckaers, "L'Espérance de l'A.T., est elle la même que la notre?" *Nouvelle Revue Théologique* (Vol. 77, 1955).

—————. "La Nature Vertueuse de l'Espérance," *Revue Théologique* (Vol. 58, 1958).

Jacques M. Pohier, O.P., "Religious Mentality and Infantile Mentality," in *Child and Adult Before God,* edited by A. Godin, S.J., (Brussels: Lumen Vitae Press, 1961).

Frederick L. Polak, *The Image of the Future* (New York: Oceana Publications, 1961).

Sandor Rado, *Psychoanalysis of Behavior* (New York: Grune and Stratton, 1956).

David Rapaport, "The Autonomy of the Ego," *Bulletin of the Menninger Clinic* (Vol. 15, 1951).

—————. "The Autonomy of the Ego," *Psychoanalytic Psychiatry and Psychology* (Clinical and Theoretical Papers) Austen Riggs Center, Vol. 1, edited by Robert P. Knight.

—————. "The Theory of Ego Autonomy: A Generalization," *Bulletin of the Menninger Clinic* (Vol. 22, 1958).

—————. *Organization and Pathology of Thought* (New York: Columbia University Press, 1951).

Theodore Reik, *Dogma and Compulsion* (New York: International Universities Press, 1951).

—————. *Myth and Guilt* (New York: Braziller, 1957).

Religion and Psychiatry Number, *Bulletin of the Menninger Clinic* (Vol. 19, 1955).

Philip Rieff, *Freud, The Mind of the Moralist* (New York: Viking Press, 1959).

Clifford J. Sager, "Freedom and Psychotherapy," *American Journal of Psychotherapy* (Vol. 13, 1959).

Leon J. Saul, "An Etymological Note on Love and Wish," *Psychoanalytic Quarterly* (Vol. 22, 1953).

Edgar H. Schein, Inge Schneier, and Curtis H. Barker, *Coercive Persuasion: A Sociopsychological Analysis of the Brainwashing of American Civilian Prisoners of the Chinese Communists* (New York: Norton, 1961).

Paul Schilder, *Medical Psychology* (New York: International Universities Press, 1953).

—————. *Psychoanalysis, Man, and Society* (New York: Norton, 1951).

Gertrude Schwing, *A Way to the Soul of the Mentally Ill* (New York: International Universities Press, 1954).

H. F. Searles, "Dependency Processes in the Psychotherapy of Schizophrenics," *Journal of the American Psychoanalytic Association* (Vol. 3, 1955).

—————. "Positive Feelings in the Relation of the Schizophrenic and his Mother," *International Journal of Psychoanalysis* (Vol. 39, 1958).

M. Sechehaye, "Principles and Methods of Symbolic Realization," *Psychiatry Res. Rep. American Psychiatric Association* (Vol. 17, 1963).

—————. *Symbolic Realization: A New Method of Psychotherapy Applied to a Case of Schizophrenia* (New York: International Universities Press, 1951).

—————. "The Transference in Symbolic Realization," *International Journal of Psychoanalysis* (Vol. 37, 1956).

John R. Seely, "The Americanization of the Unconscious," *Atlantic Monthly* (July 1961).

Martti Siirala, "Schizophrenia: A Human Situation," *The American Journal of Psychoanalysis* (Vol. 23, 1963).

Alexander Simon (ed.), *The Physiology of the Emotions* (Springfield, Mass.: John Thomas, 1961).

Karin Stephen, *The Wish to Fall Ill* (London: Cambridge, 1960).

Harry Stack Sullivan, *Clinical Studies in Psychiatry* (New York: Norton, 1956).

—————. *The Interpersonal Theory of Psychiatry* (New York: Norton, 1953).

Anthony Storr, *The Integrity of the Personality* (New York: Atheneum Publishers, 1961).

Edward A. Strecker, *Basic Psychiatry* (New York: Random House, 1952).

John D. Sutherland, *Psychoanalysis and Contemporary Thought* (London: Hogarth Press, 1958).

James Sutherland Thomson, *The Hope of the Gospel* (Greenwich, Conn.: Seabury Press, 1955).

Paul Tillich, "What is Basic in Human Nature," *The American Journal of Psychoanalysis* (Vol. 22, 1962).

John H. Weakland, "The 'Double-Bind' Hypothesis of Schizophrenia and Three-Party Interaction," *The Etiology of Schizophrenia*, edited by Don D. Jackson (New York: Basic Books, 1960).

Weaver, "Ultimate Terms in Contemporary Rhetoric," *Perspectives* (Vol. 11, 1955).

Edith Weigert, "Loneliness and Trust—Basic Factors of Human Existence," *Psychiatry: Journal for the Study of Interpersonal Processes* (Vol. 23, 1960).

—————. "The Nature of Sympathy in the Art of Psychotherapy," *Psychiatry* (Vol. 24, No. 2, May 1961).

—————. "The Psychoanalytic View of Human Personality," *Christianity and Psychoanalysis, The Journal of Pastoral Care* (Vol. 6, Winter 1952).

—————. "The Psychotherapy of the Affective Psychoses," in *Psychotherapy of the Psychoses,* edited by Arthur Burton (New York: Basic Books, 1961).

Allen Wheelis, "Will and Psychoanalysis," *Journal of the American Psychoanalytic Association* (Vol. 4, 1956).

—————. *The Quest for Identity* (New York: Norton, 1958).

Donald C. Williams, "Philosophy and Psychoanalysis," in *Psychoanalysis, Scientific Method, and Philosophy,* edited by Sidney Hook (New York: Grove Press, 1959).

D. W. Winnicott, "Dependence in Infant Care, in Child Care, and in the Psycho-analytic Setting," *International Journal of Psychoanalysis* (Vol. 44, 1963).

—————. "Psychoanalysis and the Sense of Guilt," in *Psychoanalysis and Contemporary Thought,* edited by John D. Sutherland (New York: Grove Press, 1959).

E. D. Wittkower and J. Fried, "A Cross-Cultural Approach to Mental-Health Problems," *American Journal of Psychiatry* (Vol. 116, Nov. 1959).

L. C. Wynne, I. Rychoff, J. Day, and S. H. Hersh, "Pseudo-Mutuality in the Family Relations of Schizophrenics," *Psychiatry* (Vol. 1, 1958).

Phillip Young, "Fallen From Time: The Mythic Rip Van Winkle," *The Kenyon Review* (Vol. 22, 1960).

Other MENTOR-OMEGA Books You
Will Enjoy

LEISURE: THE BASIS OF CULTURE   by Josef Pieper
In a series of astonishing essays, the author indicts the
20th century cult of "work" and hectic amusements,
which can ultimately destroy both our culture and ourselves. Introduction by T. S. Eliot.   (#MP550—60¢)

THE LITTLE FLOWERS OF ST. FRANCIS OF ASSISI
Lyric stories about the great medieval saint, composed
by his devoted followers. New translation by Serge
Hughes.   (#MT593—75¢)

**THE LOVE OF LEARNING AND THE
DESIRE FOR GOD**   by Jean Leclerq, O.S.B.
A study of the manuscripts of the medieval monasteries
reveals their role in preserving the culture of the past.
By a distinguished scholar and Benedictine monk.
(#MT432—75¢)

MARIA MONTESSORI: HER LIFE AND WORK
by E. M. Standing
A friend and colleague of the great educator writes her
biography and evaluates her contributions to modern
education. With eight pages of photographs.
(#MQ425—95¢)

OF THE IMITATION OF CHRIST   by Thomas a Kempis
The great 15th century classic of devotional literature in
a widely acclaimed modern translation by Abbot Justin
McCann.   (#MT467—75¢)

ELEMENTS OF CHRISTIAN PHILOSOPHY
by Etienne Gilson
The noted French philosopher illuminates the key ideas
of the theology of St. Thomas Aquinas. (#MT489—75¢)

THE SOCIAL TEACHINGS OF THE CHURCH
edited by Anne Fremantle
A companion volume to *The Papal Encyclicals in Their
Historical Context,* this book contains papal encyclicals
on social problems from Pope Leo XIII to Pope John
XXIII.   (#MT549—75¢)

**TWO CENTURIES OF ECUMENISM: THE SEARCH FOR
UNITY**   by George H. Tavard
A study of successive efforts at Christian reunion from
the Oxford Movement of the last century to the most
recent Council of the Church called by Pope John
XXIII.   (#MT465—75¢)

Other Books You Will Enjoy Reading in SIGNET and MENTOR Editions